For any of us to be fully conscious

intellectually we should not only be able

to detect the worldviews of others

but be aware of our own—

why it is ours and why in light of so many options

we think it is true.

OTHER BOOKS BY JAMES W. SIRE

How to Read Slowly
Scripture Twisting
Beginning with God
Discipleship of the Mind
Chris Chrisman Goes to College
Why Should Anyone Believe Anything at All?
Jesus the Reason (Bible study guide)
Habits of the Mind
Václav Havel
Naming the Elephant
Why Good Arguments Often Fail
Learning to Pray Through the Psalms
A Little Primer on Humble Apologetics
Praying the Psalms of Jesus
Deepest Differences with Carl Peraino

A Basic Worldview Catalog

THE UNIVERSE NEXT DOOR

JAMES W. SIRE

FIFTH EDITION

IVP Academic

An imprint of InterVarsity Press
Downers Grove, Illinois

InterVarsity Press, USA
P.O. Box 1400, Downers Grove, IL 60515-1426, USA
ivpress.com
email@ivpress.com

Inter-Varsity Press, England
Norton Street, Nottingham NG7 3HR, England
ivpbooks.com
ivp@ivpbooks.com

InterVarsity Press, *USA, is the book-publishing division of InterVarsity Christian Fellowship/USA*, *a movement of students and faculty active on campus at hundreds of universities, colleges and schools of nursing in the United States of America, and a member movement of the International Fellowship of Evangelical Students. For information about local and regional activities, visit intervarsity.org.*

Inter-Varsity Press, England, is closely linked with the Universities and Colleges Christian Fellowship, a student movement connecting Christian Unions in universities and colleges throughout Great Britain, and a member movement of the International Fellowship of Evangelical Students. Website: www.uccf.org.uk.

Design: Cindy Kiple

Images: deep space: Phil Morley/iStockphoto
open door: Nicolas Loran/iStockphoto

USA ISBN 978-0-8308-3850-9
UK ISBN 978-1-84474-420-6

Printed in the United States of America ♾

Library of Congress Cataloging-in-Publication Data

Sire, James W.
  The universe next door: a basic worldview catalog/James W. Sire.
  —5th ed.
    p. cm.
Includes bibliographical references and index.
ISBN 978-0-8308-3850-9 (pbk.: alk. paper)
1. Ideology. 2. Apologetics. 3. Theology, Doctrinal—Popular
works. 4. Ideology—Religious aspects—Christianity. I. Title.
B823.3.S56 2009
140—dc22
                2009026595

British Library Cataloguing in Publication Data
A catalogue record for this book is available from the British Library.

P	30	29	28	27	26	25	24	23	22	21	20	19	18	17	16	15	14	13	12
Y	34	33	32	31	30	29	28	27	26	25	24	23	22	21	20	19	18	17	16

To Marjorie

Carol, Mark and Caleb

Eugene and Lisa

Richard, Kay Dee, Derek, Hannah, Micah, Abigail and Joanna

Ann, Jeff, Aaron and Jacob

whose worlds on worlds

compose my familiar and burgeoning universe

CONTENTS

PREFACE TO
THE FIFTH EDITION

It has been more than thirty-three years since this book was first published in 1976. Much has happened both in the development of worldviews in the West and in the way others and I have come to understand the notion of worldview.

In 1976 the New Age worldview was just forming and had yet to be given a name. I called it "the new consciousness." At the same time the word *postmodern* was used only in academic circles and had yet to be recognized as an intellectually significant shift. Now, in 2009, the New Age is over thirty years old, adolescent only in character, not in years. Meanwhile postmodernism has penetrated every area of intellectual life, enough to have triggered at least a modest backlash. Pluralism, and the relativism and syncretism that have accompanied it, have muted the distinctive voice of every point of view. And though the third edition of this book noted these, there is now more to the stories of both the New Age and postmodernism. In the fourth edition I updated the chapter on the New Age and substantially revised the chapter on postmodernism.

In the fourth edition I also reformulated the entire notion of worldview. What is it, really? There have been challenges to the definition I gave in 1976 (and left unchanged in the 1988 and 1997 editions). Was it not too intellectual? Isn't a worldview more unconscious than conscious? Why does it begin with abstract ontology (the notion of being) instead of the more personal question of epistemology (how we know)? Don't we first need to have our knowledge justified before we can make claims about the nature of ultimate reality? Isn't my definition of *worldview* dependent on nineteenth-century German idealism or, perhaps, the truth of the Christian worldview itself? What about the role of behavior in forming or assessing or even identifying one's worldview? Doesn't postmodernism undermine the very notion of worldview?

I took these challenges to heart. The result was twofold. First was the writing of *Naming the Elephant: Worldview as a Concept*, published at the same time as the fourth edition of *The Universe Next Door*. Here I addressed a host of issues surrounding the concept of worldview. Readers who are interested in the intellectual tool used in the fourth edition and this one will find it analyzed at much greater depth there. To do this, I was greatly aided by the work of David Naugle, professor of philosophy at Dallas Baptist University. In *Worldview: The History of a Concept* he surveyed the origin, development and various versions of the concept from Immanuel Kant to Arthur Holmes and beyond, and he presents his own definition of the Christian worldview. It is his identification of worldview with the biblical notion of the heart that has spawned my own revised definition, which appears in chapter one of the fourth edition and the present book.

Readers of any of the first three editions will note that the new definition does four things. First, it shifts the focus from a worldview as a "set of presuppositions" to a "commitment, a fundamental orientation of the heart," giving more emphasis to the pretheoretical roots of the intellect. Second, it expands the way worldviews are expressed, adding to a set of presuppositions the notion of story. Third, it makes more explicit that the deepest root of a worldview is its commitment to and understanding of the "really real." Fourth, it acknowledges the role of behavior in assessing what anyone's worldview actually is. To further emphasize the importance of one's worldview as a commitment, in this fifth edition I have added an eighth worldview question: *What personal, life-orienting core commitments are consistent with this worldview?*

Nonetheless, most of the analysis of the first four editions of *The Universe Next Door* remains the same. Except for chapter three on deism, which has been significantly expanded to account for the diversities within this worldview, only occasional changes have been made in the presentation and analysis of the first six of the eight worldviews examined. It is my hope that with the refined definition and these modest revisions the powerful nature of every worldview will be more fully evident.

Finally, there is one major worldview now affecting the West that I have not treated in any of the previous editions. Since September 11, 2001, Islam has become a major factor of life not only in the Middle East, Africa and Southeast Asia but in Europe and North America as well. The Islamic worldview (or perhaps worldviews) now impinges on the lives of people around the globe. Moreover, the term *worldview* appears in daily newspapers when writers try to grasp and explain what is fueling the stunning events of the past few years. Unfortunately, I am not personally prepared to respond to the need for us in America to understand Islam's understanding of our world. So I have asked Dr. Winfried Corduan, professor of philosophy and religion at Taylor University and author of a number of books but especially of *Neighboring Faiths*, to contribute a chapter on Islamic worldviews.[1]

One final comment on my motivation for the first edition. It has triggered numerous negative comments especially among Amazon.com reviewers who complain that the book displays a pro-Christian bias. They want an unbiased study. There is no such thing as an unbiased study of any significant intellectual idea or movement. Of course an analysis of worldviews will display some sort of bias. Even the idea of an objective account assumes that objectivity is possible or more valuable than an account from a committed and acknowledged perspective. C. S. Lewis, writing about his interpretation of Milton's *Paradise Lost*, once commented that his Christian faith was an advantage. "What would you not give," he asked, "to have a real live Epicurean at your elbow while reading Lucretius?"[2] Here you have a real live Christian's guide to the Christian worldview and its alternatives.

Furthermore, I first wrote the book for Christian students in the mid 1970s; it was designed to help them identify why they often felt so "out of it" when their professors assumed the truth of ideas they deemed odd or even false. I wanted these students to know the outlines of a "merely" Christian worldview, how it provided the foundation for much of the modern Western world's understanding of reality and what the differences were between the Christian worldview and the various worldviews that either stemmed from Christianity by variation and decay or countered Christianity at its very intellectual roots. The book was immedi-

---

[1]Winfried Corduan, *Neighboring Faiths* (Downers Grove, Ill.: InterVarsity Press, 1998).
[2]C. S. Lewis, *Preface to Paradise Lost* (London: Oxford University Press, 1960), p. 65.

ately adopted as a text in both secular institutions—Stanford, the University of Rhode Island and North Texas State, for example—and Christian colleges. Subsequent editions have been edited to acknowledge readers with other worldviews, but the Christian perspective has, without apology, not been changed.

In fact, the continued interest of readers in this book continues to surprise and please me. It has been translated into nineteen languages, and each year it finds its way into the hands of many students at the behest of professors in courses as widely divergent as apologetics, history, English literature, introduction to religion, introduction to philosophy and even one on the human dimensions of science. Such a range of interests suggests that one of the assumptions on which the book is based is indeed true: the most fundamental issues we as human beings need to consider have no departmental boundaries. What is prime reality? Is it God or the cosmos? What is a human being? What happens at death? How should we then live? These questions are as relevant to literature as to psychology, to religion as to science.

On one issue I remain constant: I am convinced that for any of us to be fully conscious intellectually we should not only be able to detect the worldviews of others but be aware of our own—why it is ours and why, in light of so many options, we think it is true. I can only hope that this book becomes a steppingstone for others toward their self-conscious development and justification of their own worldview.

In addition to the many acknowledgments contained in the footnotes, I would especially like to thank C. Stephen Board, who many years ago invited me to present much of this material in lecture form at the Christian Study Project, sponsored by InterVarsity Christian Fellowship and held at Cedar Campus in Michigan. He and Thomas Trevethan, also on the staff of that program, have given excellent counsel in the development of the material and in the continued critique of my worldview thinking since the first publication of this book.

Other friends who have read the manuscript and helped polish some of the rough edges are C. Stephen Evans (who contributed the section on Marxism), Winfried Corduan (who contributed the chapter on Islam), Os Guinness, Charles Hampton, Keith Yandell, Douglas Groothuis, Richard H. Bube, Rodney Clapp, Gary Deddo, Chawkat Moucarry and Colin Chapman. Dan Synnestvedt's review of the fourth edition sparked my vision for a fifth and provided guidance, especially for the chapter on deism. Recognition, too, goes to David Naugle, without whom my definition of a worldview would have remained unchanged. To them and to the editor of this edition, James Hoover, goes my sincere appreciation. I would also like to acknowledge the feedback from the many students who have weathered worldview criticism in my classes and lectures. Finally, which rightly should be firstly, I must thank my wife Marjorie, who not only proofed draft after draft of edition after edition, but who suffered my attention to the manuscript when I had best attended to her and our family. Love gives no better gift than suffering for others.

Responsibility for the continued infelicities and the downright errors in this book is, alas, my own.

Chapter 1

A WORLD OF DIFFERENCE

INTRODUCTION

But often, in the world's most crowded streets,
But often, in the din of strife,
There rises an unspeakable desire
After the knowledge of our buried life:
A thirst to spend our fire and restless force
In tracking out our true, original course;
A longing to inquire
Into the mystery of this heart which beats
So wild, so deep in us—to know
Whence our lives come and where they go.

MATTHEW ARNOLD, "THE BURIED LIFE"

In the late nineteenth century Stephen Crane captured our plight as we in the early twenty-first century face the universe.

A man said to the universe:
"Sir, I exist."
"However," replied the universe,
"The fact has not created in me
A sense of obligation."[1]

---

[1]From Stephen Crane, *War Is Kind and Other Lines* (1899), frequently anthologized. The Hebrew poem that follows is Psalm 8.

How different this is from the words of the ancient psalmist, who
looked around himself and up to God and wrote:

O LORD, our Lord,
 how majestic is your name in all the earth!

You have set your glory
 above the heavens.
From the lips of children and infants
 you have ordained praise
because of your enemies,
 to silence the foe and the avenger.

When I consider your heavens,
 the work of your fingers,
the moon and the stars,
 which you have set in place,
what is man that you are mindful of him,
 the son of man that you care for him?
You made him a little lower than the heavenly beings
 and crowned him with glory and honor.

You made him ruler over the works of your hands;
 you put everything under his feet:
all flocks and herds,
 and the beasts of the field,
the birds of the air,
 and the fish of the sea,
 all that swim the paths of the seas.

O LORD, our Lord,
 how majestic is your name in all the earth! (Ps 8)

There is a world of difference between the worldviews of these two
poems. Indeed, they propose alternative universes. Yet both poems rever-
berate in the minds and souls of people today. Many who stand with Stephen Crane have more than a memory of the psalmist's great and glorious assurance of God's hand in the cosmos and God's love for his people.
They long for what they no longer can truly accept. The gap left by the
loss of a center to life is like the chasm in the heart of a child whose father
has died. How those who no longer believe in God wish something could
fill this void!

And many who yet stand with the psalmist and whose faith in the Lord God Jehovah is vital and brimming still feel the tug of Crane's poem. Yes, that is exactly how it is to lose God. Yes, that is just what those who do not have faith in the infinite-personal Lord of the Universe must feel—alienation, loneliness, even despair.

We recall the struggles of faith in our nineteenth-century forebears and know that for many, faith was the loser. As Alfred, Lord Tennyson wrote in response to the death of his close friend,

> Behold, we know not anything;
>   I can but trust that good shall fall
>   At last—far off—at last, to all
> And every winter change to spring.
> So runs my dream; but what am I?
>   An infant crying in the night;
>   An infant crying for the light;
> And with no language but a cry.[2]

For Tennyson, faith eventually won out, but the struggle was years in being resolved.

The struggle to discover our own faith, our own worldview, our beliefs about reality, is what this book is all about. Formally stated, the purposes of this book are (1) to outline the basic worldviews that underlie the way we in the Western world think about ourselves, other people, the natural world, and God or ultimate reality; (2) to trace historically how these worldviews have developed from a breakdown in the theistic worldview, moving in turn into deism, naturalism, nihilism, existentialism, Eastern mysticism, the new consciousness of the New Age and Islam, a recent infusion from the Middle East; (3) to show how postmodernism puts a twist on these worldviews; and (4) to encourage us all to think in terms of worldviews, that is, with a consciousness of not only our own way of thought but also that of other people, so that we can first understand and then genuinely communicate with others in our pluralistic society.

That is a large order. In fact it sounds very much like the project of a lifetime. My hope is that it will be just that for many who read this book and take seriously its implications. What is written here is only an introduction to what might well become a way of life.

---

[2]From Alfred, Lord Tennyson, *In Memoriam* (1850), poem 54.

In writing this book I have found it especially difficult to know what to include and what to leave out. But because I see the whole book as an introduction, I have tried rigorously to be brief—to get to the heart of each worldview, suggest its strengths and weaknesses, and move to the next. I have, however, indulged my own interest by including textual and bibliographical footnotes that will, I trust, lead readers into greater depths than the chapters themselves. Those who wish first to get at

---

A worldview (or vision of life) is a framework or set of fundamental beliefs through which we view the world and our calling and future in it. This vision need not be fully articulated: it may be so internalized that it goes largely unquestioned; it may not be explicitly developed into a systematic conception of life; it may not be theoretically deepened into a philosophy; it may not even be codified into creedal form; it may be greatly refined through cultural-historical development. Nevertheless, this vision is a channel for the ultimate beliefs which give direction and meaning to life. It is the integrative and interpretative framework by which order and disorder are judged; it is the standard by which reality is managed and pursued; it is the set of hinges on which all our everyday thinking and doing turns.

JAMES H. OLTHUIS
"On Worldviews," in *Stained Glass: Worldviews and Social Science*

---

what I take to be the heart of the matter can safely ignore them. But those who wish to go it on their own (may their name be legion!) may find the footnotes helpful in suggesting further reading and further questions for investigation.

WHAT IS A WORLDVIEW?

Despite the fact that such philosophical names as Plato, Kant, Sartre, Camus and Nietzsche will appear on these pages, this book is not a work of professional philosophy. And though I will refer time and again to concepts made famous by the apostle Paul, Augustine, Aquinas and Calvin, this is not a work of theology. Furthermore, though I will frequently point out how various worldviews are expressed in various religions, this is not a book on comparative religion.[3] Each religion has its own rites and liturgies, its own peculiar practices and aesthetic character, its own doctrines and turns of expression. Rather, this is a book of worldviews—in some ways more basic, more foundational than formal studies in philosophy, theology or comparative religion.[4] To put it yet another way, it is a book of universes fashioned by words and concepts that work together to provide a more or less coherent frame of reference for all thought and action.[5]

Few people have anything approaching an articulate philosophy—at least as epitomized by the great philosophers. Even fewer, I suspect, have a carefully constructed theology. But everyone has a worldview. Whenever any of us thinks about anything—from a casual thought *(Where did I leave my watch?)* to a profound question *(Who am I?)*—we are operating within such a framework. In fact, it is only the assumption of a worldview—however basic or simple—that allows us to think at all.[6]

What, then, is this thing called a worldview that is so important to all of us? I've never even heard of one. How could I have one? That may well

---

[3]For a phenomenological and comparative religion approach, see Ninian Smart, *Worldviews: Crosscultural Explorations of Human Beliefs*, 3rd ed. (Upper Saddle River, N.J.: Prentice-Hall, 2000); see also David Burnett's *Clash of Worlds* (Grand Rapids: Monarch Books, 2002), which focuses on religious worldviews.

[4]A helpful collection of essays on the notion of worldviews is found in Paul A. Marshall, Sander Griffioen and Richard Mouw, eds., *Stained Glass: Worldviews and Social Science* (Lanham, Md.: University Press of America, 1989); the essay by James H. Olthuis, "On Worldviews," pp. 26-40, is especially insightful. Worldview analysis in general has recently been criticized not only for overemphasizing the intellectual and abstract nature of worldviews but for the implicit assumption that there is such a thing as *the* Christian worldview. Because any expression of a worldview, Christian or not, is deeply imbedded in the flow of history and the varying characteristics of language, this criticism is sound. Each expression of any general worldview will bear the marks of the culture out of which it comes. Nonetheless, Christians, especially Christians, in every time and place should be seeking for the clearest expression and the closest approximation of what the Bible and Christian tradition have basically affirmed. See Roger P. Ebertz, "Beyond Worldview Analysis: Insights from Hans-Georg Gadamer on Christian Scholarship," *Christian Scholar's Review* 36 (Fall 2006): 13-28. Ebertz remarks: "The resulting worldview . . . is not absolute and ahistorical. Nor is it a set of bare theological claims. It is rather a richly fleshed-out perspective that incorporates discoveries from the past and the present, as well as insights from believers and non-believers" (p. 27). The description of the Christian worldview that constitutes the next chapter should be understood in that light.

[5]In the third edition of *The Universe Next Door* I confessed that long ago I took T. S. Eliot to heart. He is credited with saying, "Mediocre poets imitate; good poets steal." The title for this book comes from the two last lines of an e. e. cummings poem, "pity this busy monster, manunkind: listen: there's a hell/of a good universe next door; let's go." See e. e. Cummings, *Poems: 1923-1954* (New York: Harcourt Brace, 1954), p. 397.

[6]As Charles Taylor says, "[A]ll beliefs are held within a context or framework of the taken-for-granted, which usually remains tacit, and may even be as yet unacknowledged by the agent, because never before formulated" (*A Secular Age* [Cambridge, Mass.: Belknap, 2007], p. 13).

be the response of many people. One is reminded of M. Jourdain in Jean Baptiste Molière's *The Bourgeois Gentleman,* who suddenly discovered he had been speaking prose for forty years without knowing it. But to discover one's own worldview is much more valuable. In fact, it is a significant step toward self-awareness, self-knowledge and self-understanding.

So what is a worldview? Essentially this:

A worldview is a commitment, a fundamental orientation of the heart, that can be expressed as a story or in a set of presuppositions (assumptions which may be true, partially true or entirely false) that we hold (consciously or subconsciously, consistently or inconsistently) about the basic constitution of reality, and that provides the foundation on which we live and move and have our being.

This succinct definition needs to be unpacked. Each phrase represents a specific characteristic that deserves more elaborate comment.[7]

Worldview as a commitment. The essence of a worldview lies deep in the inner recesses of the human self. A worldview involves the mind, but it is first of all a commitment, a matter of the soul. It is a spiritual orientation more than it is a matter of mind alone.

Worldviews are, indeed, a matter of the heart. This notion would be easier to grasp if the word *heart* bore in today's world the weight it bears in Scripture. The biblical concept includes the notions of wisdom (Prov 2:10), emotion (Ex 4:14; Jn 14:1), desire and will (1 Chron 29:18), spirituality (Acts 8:21) and intellect (Rom 1:21).[8] In short, and in biblical terms, the heart is "the central defining element of the human person."[9] A worldview, therefore, is situated in the self—the central operating chamber of every human being. It is from this *heart* that all one's thoughts and actions proceed.

Expressed in a story or a set of presuppositions. A worldview *is not* a story or a set of presuppositions, but it can be expressed in these ways. When I reflect on where I and the whole of the human race have come from or where my life or humanity itself is headed, my worldview is being

---

[7]See my *Naming of the Elephant: Worldview as a Concept* (Downers Grove, Ill.: InterVarsity Press, 2004), especially chap. 7, for an extended development and justification of this definition.

[8]See David Naugle's extended description of the biblical concept of heart (*Worldview: The History of a Concept* [Grand Rapids: Eerdmans, 2002], pp. 267-74). The NRSV translates *kardia* as "mind"; the NIV translates it as "heart."

[9]Ibid., p. 266.

expressed as a story. One story told by science begins with the big bang and proceeds through the evolution of the cosmos, formation of the galaxies, stars and planets, the appearance of life on earth and on to its disappearance as the universe runs down. Christians tell the story of creation, Fall, redemption, glorification—a story in which Jesus' birth, death and resurrection are the centerpiece. Christians see their lives and the lives of others as tiny chapters in that master story. The meaning of those little stories cannot be divorced from the master story, and some of this meaning is propositional. When, for example, I ask myself what I am really assuming about God, humans and the universe, the result is a set of presuppositions that I can express in propositional form.

When they are expressed that way, they answer a series of basic questions about the nature of fundamental reality. I will list and examine these questions shortly. But consider first the nature of those assumptions.

Assumptions that may be true, conscious, consistent. The presuppositions that express one's commitments may be true, partially true or entirely false. There is, of course, a *way things are*, but we are often mistaken about the way things are. In other words, reality is not endlessly plastic. A chair remains a chair whether we recognize it as a chair or not. Either there is an infinitely personal God or there is not. But people disagree on which is true. Some assume one thing; others assume another.

Second, sometimes we are aware of what our commitments are, sometimes not. Most people, I suspect, do not go around consciously thinking of people as organic machines, yet those who do not believe in any sort of God actually assume, consciously or not, that that is what they are. Or they assume that they do have some sort of immaterial soul and treat people that way, and are thus simply inconsistent in their worldview. Some people who do not believe in anything supernatural at all wonder whether they will be reincarnated. So, third, sometimes our worldviews— both those characterizing small or large communities and those we hold as individuals—are inconsistent.

The foundation on which we live. It is important to note that our own worldview may not be what we think it is. It is rather what we show it to be by our words and actions. Our worldview generally lies so deeply embedded in our subconscious that unless we have reflected long and hard, we are unaware of what it is. Even when think we know what it is and lay it out clearly in neat propositions and clear stories, we may well be wrong. Our very actions may belie our self-knowledge.

Because this book focuses on the main worldview systems held by very large numbers of people, this private element of worldview analysis will not receive much further commentary. If we want clarity about our own worldview, however, we must reflect and profoundly consider how we actually behave.

SEVEN BASIC QUESTIONS

If a worldview can be expressed in propositions, what might they be? Essentially, they are our basic, rock-bottom answers to the following seven questions:

1. *What is prime reality—the really real?* To this we might answer: God, or the gods, or the material cosmos. Our answer here is the most fundamental.[10] It sets the boundaries for the answers that can consistently be given to the other six questions. This will become clear as we move from worldview to worldview in the chapters that follow.

2. *What is the nature of external reality, that is, the world around us?* Here our answers point to whether we see the world as created or autonomous, as chaotic or orderly, as matter or spirit; or whether we emphasize our subjective, personal relationship to the world or its objectivity apart from us.

3. *What is a human being?* To this we might answer: a highly complex machine, a sleeping god, a person made in the image of God, a naked ape.

4. *What happens to a person at death?* Here we might reply: personal extinction, or transformation to a higher state, or reincarnation, or departure to a shadowy existence on "the other side."

5. *Why is it possible to know anything at all?* Sample answers include the idea that we are made in the image of an all-knowing God or that consciousness and rationality developed under the contingencies of survival in a long process of evolution.

6. *How do we know what is right and wrong?* Again, perhaps we are made in the image of a God whose character is good, or right and wrong are determined by human choice alone or what feels good, or

---

[10]Sire, *Naming the Elephant*, chap. 3.

the notions simply developed under an impetus toward cultural or physical survival.

7. *What is the meaning of human history?* To this we might answer: to realize the purposes of God or the gods, to make a paradise on earth, to prepare a people for a life in community with a loving and holy God, and so forth.

Earlier editions of this book listed only seven questions, but these do not adequately encompass the notion of a worldview as a *commitment* or *a matter of the heart.* So I am adding the following question to flesh out the personal implications of the rather intellectual and abstract character of the first seven questions.

8. *What personal, life-orienting core commitments are consistent with this worldview?* Within any given worldview, core commitments may vary widely. For example, a Christian might say, to fulfill the will of God, or to seek first the kingdom of God, or to obey God and enjoy him forever, or to be devoted to knowing God or loving God. Each will lead to a somewhat different specific grasp of the Christian worldview. A naturalist might say to realize their personal potential for experiencing life, or to do as much good as they can for others, or to live in a world of inner peace in a world of social diversity and conflict. The question and its answers reveal the variety of ways the intellectual commitments are worked out in individual lives. They recognize the importance of seeing one's own worldview not only within the context of vastly different worldviews but within the community of one's own worldview. Each person, in other words, ends up having his or her own take on reality. And though it is extremely useful to identify the nature of a few (say, five to ten) generic worldviews, it is necessary in identifying and assessing one's own worldview to pay attention to its unique features, the most important of which is one's own answer to this eighth question.[11]

Within various basic worldviews other issues often arise. For example: Who is in charge of this world—God or humans or no one at all? Are we as

---

[11]For an approach to worldview analysis with an even more individual and personal focus, see J. H. Bavinck, *The Church Between Temple and Mosque* (Grand Rapids: Eerdmans, n.d. [reprinted 1981]). Bavinck examines alternate worldviews from five foci: (1) I and the cosmos, (2) I and the norm, (3) I and the riddle of my existence, (4) I and salvation, and (5) I and the Supreme power.

human beings determined or free? Are we alone the maker of values? Is God really good? Is God personal or impersonal? Or does he, she or it exist at all?

When stated in such a sequence, these questions boggle the mind. Either the answers are obvious to us and we wonder why anyone would bother to ask such questions, or else we wonder how any of them can be answered with any certainty. If we feel the answers are too obvious to consider, then we have a worldview, but we have no idea that many others do not share it. We should realize that we live in a pluralistic world. What is obvious to us may be "a lie from hell" to our neighbor next door. If we do not recognize that, we are certainly naive and provincial, and we have much to learn about living in today's world. Alternatively, if we feel that none of the questions can be answered without cheating or committing intellectual suicide, we have already adopted a sort of worldview. The latter is a form of skepticism which in its extreme form leads to nihilism.

The fact is that we cannot avoid assuming some answers to such questions. We will adopt either one stance or another. Refusing to adopt an explicit worldview will turn out to be itself a worldview, or at least a philosophic position. In short, we are caught. So long as we live, we will live either the examined or the unexamined life. It is the assumption of this book that the examined life is better.

So the following chapters—each of which examines a major worldview—are designed to illuminate the possibilities. We will examine the answers each worldview gives to the eight basic questions. This will give us a consistent approach to each one, help us see their similarities and differences, and suggest how each might be evaluated within its own frame of reference as well as from the standpoint of other competing worldviews.

The worldview I have adopted will be detected early in the course of the argument. But to waylay any guessing, I will declare now that it is the subject of the next chapter. Nonetheless, the book is not intended as a revelation of my worldview but an exposition and critique of the options. If in the course of this examination readers find, modify or make more explicit their own individual worldview, a major goal of this book will have been reached.

There are many verbal or conceptual universes. Some have been around a long time; others are just now forming. Which is your universe? Which are the universes next door?

Chapter 2

A UNIVERSE CHARGED WITH THE GRANDEUR OF GOD

CHRISTIAN THEISM

The world is charged with the grandeur of God.
It will flame out, like shining from shook foil;
It gathers to a greatness, like the ooze of oil
Crushed. Why do men then now not reck his rod?

GERARD MANLEY HOPKINS, "GOD'S GRANDEUR"

In the Western world up to the end of the seventeenth century, the theistic worldview was clearly dominant. Intellectual squabbles—and there were as many then as now—were mostly family squabbles. Dominicans might disagree with Jesuits, Jesuits with Anglicans, Anglicans with Presbyterians, ad infinitum, but all these parties subscribed to the same set of basic presuppositions. The triune personal God of the Bible existed; he had revealed himself to us and could be known; the universe was his creation; human beings were his special creation. If battles were fought, the lines were drawn within the circle of theism.

How, for example, do we know God? By reason, by revelation, by faith, by contemplation, by proxy, by direct access? This battle was fought on many fronts over a dozen centuries and is still an issue with those remaining on the theistic field. Or take another issue: Is the basic stuff of the universe matter only, form only or a combination? Theists have differed on this too. What role does human freedom play in a universe where God is sovereign? Again, a family squabble.

During the period from the early Middle Ages to the end of the seventeenth century, very few challenged the existence of God or held that ultimate reality was impersonal or that death meant individual extinction. The reason is obvious. Christianity had so penetrated the Western world that whether or not people believed in Christ or acted as Christians should, they all lived in a context of ideas influenced and informed by the Christian faith. Even those who rejected the faith often lived in fear of hellfire or the pangs of purgatory. Bad people may have rejected Christian goodness, but they knew themselves to be bad by basically Christian standards—crudely understood, no doubt, but Christian in essence. The theistic presuppositions that lay behind their values came with their mother's milk.

This, of course, is no longer true. Being born in the Western world now guarantees nothing. Worldviews have proliferated. Walk down a street of any major city in Europe or North America and the next person you meet could adhere to any one of a dozen distinctly different patterns of understanding what life is all about. Little seems bizarre to us, which makes it more and more difficult for talk-show hosts to get good ratings by shocking their television audiences.

Consider the problem of growing up today. Baby Jane, a twentieth- and twenty-first-century child of the Western world, often gets reality defined in two widely divergent forms—her mother's and father's. Then if the family breaks apart, the court may enter with a third definition of human reality. This poses a distinct problem for deciding what the shape of the world actually is.

Baby John, a child of the seventeenth century, was cradled in a cultural consensus that gave a sense of place. The world around was really there—created to be there by God. As God's vice regent, young John sensed that he and other human beings had been given dominion over the world. He was required to worship God, but God was eminently worthy of worship. He was required to obey God, but then obedience to God was true freedom since that was what people were made for. Besides, God's yoke was easy and his burden light. Furthermore, God's rules were seen as primarily moral, and people were free to be creative over the external universe, free to learn its secrets, free to shape and fashion it as God's stewards cultivating God's garden and offering up their work as true worship before a God who honors his creation with freedom and dignity.

There was a basis for both meaning and morality and also for the question of identity. The apostles of absurdity were yet to arrive. Even Shakespeare's King Lear (perhaps the English Renaissance's most "troubled" hero) does not end in total despair. And Shakespeare's later plays suggest that he himself had passed well beyond the moment of despair and found the world to be ultimately meaningful.

It is fitting, therefore, that we begin a study of worldviews with theism. It is the foundational view, the one from which all others developing between 1700 and 1900 essentially derive. It would be possible to go behind theism to Greco-Roman classicism, but even this as it was reborn in the Renaissance was seen almost solely within the framework of theism.[1]

BASIC CHRISTIAN THEISM

As the core of each chapter I will try to express the essence of each worldview in a minimum number of succinct propositions. Each worldview considers the following basic issues: the nature and character of God or ultimate reality, the nature of the universe, the nature of humanity, the question of what happens to a person at death, the basis of human knowing, the basis of ethics and the meaning of history.[2] In the case of theism, the prime proposition concerns the nature of God. Since this first proposition is so important, we will spend more time with it than with any other.

---

[1]One of the most fascinating studies of this is Jean Seznec, *The Survival of the Pagan Gods* (New York: Harper & Row, 1961), which argues that the Greek gods became "Christianized"; that, as Julian the Apostate said, "Thou hast conquered, O Pale Galilean."

[2]Several books on the Christian worldview have been published since the earlier editions of the present book. Especially notable are Arthur F. Holmes, *Contours of a Christian World View* (Grand Rapids: Eerdmans, 1983); Arthur F. Holmes, ed., *The Making of a Christian Mind* (Downers Grove, Ill.: InterVarsity Press, 1985); W. Gary Phillips and William E. Brown, *Making Sense of Your World from a Biblical Viewpoint* (Chicago: Moody Press, 1991); Brian Walsh and Richard Middleton, *The Transforming Vision: Shaping a Christian World View* (Downers Grove, Ill.: InterVarsity Press, 1984); and Richard Middleton and Brian Walsh, *Truth Is Stranger Than It Used to Be* (Downers Grove, Ill.: InterVarsity Press, 1995). My own *Discipleship of the Mind* (Downers Grove, Ill.: InterVarsity Press, 1990) elaborates themes from the present chapter. Most recent are David Naugle, *Worldview: The History of a Concept* (Grand Rapids: Eerdmans, 2002); Nancy Pearcey, *Total Truth: Liberating Christianity from Its Cultural Captivity* (Wheaton, Ill.: Crossway, 20040; J. Mark Bertrand, *(Re)thinking Worldview: Learning to Think, Live and Speak in This World* (Wheaton, Ill.: Crossway, 2007); Charles H. Kraft, *Worldview for Christian Witness* (Pasadena, Calif.: William Carey Library Publishers, 2008); and Paul G. Hiebert, *Transforming Worldviews: An Anthropological Understanding of How People Change* (Grand Rapids: Baker Academic, 2008).

1. Worldview Question 1: *Prime reality is the infinite, personal God revealed in the Holy Scriptures. This God is triune, transcendent and immanent, omniscient, sovereign, and good.*[3]

Let's break this proposition down into its parts.

God is infinite. This means that he is beyond scope, beyond measure, as far as we are concerned. No other being in the universe can challenge him in his nature. All else is secondary. He has no twin but is alone the be-all and end-all of existence. He is, in fact, the only self-existent being,[4] as he spoke to Moses out of the burning bush: "I AM WHO I AM" (Ex 3:14). He *is* in a way that none else is. As Moses proclaimed, "Hear, O Israel: The LORD our God is one LORD" (Deut 6:4 KJV). So God is the one prime existent, the one prime reality and, as will be discussed at some length later, the one source of all other reality.

God is personal. This means God is not mere force or energy or existent "substance." God is personal. Personality requires two basic characteristics: self-reflection and self-determination. In other words, God is personal in that he knows himself to be (he is self-conscious) and he possesses the characteristics of self-determination (he "thinks" and "acts").

One implication of the personality of God is that he is like us. In a way, this puts the cart before the horse. Actually, we are like him, but it is helpful to put it the other way around at least for a brief comment. He is like us. That means there is Someone ultimate who is there to ground our highest aspirations, our most precious possession—personality. But more on this under proposition 3.

Another implication of the personality of God is that God is not a simple unity, an integer. He has attributes, characteristics. He is a unity, yes, but a unity of complexity.

Actually, in Christian theism (not Judaism or Islam) *God is not only personal but triune.* That is, "within the one essence of the Godhead we

---

[3]One classic Protestant definition of God is found in the Westminster Confession 2.1.
[4]For a consideration of the theistic concept of God from the standpoint of academic philosophy, see Étienne Gilson, *God and Philosophy* (New Haven: Yale University Press, 1941); E. L. Mascall, *He Who Is: A Study in Traditional Theism* (London: Libra, 1943); H. P. Owen, *Concepts of Deity* (London: Macmillan, 1971), pp. 1-48. Other metaphysical issues dealt with here are discussed in William Hasker, *Metaphysics* (Downers Grove, Ill.: InterVarsity Press, 1983); C. Stephen Evans, *Philosophy of Religion* (Downers Grove, Ill.: InterVarsity Press, 1985);Thomas V. Morris, *Our Idea of God* (Downers Grove, Ill.: InterVarsity Press, 1991); J. P. Moreland and William Lane Craig, *Philosophical Foundations for a Christian Worldview* (Downers Grove, Ill: InterVarsity Press, 2003).

have to distinguish three 'persons' who are neither three gods on the one side, not three parts or modes of God on the other, but coequally and coeternally God."[5] The Trinity is certainly a great mystery, and I cannot even begin to elucidate it now. What is important here is to note that the

---

There is but one living and true God, who is infinite in being and perfection, a most pure spirit, invisible, without body, parts or passions, immutable, immense, eternal, incomprehensible, almighty; most wise, most holy, most free, most absolute, working all things according to the counsel of his own immutable and most righteous will, for his own glory; most loving, gracious, merciful, long-suffering, abundant in goodness and truth, forgiving iniquity, transgression and sin; the rewarder of them that diligently seek him; and withal most just and terrible in his judgments; hating all sin, and who will by no means clear the guilty.
WESTMINSTER CONFESSION 2.1

Trinity confirms the communal, "personal" nature of ultimate being. God is not only there—an actually existent being; he is personal and we can relate to him in a personal way. To know God, therefore, means knowing more than that he exists. It means knowing him as we know a brother or, better, our own father.

God is transcendent. This means God is beyond us and our world. He is *otherly.* Look at a stone: God is not it; God is beyond it. Look at a man: God is not he; God is beyond him. Yet God is not so beyond that he bears no relation to us and our world. It is likewise true that *God is immanent,* and this means that he is with us. Look at a stone: God is present. Look at a person: God is present. Is this, then, a contradiction? Is theism nonsense at this point? I think not.

My daughter Carol, when she was five years old, taught me a lot here. She and her mother were in the kitchen, and her mother was teaching her about God's being everywhere. So Carol asked, "Is God in the living room?"

"Yes," her mother replied.

"Is he in the kitchen?"

---

[5]Geoffrey W. Bromiley, "The Trinity," in *Baker's Dictionary of Theology,* ed. Everett F. Harrison (Grand Rapids: Baker, 1960), p. 531.

"Yes," she said.

"Am I stepping on God?"

My wife was speechless. But look at the point that was raised. Is God *here* in the same way a stone or a chair or a kitchen is here? No, not quite. God is immanent, here, everywhere, in a sense completely in line with his transcendence. For God is not matter like you and me, but Spirit. And yet he is here. In the New Testament book of Hebrews Jesus Christ is said to be "sustaining all things by his powerful word" (Heb 1:3). That is, God is beyond all, yet in all and sustaining all.

God is omniscient. This means that God is all-knowing. He is the alpha and the omega and knows the beginning from the end (Rev 22:13). He is the ultimate source of all knowledge and all intelligence. He is *He Who Knows*. The author of Psalm 139 expresses beautifully his amazement at God's being everywhere, preempting him—knowing him even as he was being formed in his mother's womb.

God is sovereign. This is really a further ramification of God's infiniteness, but it expresses more fully his concern to rule, to pay attention, as it were, to all the actions of his universe. It expresses the fact that nothing is beyond God's ultimate interest, control and authority.

God is good. This is the prime statement about God's character.[6] From it flow all others. To be good means to *be* good. God *is* goodness. That is, *what* he is is good. There is no sense in which goodness surpasses God or God surpasses goodness. As being is the essence of his nature, goodness is the essence of his character.

God's goodness is expressed in two ways, through holiness and through love. Holiness emphasizes his absolute righteousness, which brooks no shadow of evil. As the apostle John says, "God is light; in him there is no darkness at all" (1 Jn 1:5). God's holiness is his separateness from all that smacks of evil. But God's goodness is also expressed as love. In fact, John says, "God is love" (1 Jn 4:16), and this leads God to self-sacrifice and the full extension of his favor to his people, called in the Hebrew Scriptures "the sheep of his pasture" (Ps 100:3).

---

[6]Many people puzzle over the issue of evil. Given both the omniscience and the goodness of God, what is evil and why does it exist? For an extended analysis of the issue, see Peter Kreeft, *Making Sense out of Suffering* (Ann Arbor, Mich.: Servant, 1986), and Henri Blocher, *Evil and the Cross* (Downers Grove, Ill.: InterVarsity Press, 1994). I have addressed this issue in chapters 12 and 13 of *Why Should Anyone Believe Anything at All?* (Downers Grove, Ill.: InterVarsity Press, 1994).

God's goodness means then, first, that there is an absolute and personal standard of righteousness (it is found in God's character) and, second, that there is hope for humanity (because God is love and will not abandon his creation). These twin observations will become especially significant as we trace the results of rejecting the theistic worldview.

2. Worldview Question 2: *External reality is the cosmos God created ex nihilo to operate with a uniformity of cause and effect in an open system.*

God created the cosmos ex nihilo. God is He Who Is, and thus he is the source of all else. Still, it is important to understand that God did not make the universe out of himself. Rather, God spoke it into existence. It came into being by his word: "God said, 'Let there be light,' and there was light" (Gen 1:3). Theologians thus say God "created" (Gen 1:1) the cosmos ex nihilo—out of nothing, not out of himself or from some preexistent chaos (for if it were really "preexistent," it would be as eternal as God).

Second, God created the cosmos as *a uniformity of cause and effect in an open system.* This phrase is a useful piece of shorthand for two key conceptions.[7] First, it signifies that the cosmos was not created to be chaotic. Isaiah states this magnificently:

> For this is what the LORD says—
> he who created the heavens,
>   he is God;
> he who fashioned and made the earth,
>   he founded it;
> he did not create it to be empty [a chaos],[8]
>   but formed it to be inhabited—
> he says:
> "I am the LORD,
>   and there is no other.
> I have not spoken in secret,
>   from somewhere in a land of darkness;
> I have not said to Jacob's descendants,

---

[7]This phrase comes from Francis A. Schaeffer, *He Is There and He Is Not Silent* (Wheaton, Ill.: Tyndale House, 1972), p. 43. Chap. 8 of C. S. Lewis, *Miracles* (London: Fontana, 1960), p. 18, also contains an excellent description of what an open universe involves. Other issues involving a Christian understanding of science are discussed in Del Ratzsch, *Science and Its Limits* (Downers Grove, Ill.: InterVarsity Press, 2000), and Nancy R. Pearcey and Charles Thaxton, *The Soul of Science* (Wheaton, Ill.: Crossway, 1994).

[8]NRSV translation.

'Seek me in vain.'
I, the LORD, speak the truth,
    I declare what is right." (Is 45:18-19)

The universe is orderly, and God does not present us with confusion but with clarity. The nature of God's universe and God's character are thus closely related. This world is as it is at least in part because God is who he is. We will see later how the Fall qualifies this observation. Here it is sufficient to note that there is an orderliness, a regularity, to the universe. We can expect the earth to turn so the sun will "rise" every day.

But another important notion is buried in this shorthand phrase. The system is *open*, and that means it is not programmed. God is constantly involved in the unfolding pattern of the ongoing operation of the universe. And so are we human beings! The course of the world's operation is open to reordering by either. So we find it dramatically reordered in the Fall. Adam and Eve made a choice that had tremendous significance. But God made another choice in redeeming people through Christ.

The world's operation is also reordered by our continued activity after the Fall. Each action of each of us, each decision to pursue one course rather than another, changes or rather "produces" the future. By dumping pollutants into fresh streams, we kill fish and alter the way we can feed ourselves in years to come. By "cleaning up" our streams, we again alter our future. If the universe were not orderly, our decisions would have no effect. If the course of events were determined, our decisions would have no significance. So theism declares that the universe is orderly but not determined. The implications of this become clearer as we consider humanity's place in the cosmos. *The universe is orderly but not determined*

3. Worldview Question 3: *Human beings are created in the image of God and thus possess personality, self-transcendence, intelligence, morality, gregariousness and creativity.*

The key phrase here is "the image of God," a conception highlighted by the fact that it occurs three times in the short space of two verses in Genesis:

Then God said, "Let us make man in our image, in our likeness, and let them rule over the fish of the sea and the birds of the air, over the livestock, over all the earth, and over all the creatures that move along the ground."

So God created man in his own image
in the image of God he created him;
male and female he created them.
(Gen 1:26-27; compare Gen 5:3; 9:6)

That people are made in the image of God means we are like God. We have already noted that God is like us. But the Scriptures really say it the other way. "We are like God" puts the emphasis where it belongs—on the primacy of God.

We are personal because God is personal. That is, we know ourselves to be (we are self-conscious), and we make decisions uncoerced (we pos-

We know ourselves to be (we are self-conscious)

When I look at your heavens, the work of your fingers,
   the moon and the stars that you have established;
what are human beings that you are mindful of them,
   mortals that you care for them?
Yet you have made them a little lower than God,
   and crowned them with glory and honor.

We make decisions uncoerced (we possess self-determination)

You have given them dominion over the works of your hands;
   you have put all things under their feet,
all sheep and oxen,
   and also the beasts of the field,
the birds of the air, and the fish of the sea,
   whatever passes along the paths of the seas. (Ps 8:3-8 NRSV)

---

sess self-determination). We are capable of acting on our own. We do not merely react to our environment but can act according to our own character, our own nature.

No two people are alike, we say. And this is not just because no two people have shared exactly the same heredity and environment but because each of us possesses a unique character out of which we think, desire, weigh consequences, refuse to weigh consequences, indulge, refuse to indulge—in short, choose to act.

In this each person reflects (as an image) the transcendence of God over his universe. God is totally unconstrained by his environment. God is limited (we might say) only by his character. God, being good, cannot lie, be deceived, act with evil intent and so forth. But nothing external to God can possibly constrain him. If he chooses to restore a broken universe, it is because he "wants" to, because, for example, he loves it and wants the best for it. But he is free to do as he wills, and his character (*Who* He Is) controls his will.

So we participate *in part* in a transcendence over our environment. Except at the very extremities of existence—in sickness or physical deprivation (utter starvation, cooped up in darkness for days on end, for example)—a person is not forced to any necessary reaction.

Step on my toe. Must I curse? I may. Must I forgive you? I may. Must I yell? I may. Must I smile? I may. What I do will reflect my character, but it is "I" who will act and not just react like a bell ringing when a button is pushed.

In short, people have personality and are capable of transcending the cosmos in which they are placed in the sense that they can know something of that cosmos and can act significantly to change the course of both human and cosmic events. This is another way of saying that the cosmic system God made is *open* to reordering by human beings.

Personality is the chief thing about human beings, as, I think it is fair to say, it is the chief thing about God, who is infinite both in his personality and in his being. Our personality is grounded in the personality of God. That is, we find our true home in God and in being in close relationship with him. "There is a God-shaped vacuum in the heart of every man," wrote Pascal.[9] "Our hearts are restless till they rest in thee," wrote Augustine.[10]

How does God fulfill our ultimate longing? He does so in many ways: by being the perfect fit for our very nature, by satisfying our longing for interpersonal relationship, by being in his omniscience the end to our search for knowledge, by being in his infinite being the refuge from all fear, by being in his holiness the righteous ground of our quest for justice, by being in his infinite love the cause of our hope for salvation, by being in his infinite creativity both the source of our creative imagination and the ultimate beauty we seek to reflect as we ourselves create.

We can summarize this conception of humankind in God's image by saying that, like God, we have *personality, self-transcendence, intelli-*

---

[9]Pascal *Pensées* 10.148.
[10]Augustine *Confessions* 1.1.1.

gence (the capacity for reason and knowledge), *morality* (the capacity for recognizing and understanding good and evil), *gregariousness* or social capacity (our characteristic and fundamental desire and need for human companionship—community—especially represented by the "male and female" aspect) and *creativity* (the ability to imagine new things or to endow old things with new significance).

We will consider the root of human intelligence below. Here I want to comment on human creativity—a characteristic often lost sight of in popular theism. Human creativity is borne as a reflection of the infinite creativity of God himself. Sir Philip Sidney (1554-1586) once wrote about the poet who, "lifted up with the vigor of his own invention, doth grow, in effect, into another nature, in making things either better than nature bringeth forth, or quite anew, forms such as never were in nature, . . . freely ranging within the zodiac of his own wit." To honor human creativity, Sidney argued, is to honor God, for God is the "heavenly Maker of that maker."[11]

Artists operating within the theistic worldview have a solid basis for their work. Nothing is more freeing than for them to realize that because they are like God they can really invent. Artistic inventiveness is a reflection of God's unbounded capacity to create.

In Christian theism human beings are indeed dignified. In the psalmist's words, they are "a little lower than the heavenly beings," for God himself has made them that way and has crowned them "with glory and honor" (Ps 8:5). Human dignity is in one way not our own; contrary to Protagoras, humanity is not the measure. Human dignity is derived from God. But though it is derived, people do possess it, even if as a gift. Helmut Thielicke says it well: "His [humankind's] greatness rests solely on the fact that God in his incomprehensible goodness has bestowed his love upon him. God does not love us because we are so valuable; we are valuable because God loves us."[12]

So human dignity has two sides. As human beings we are dignified, but we are not to be proud of it, for our dignity is borne as a reflection of the Ultimately Dignified. Yet it *is* a reflection. So people who are theists

[11]Sir Philip Sidney, *The Defense of Poesy*. See also Dorothy L. Sayers, *The Mind of the Maker* (New York: Meridian, 1956), and J. R. R. Tolkien, "On Fairy Stories," in *The Tolkien Reader* (New York: Ballantine, 1966), p. 37.

[12]Helmut Thielicke, *Nihilism*, trans. John W. Doberstein (London: Routledge and Kegan Paul, 1962), p. 110.

see themselves as a sort of midpoint—above the rest of creation (for God has given them dominion over it—Gen 1:28-30; Ps 8:6-8) and below God (for people are not autonomous, not on their own).

This is then the ideal balanced human status. It is in failing to remain in that balance that our troubles arose, and the story of how that happened is very much a part of Christian theism. But before we see what tipped the balanced state of humanity, we need to understand a further implication of being created in the image of God.

4. Worldview Question 5: *Human beings can know both the world around them and God himself because God has built into them the capacity to do so and because he takes an active role in communicating with them.*

The foundation of human knowledge is the character of God as Creator. We are made in his image (Gen 1:27). As he is the all-knowing knower of all things, so we can be the sometimes knowing knowers of some things. The Gospel of John puts the concept this way:

> In the beginning was the Word, and the Word was with God, and the Word was God. He was with God in the beginning
>
> Through him all things were made; without him nothing was made that has been made. In him was life, and that life was the light of men. (Jn 1:1-4)

The Word (in Greek *Logos*, from which our word *logic* comes) is eternal, an aspect of God himself.[13] That is, logicality, intelligence, rationality, meaning are all inherent in God. It is out of this intelligence that the world, the universe, came to be. And therefore, because of this source the universe has structure, order and meaning.

Moreover, in the Word—this inherent intelligence—is the "light of men," light being in the book of John a symbol for both moral capacity and intelligence. Verse 9 adds that the Word, "the true light . . . gives light to every man." God's own intelligence is thus the basis of human intelligence. Knowledge is possible because there is something to be known (God and his creation) and someone to know (the omniscient

---

[13]The word *logos* as used in John and elsewhere has a rich context of meaning. See, for example, J. N. Birdsall, "Logos," in *New Bible Dictionary*, 3rd ed. (Downers Grove, Ill.: InterVarsity Press, 1996), pp. 744-45.

God and human beings made in his image).[14]

Of course, God himself is forever so beyond us that we cannot have anything approaching total comprehension of him. In fact, if God desired, he could remain forever hidden. But God wants us to know him, and he takes the initiative in this transfer of knowledge.

In theological terms, this initiative is called revelation. God reveals, or discloses, himself to us in two basic ways: by general revelation and by special revelation. In general revelation God speaks through the created order of the universe. The apostle Paul wrote, "What may be known about God is plain to them [all people], because God has made it plain to them. For since the creation of the world God's invisible qualities—his eternal power and divine nature—have been clearly seen, being understood from what has been made" (Rom 1:19-20). Centuries before that the psalmist wrote,

The heavens declare the glory of God;
    the skies proclaim the work of his hands.
Day after day they pour forth speech;
    night after night they display knowledge. (Ps 19:1-2)

In other words, God's existence and his nature as Creator and powerful sustainer of the universe are revealed in God's prime "handiwork," his universe. As we contemplate the magnitude of this—its orderliness and its beauty—we can learn much about God. When we turn from the universe at large to look at humanity, we see something more, for human beings add the dimension of personality. God, therefore, must be at least as personal as we are.

Thus far can general revelation go, but little further. As Thomas Aquinas said, we can know that God exists through general revelation, but we could never know that God is triune except for special revelation.

Special revelation is God's disclosure of himself in extranatural ways. Not only did he reveal himself by appearing in spectacular forms such as a bush that burns but is not consumed, but he also spoke to people in their own language. To Moses he defined himself as "I AM WHO I AM" and identified himself as the same God who had acted before on behalf of the Hebrew people. He called himself the God of Abraham, Isaac and

---

[14]For more extensive treatments of epistemology from a Christian perspective see Arthur F. Holmes, *All Truth Is God's Truth* (Downers Grove, Ill.: InterVarsity Press, 1977); W. Jay Wood, *Epistemology: Becoming Intellectually Virtuous* (Downers Grove, Ill.: InterVarsity Press, 1998); and chaps. 5-6 in my *Discipleship of the Mind*.

Jacob (Ex 3:1-17). In fact, God carried on a dialogue with Moses in which genuine two-way communication took place. This is one way special revelation occurred.

Later God gave Moses the Ten Commandments and revealed a long code of laws by which the Hebrews were to be ruled. Later yet God revealed himself to prophets from a number of walks of life. His word came to them, and they recorded it for posterity. The New Testament writer of the letter to the Hebrews summed it up this way: "In the past God spoke to our forefathers through the prophets at many times and in various ways" (Heb 1:1). In any case, the revelations to Moses, David and the various prophets were, by command of God, written down and kept to be read over and over to the people (Deut 6:4-8; Ps 119). The cumulative writings grew to become the Old Testament, which was affirmed by Jesus himself as an accurate and authoritative revelation of God.[15]

The writer of the letter to the Hebrews did not end with the summary of God's past revelation. He went on to say, "But in these last days he has spoken to us by his Son, whom he appointed heir of all things. . . . The Son is the radiance of God's glory and the exact representation of his being" (Heb 1:2-3). Jesus Christ is God's ultimate special revelation. Because Jesus Christ was very God of very God, he showed us what God is like more fully than any other form of revelation can. Because Jesus was also completely human, he spoke more clearly to us than any other form of revelation can.

Again the opening of the Gospel of John is relevant. "The Word became flesh and made his dwelling among us, . . . full of grace and truth" (Jn 1:14). That is, the Word is Jesus Christ. "We have seen his glory," John continues, "the glory of the One and Only, who came from the Father." Jesus has made God known to us in very fleshly terms.

The main point for us is that theism declares that God can and has clearly communicated with us. Because of this we can know much about who God is and what he desires for us. That is true for people at all times and all places, but it was especially true before the Fall, to which we now turn.

5. Worldview Question 3: *Human beings were created good, but through the Fall the image of God became defaced, though not so ruined as not to*

---

[15]See John Wenham, *Christ and the Bible*, 2nd ed. (Grand Rapids: Baker, 1984).

be capable of restoration; through the work of Christ, God redeemed humanity and began the process of restoring people to goodness, though any given person may choose to reject that redemption.

Human "history" can be subsumed under four words—*creation, Fall, redemption, glorification.* We have just seen the essential human characteristics. To these we must add that human beings and all the rest of creation were created good. As Genesis records, "God saw all that he had made, and it was very good" (Gen 1:31). Because God by his character sets the standards of righteousness, human goodness consisted in being what God wanted people to be—beings made in the image of God and acting out that nature in their daily life. The tragedy is that we did not stay as we were created.

As we have seen, human beings were created with a capacity for self-determination. God gave them the freedom to remain or not to remain in the close relationship of image to original. As Genesis 3 reports, the original pair, Adam and Eve, chose to disobey their Creator at the only point where the Creator put down limitations. This is the essence of the story of the Fall. Adam and Eve chose to eat the fruit God had forbidden them to eat, and hence they violated the personal relationship they had with their Creator.

In this manner people of all eras have attempted to set themselves up as autonomous beings, arbiters of their own way of life. They have chosen to act as if they had an existence independent from God. But that is precisely what they do not have, for they owe everything—both their origin and their continued existence—to God.

The result of this act of rebellion was death for Adam and Eve. And their death has involved for subsequent generations long centuries of personal, social and natural turmoil. In brief summary, we can say that the image of God in humanity was defaced in all its aspects. In *personality,* we lost our capacity to know ourselves accurately and to determine our own course of action freely in response to our intelligence.

Our *self-transcendence* was impaired by alienation from God, for as Adam and Eve turned from God, God let them go. And as we, humankind, slipped from close fellowship with the ultimately transcendent One, we lost our ability to stand over against the external universe, understand it, judge it accurately and thus make truly "free" decisions. Rather, humanity became more a servant to nature than to God. And our status as God's vice regent over nature (an aspect of the image of God) was reversed.

Human *intelligence* also became impaired. Now we can no longer gain a fully accurate knowledge of the world around us, nor are we able to reason without constantly falling into error. *Morally,* we became less able to discern good and evil and less able to live by the standards we do perceive. *Socially,* we began to exploit other people. *Creatively,* our imagination became separated from reality; imagination became illusion, and artists who created gods in their own image led humanity further and further from its origin. The vacuum in each human soul created by this string of consequences is ominous indeed. (The fullest biblical expression of these ideas is Rom 1–2.)

Theologians have summed it up this way: we have become alienated from God, from others, from nature and even from ourselves. This is the essence of *fallen* humanity.[16]

But humanity is redeemable and has been redeemed. The story of creation and fall is told in three chapters of Genesis. The story of redemption takes up the rest of the Scriptures. The Bible records God's love for us in searching us out, finding us in our lost, alienated condition, and redeeming us by the sacrifice of his own Son, Jesus Christ, the Second Person of the Trinity. God, in unmerited favor and great grace, has granted us the possibility of a new life, a life involving substantial healing of our alienations and restoration to fellowship with God.

> We all, like sheep, have gone astray;
>   each of us has turned to his own way;
> And the LORD has laid on him
>   the iniquity of us all. (Is 53:6)

That God has provided a way back for us does not mean we play no role. Adam and Eve were not forced to fall. We are not forced to return. While it is not the purpose of this description of theism to take sides in a famous family squabble within Christian theism (predestination versus free will), it is necessary to note that Christians disagree on precisely what role God takes and what role he leaves us. Still, most would agree that God is the primary agent in salvation. Our role is to respond by repentance for our wrong attitudes and acts, to accept God's provi-

---

[16]See, for example, the discussion of the Fall and its effects in Francis A. Schaeffer's *Genesis in Space and Time* (Downers Grove, Ill.: InterVarsity Press, 1972), pp. 69-101.

sions and to follow Christ as Lord as well as Savior.

Redeemed humanity is humanity on the way to restoration of the defaced image of God, in other words, substantial healing in every area—personality, self-transcendence, intelligence, morality, social capacity and creativity. *Glorified* humanity is humanity totally healed and at peace with God, and individuals at peace with others and themselves. But this happens only on the other side of death and the bodily resurrection, the importance of which is stressed by Paul in 1 Corinthians 15. Individual people are so important that they retain uniqueness—a personal and individual existence—forever. Glorified humanity is humanity transformed into a purified personality in fellowship with God and God's people. In short, in theism human beings are seen as significant because they are essentially godlike and though fallen can be restored to original dignity.

6. Worldview Question 4: *For each person death is either the gate to life with God and his people or the gate to eternal separation from the only thing that will ultimately fulfill human aspirations.*

The meaning of death is really part of proposition 5, but it is singled out here because attitudes to death are so important in every worldview. What happens when a person dies? Let's put it personally, for this aspect of one's worldview is indeed most personal. Do I disappear—personal extinction? Do I hibernate and return in a different form—reincarnation? Do I continue in a transformed existence in heaven or hell?

Christian theism clearly teaches the last of these. At death people are transformed. Either they enter an existence with God and his people—a glorified existence—or they enter an existence forever separated from God, holding their uniqueness in awful loneliness apart from precisely that which would fulfill them.

And that is the essence of hell. G. K. Chesterton once remarked that hell is a monument to human freedom—and, we might add, human dignity. Hell is God's tribute to the freedom he gave each of us to choose whom we would serve; it is a recognition that our decisions have a significance that extends far down into the reaches of foreverness.[17]

Those who respond to God's offer of salvation, however, people the plains of eternity as glorious creatures of God—completed, fulfilled but

---

[17]To pursue the biblical teaching on this subject see John Wenham, *The Enigma of Evil* (Grand Rapids: Zondervan, 1985), pp. 27-41.

not sated, engaged in the ever-enjoyable communion of the saints. The Scriptures give little detail about this existence, but its glimpses of heaven in Revelation 4–5 and 21, for example, create a longing Christians expect to be fulfilled beyond their fondest desires.

7. Worldview Question 6: *Ethics is transcendent and is based on the character of God as good (holy and loving).*

This proposition has already been considered as an implication of proposition 1. God is the source of the moral world as well as the physical world. God is good and expresses this in the laws and moral principles he has revealed in Scripture.

Made in God's image, we are essentially moral beings, and thus we cannot refuse to bring moral categories to bear on our actions. Of course, our sense of morality has been flawed by the Fall, and now we only brokenly reflect the truly good. Yet even in our moral relativity, we cannot get rid of the sense that some things are "right" or "natural" and others not.

For years homosexual behavior was considered immoral by most of society. Now a large number of people challenge this. But they do so not on the basis that no moral categories exist but that this one area—homosexuality—really ought to have been on the other side of the line dividing the moral from the immoral. Homosexuals do not usually condone incest! So the fact that people differ in their moral judgments does nothing to alter the fact that we continue to make, to live by and to violate moral judgments. Everyone lives in a moral universe, and virtually everyone—if they reflect on it—recognizes this and would have it no other way.

Theism, however, teaches that not only is there a moral universe but there is an absolute standard by which all moral judgments are measured. God himself—his character of goodness (holiness and love)—is the standard. Furthermore, Christians and Jews hold that God has revealed his standard in the various laws and principles expressed in the Bible. The Ten Commandments, the Sermon on the Mount, the apostle Paul's ethical teaching—in these and many other ways God has expressed his character to us. There is thus a standard of right and wrong, and people who want to know it can know it.

The fullest embodiment of the good, however, is Jesus Christ. He is the complete man, humanity as God would have it be. Paul calls him the second Adam (1 Cor 15:45-49). And in Jesus we see the good life incarnate. Jesus' good life was supremely revealed in his death—an act of infinite love, for as Paul says, "Very rarely will anyone die for a righteous man. . . . But God demonstrates his own love for us in this: While we were still sinners, Christ died for us" (Rom 5:7-8). And the apostle John echoes, "This is love: not that we loved God, but that he loved us and sent his Son as an atoning sacrifice for our sins" (1 Jn 4:10).

So ethics, while very much a human domain, is ultimately the business of God. We are not the measure of morality. God is.

8. Worldview Question 7: *History is linear, a meaningful sequence of events leading to the fulfillment of God's purposes for humanity.*

"History is linear" means that the actions of people—as confusing and chaotic as they appear—are part of a meaningful sequence that has a beginning, a middle and an end. History is not reversible, not repeatable, not cyclic; history is not meaningless. Rather, history is teleological, going somewhere, directed toward a known end. The God who knows the end from the beginning is aware of and sovereign over the actions of humankind.

Several basic turning points in the course of history are singled out for special attention by biblical writers, and these form the background for the theistic understanding of human beings in time. These turning points include the creation, the fall into sin, the revelation of God to the Hebrews (which includes the calling of Abraham from Ur to Canaan, the exodus from Egypt, the giving of the law, the witness of the prophets), the incarnation, the life of Jesus, the crucifixion and resurrection, Pentecost, the spread of the good news via the church, the second coming of Christ and the final judgment. This is a slightly more detailed list of events paralleling the pattern of human life: creation, fall, redemption, glorification.

Looked at in this way, history itself is a form of revelation. That is, not only does God reveal himself in history *(here, there, then)*, but the very sequence of events is revelation. One can say, therefore, that history (especially as localized in the Jewish people) is the record of the involvement and concern of God in human events. History is the divine purpose of God in concrete form.

This pattern is, of course, dependent on the Christian tradition. It does not at first appear to take into account people other than Jews and Christians. Yet the Old Testament has much to say about the nations surrounding Israel and about God-fearers (non-Jewish people who adopted Jewish beliefs and were considered a part of God's promise). And the New Testament stresses even more the international dimension of God's purposes and his reign.

The revelation of God's design took place primarily through one people—the Jews. And while we may say with William Ewer, "How odd / Of God / To choose / The Jews," we need not think that doing so indicates favoritism on God's part. Peter once said, "God does not show favoritism but accepts men from every nation who fear him and do what is right" (Acts 10:34-35).

Theists look forward, then, to history's being closed by judgment and a new age inaugurated beyond time. But prior to that new age, time is irreversible and history is localized in space. This conception needs to be stressed, since it differs dramatically from the typically Eastern notion. To much of the East, time is an illusion; history is eternally cyclic. Reincarnation brings a soul back into time again and again; progress in the soul's journey is long, arduous, perhaps eternal. But in Christian theism, "man is destined to die once, and after that to face judgment" (Heb 9:27). An individual's choices have meaning to that person, to others and to God. History is the result of those choices that, under the sovereignty of God, bring about God's purposes for this world.

In short, the most important aspect of the theistic concept of history is that history has meaning because God—the Logos, meaning itself—is behind all events, not only "sustaining all things by his powerful word" (Heb 1:3) but also "in all things . . . [working] for the good of those who love him, who have been called according to his purpose" (Rom 8:28). Behind the apparent chaos of events stands the loving God sufficient for all.

CORE COMMITMENT

What then fuels the fire of consistent Christian theists? What provides the driving motive for their lives?

9. Worldview Question 8: *Christian theists live to seek first the kingdom of God, that is, to glorify God and enjoy him forever.*

The Christian worldview is unique in many ways, but not the least of which is the way in which it serves as the focus for the ultimate meaning of life, not just the meaning of human history or human existence in the abstract, but the meaning of life for each Christian. As God himself is the really real, the ultimate ground of being and the creator of all being other than himself, so devoted Christians live not for themselves but for God. "What is the chief end of man?" asks the Westminster Shorter Catechism.[18] And the answer is "to glorify God and enjoy him forever." To glorify God is not just to do so in religious worship, singing praise and enacting the traditional rites of the church. To glorify God is to reveal his character by being who we were created to be—the embodiment of the image of God in human form. When we are like him, we glorify him. And what is he like? He is not just the awesome I AM, shaking the heavens and the earth with his thunderous voice and transcendent being. He is Jesus. He is Immanuel, "God with us." To be like Jesus, then, is to be like God who is himself all the glory there is.

Jesus came proclaiming the kingdom of God, embodying in his earthly existence the presence of the Father's kingdom (Mk 1:14). We are to imitate him, to obey his command to "seek first his kingdom and his righteousness" (Mt 6:33). Lo and behold, when we do this we both avoid the tragic consequences of selfishness and pride and receive what really fulfills our lives. All the happiness and joy we seek when we substitute our desires for God's glory comes to us as a result of yielding our will to his. Human flourishing, then, while not being a primary goal, is a result of turning one's attention toward God and his glory.[19] "All these things will be given to you as well," Jesus said in the Sermon on the Mount (Mt 6:33). To glorify God then, as the catechism says, is to enjoy him forever.

There are, of course, other ways to personalize this core commitment. Some Christians say it is to obey God; or to love God with all their heart, mind, soul and strength and their neighbors as themselves; or to lose their lives for the sake of the gospel. Others may cast their answers in rather unique ways, but if these answers truly reflect a grasp and commitment to the Christian understanding of reality, they will emphasize the centrality of God and his good pleasure in what they say. They will not point first of all to happiness; happiness or joy will be a consequence, not a goal. Life is all about God, they will say, not about themselves.

---

[18]Westminster Shorter Catechism, Question 1.

[19]*Human flourishing* is a term frequently used today to describe the proper end toward which human life should be directed. Each worldview, however, has a different conception of just what human flourishing involves and whether it is in any way tied to transcendence. See Charles Taylor, *A Secular Age* (Cambridge, Mass.: Belknap, 2007), pp. 16-20.

THE GRANDEUR OF GOD

It should by now be obvious that Christian theism is primarily dependent on its concept of God, for theism holds that everything stems from him. Nothing is prior to God or equal to him. He is *He Who Is.* Thus theism has a basis for metaphysics. Since He Who Is also has a worthy character and is thus *The Worthy One,* theism has a basis for ethics. Since He Who Is also is *He Who Knows,* theism has a basis for epistemology. In other words, theism is a complete worldview.

So the greatness of God is the central tenet of Christian theism. When a person recognizes this and consciously accepts and acts on it, this central conception is the rock, the transcendent reference point, that gives life meaning and makes the joys and sorrows of daily existence on planet earth significant moments in an unfolding drama in which one expects to participate forever, not always with sorrows but someday with joy alone. Even now, though, the world is, as Gerard Manley Hopkins once wrote, "charged with the grandeur of God."[20] That there are "God adumbrations in many daily forms" signals to us that God is not just in his heaven but with us—sustaining us, loving us and caring for us.[21] Fully cognizant Christian theists, therefore, do not just believe and proclaim this view as true. Their first act is toward God—a response of love, obedience and praise to the Lord of the Universe, their maker, sustainer and, through Jesus Christ, their redeemer and friend.

---

[20]"God's Grandeur," in *The Poems of Gerard Manley Hopkins,* 4th ed., ed. W. H. Gardner and N. H. MacKenzie (New York: Oxford University Press, 1967), p. 66.
[21]Saul Bellow, *Mr. Sammler's Planet* (Greenwich, Conn.: Fawcett, 1970), p. 216.

Chapter 3

THE CLOCKWORK UNIVERSE

DEISM

Say first, of God above or man below,
What can we reason but from what we know?
Of man what see we but his station here
From which to reason, or to which refer?
Through worlds unnumbered though the God be known,
'Tis ours to trace him only in our own.

ALEXANDER POPE, *ESSAY ON MAN*

If theism lasted so long, what could possibly have happened to undermine it? If it satisfactorily answered all our basic questions, provided a refuge for our fears and hope for our future, why did anything else come along? Answers to these questions can be given on many levels. The fact is that many forces operated to shatter the basic intellectual unity of the West.[1]

Deism developed, some say, as an attempt to bring unity out of a chaos of theological and philosophical discussion which in the seventeenth century became bogged down in interminable quarrels over what began to seem even to the disputants like trivial questions. Perhaps John Milton

---

[1] A brief but helpful sketch of the transition from Christian theism to deism can be found in Jonathan Hill, *Faith in the Age of Reason* (Downers Grove, Ill.: InterVarsity Press, 2004). See Charles Taylor's massive *A Secular Age* (Cambridge, Mass.: Belknap, 2007) for a detailed study of the transition from Christian theism through deism to naturalism.

had such questions in mind when he envisioned the fallen angels making
an epic game of philosophical theology:

> Others apart sat on a Hill retir'd
> In thoughts more elevate, and reason'd high
> Of Providence, Foreknowledge, Will and Fate,
> Fixt Fate, Free will, Foreknowledge absolute,
> And found no end, in wandering mazes lost.[2]

After decades of wearying discussion, Lutheran, Puritan and Anglican
divines might well have wished to look again at points of agreement. Deism to some extent is a response to this, though the direction such agreement took put deism rather beyond the limits of traditional Christianity.

Another factor in the development of deism was a change in the location of the authority for knowledge about the divine; it shifted from the
special revelation found in Scripture to the presence of Reason, "the can-
dle of God," in the human mind or to intuition, "the inner light."[3] Why
should such a shift in authority take place?

One of the reasons is especially ironic. It is linked with an implication
of theism which, when it was discovered, was very successfully developed. Through the Middle Ages, due in part to the rather Platonic theory
of knowledge that was held, the attention of theistic scholars and intellectuals was directed toward God. The idea was that knowers in some
sense *become* what they know. And since one should become in some
sense good and holy, one should study God. Theology was thus considered the queen of the *sciences* (which at that time simply meant knowledge), for theology was the science of God.

If people studied animals or plants or minerals (zoology, biology,
chemistry and physics), they were lowering themselves. This hierarchical
view of reality is really more Platonic than theistic or Christian, because
it picks up from Plato the notion that matter is somehow, if not evil, then
at least irrational and certainly not good. Matter is something to be transcended, not to be understood.

But as more biblically oriented minds began to recognize, this is
God's world—all of it. And though it is a fallen world, it has been created by God and has value. It is indeed worth knowing and understand-

---

[2]John Milton *Paradise Lost* 2.557-61.
[3]Avery Cardinal Dulles, in "The Deist Minimum" (*First Things* [January 2005], pp. 25-30),
  gives a remarkably lucid account of the rise and decline of deism.

ing. Furthermore, God is a rational God, and his universe is thus rational, orderly, knowable. Operating on this basis, scientists began investigating the *form* of the universe. A picture of God's world began to emerge; it was seen to be like a huge, well-ordered mechanism, a giant clockwork, whose gears and levers meshed with perfect mechanical precision. Such a picture seemed both to arise from scientific inquiry and to prompt more inquiry and stimulate more discovery about the makeup of the universe. In other words, science as we now know it was born and was amazingly successful.

At the same time, of course, there were those who distrusted the findings of the scientists. The case of Galileo Galilei (1564-1642) is famous and, in a quite distorted form, is often cited today as proof of the antiscientific nature of Christian theism. In fact, Galileo as well as other renaissance scientists such as Nicolaus Copernicus (1473-1543), Francis Bacon (1561-1626) and Johannes Kepler (1571-1630) held fully Christian worldviews.[4] Moreover, in Bacon's words, knowledge became power, power to manipulate and bring creation more fully under human dominion. This view is echoed in modern parlance by J. Bronowski: "I define science as the organization of our knowledge in such a way that it commands more of the hidden potential in nature."[5] If this way of obtaining knowledge about the universe was so successful, why not apply the same method to knowledge about God?

In Christian theism, of course, such a method was already given a role to play, for God was said to reveal himself in nature. The depth of content, however, that was conveyed in such general revelation was considered limited; much more was made known about God in special revelation. But deism denies that God can be known by revelation, by special acts of God's self-expression in, for example, Scripture or the incarnation. Having cast out Aristotle as an authority in matters of science, deism began to cast out Scripture as an authority in theology and to allow only the application of "human" reason. As Peter Medawar says, "The 17th-century doctrine of the *necessity* of reason was slowly giving way to a

---

[4]Nancy R. Pearcey and Charles B. Thaxton point out that "on the whole the Catholic church had no argument with Galileo's theories as science." Rather, it was actually more opposed to "Galileo's attack on Aristotelian philosophy" than to any undermining of Christian belief. See *The Soul of Science: Christian Faith and Natural Philosophy* (Wheaton, Ill.: Crossway Books, 1994), pp. 38-40.

[5]J. Bronowski, *Science and Human Values* (New York: Harper & Row, 1965), p. 7.

belief in the *sufficiency* of reason."[6] Deism thus sees God only in "Nature," by which was meant the system of the universe. And since the system of the universe is seen as a giant clockwork, God is seen as the clockmaker.

In some ways, we can say that limiting knowledge about God to general revelation is like finding that eating eggs for breakfast makes the morning go well, and then eating *only* eggs for breakfast (and maybe lunch and dinner too) for the rest of one's life (which now unwittingly becomes rather shortened!). To be sure, theism assumes that we can know something about God from nature. But it also holds that there is much *more to know* than can be known that way and that there are *other ways to come to know.*

BASIC DEISM

As Frederick Copleston explains, deism historically is not really a "school" of thought. In the late seventeenth and the eighteenth century more than a few thinkers came to be called deists or called themselves

> Whatever God hath revealed is certainly true: no doubt can be made of it. This is the proper object of faith: but whether it be a divine revelation or no, reason must judge; which can never permit the mind to reject a greater evidence to embrace what is less evident, nor allow it to entertain probability in opposition to knowledge and certainty. There can be no evidence that any traditional revelation is of divine original, in the words we receive it, and in the sense we understand it, so clear and so certain as that of the principles of reason: and therefore Nothing that is contrary to, and inconsistent with, the clear and self-evident dictates of reason, has a right to be urged or assented to as a matter of faith, wherein reason hath nothing to do.
>
> **JOHN LOCKE,** *Essay Concerning Human Understanding* 4.18

deists. These men held a number of related views, but not all held every doctrine in common. John Locke (1632-1704), for example, did not re-

[6]Peter Medawar, "On 'The Effecting of All Things Possible,'" *The Listener,* October 2, 1969, p. 438.

ject the idea of revelation, but he did insist that human reason was to be used to judge it.[7] Some *cold* deists, like Voltaire (1694-1778), were hostile to Christianity; some *warm* deists, like Locke, were not.[8] Some, like Benjamin Franklin (1706-1790), believed in the immortality of the soul; some did not. Some believed God left his creation to function on its own; some believed in providence. Some believed in a mildly personal God; others did not. So deists were much less united on basic issues than were theists.[9] Moreover, as we will see below, some forms of popular deism, such as *moralistic therapeutic deism,* are thought of by some people as fully Christian.

Still, it is helpful to think of deism as a system and to state that system in a relatively extreme form, for in that way we will be able to grasp the implications the various "reductions" of theism were beginning to have in the eighteenth century. Naturalism, as we shall see, pushes these implications even further.

1. Worldview Question 1: *A transcendent God, as a First Cause, created the universe but then left it to run on its own. God is thus not immanent, not triune, not fully personal, not sovereign over human affairs, not providential.*

As in theism, the most important proposition regards the existence and character of God. *Warm* deism, such as that of Franklin, who confessed, "I believe in one God, Creator of the Universe. That he governs it by his Providence," retains enough sense of God's personality that Franklin thought this God "ought to be worshipped."[10] But *cold* deism eliminates most features of personality God is said to display. He is only a transcendent force or energy, a Prime Mover or First Cause, a beginning to the otherwise infinite regress of past causes. But he is really not a *he,* though the personal pronoun remains in the language used about him. He does not care for his creation; he does not love it. He has no "personal" relationship to it at all. Certainly he did not become incarnate in Jesus. He is purely monotheistic. As Thomas Paine said, "The only idea man can affix

---

[7]Frederick Copleston, *A History of Philosophy* (London: Burns and Oates, 1961), 5:162-63.

[8]I owe the terms *cold* and *warm* to philosopher Daniel Synnestvedt (private correspondence).

[9]Peter Gay's *Deism: An Anthology* (Princeton, N.J.: D. Van Nostrand, 1968) is a useful collection of writings from a wide variety of deist writers.

[10]Benjamin Franklin, Letter to Ezra Stiles, March 9, 1790 <http://www.franklinpapers.org/franklin/framedNames.jsp>.

to the name of God is *first cause*, the cause of all things."[11]

A modern deist of sorts, Buckminster Fuller, expressed his faith this way: "I have faith in the integrity of the anticipatory intellectual wisdom which we may call 'God.'"[12] But Fuller's God is not a person to be worshiped, merely an intellect or force to be recognized.

To the deist, then, God is distant, foreign, alien. The lonely state this leaves humanity in was, however, not seemingly felt by early deists. Almost two centuries passed before this implication was played out on the field of human emotions.

2. Worldview Question 2: *The cosmos God created is determined, because it is created as a uniformity of cause and effect in a closed system; no miracle is possible.*

In *cold* deism the system of the universe is closed in two senses. First, it is closed to God's reordering, for he is not "interested" in it. He merely brought it to be. Therefore, no miracles or events that reveal any special interests of God are possible. Any tampering or apparent tampering with the machinery of the universe would suggest that God had made a mistake in the original plan, and that would be beneath the dignity of an all-competent deity.

Second, the universe is closed to human reordering because it is locked up in a clocklike fashion. To be able to reorder the system, any human being alone or with others would have to be able to transcend it, get out of the chain of cause and effect. But this we cannot do. We should note, however, that this second implication is not much recognized by deists. Most continue to assume, as we all do apart from reflection, that we can act to change our environment.

3. Worldview Question 3: *Human beings, though personal, are a part of the clockwork of the universe.*

To be sure, deists do not deny that humans are personal. Each of us has self-consciousness and, at least on first glance, self-determination. But these

[11]Thomas Paine, *The Age of Reason*, part 1, chapter 10, first sentence <http://www.infidels.org/library/historical/thomas_paine/age_of_reason/part1.html#10>.

[12]Buckminster Fuller, *Ideas and Integrities*, quoted by Sara Sanborn ("Who Is Buckminster Fuller?" *Commentary*, October 1973, p. 60), who comments that "Fuller's Benevolent Intelligence seems compounded out of the Great Watchmaker of the Deists and Emerson's Over-Soul" (p. 66).

have to be seen in the light of human dimensions only. That is, as human beings we have no essential relation to God—as image to original—and thus we have no way to transcend the system in which we find ourselves.

Bishop François Fénelon (1651-1715), criticizing the deists of his day, wrote, "They credit themselves with acknowledging God as the creator whose wisdom is evident in his works; but according to them, God would be neither good nor wise if he had given man free will—that is, the power to sin, to turn away from his final goal, to reverse the order and be forever lost."[13] Fénelon put his finger on a major problem within deism: human beings have lost their ability to act significantly. If we cannot "reverse the order," then we cannot be significant. We can only be puppets. If an individual has personality, it must then be a type that does not include the element of self-determination.

Deists, of course, recognize that human beings have intelligence (to be sure, they emphasize human reason), a sense of morality (deists are very interested in ethics), a capacity for community and for creativity. But none of these, while built into us as created beings, is grounded in God's character. None has any special relationship to God; each is on its own.

4. Worldview Question 4: *Human beings may or may not have a life beyond their physical existence.*

Here there is a distinction between *warm* and *cold* deists. Deism is the historical result of the decay of robust Christian theism. That is, specific commitments and beliefs of traditional Christianity are gradually abandoned. The first and most significant belief to be eroded was the full personhood and trinitarian nature of God. Reducing God to a force or ultimate intelligence eventually had catastrophic results. In fact, as we shall see, not only naturalism but nihilism is the final result. Were the history of worldviews a matter of the immediate working out of rational implications of a change in the idea of the really real, a belief in an afterlife would have immediately disappeared. But it didn't. Nor did a belief in morality; that took another century. So *warm* deists, those closest to Christian theists, persisted in the notion of an afterlife, and *cold* deists, those further away, did not.

---

[13]François Fénelon, *Lettres sur divers sujets, metaphysique et de religion*, letter 5. Quoted in Émile Bréhier, *The History of Philosophy*, trans. Wade Baskin (Chicago: University of Chicago Press, 1967), 5:14.

5. Worldview Question 5: *Through our innate and autonomous human reason and the methods of science, we can not only know the universe but we can infer at least something of what God is like. The cosmos, this world, is understood to be in its normal state; it is not fallen or abnormal.*

In deism human reason becomes autonomous. That is, without relying on any revelation from the outside—no Scripture, no messages from God via living prophets or dreams and visions—human beings have the ability to know themselves, the universe and even God. As John Locke put it,

> Nothing that is contrary to, and inconsistent with, the clear and self-evident dictates of reason, has a right to be urged or assented to as a matter of faith, wherein reason has nothing to do.[14]

Because the universe is essentially as God created it, and because people have the intellectual capacity to understand the world around them, they can learn about God from a study of his universe. The Scriptures, as we saw above, give a basis for it, for the psalmist wrote, "The heavens declare the glory of God; the skies proclaim the work of his hands" (Ps 19:1). Of course, theists too maintain that God has revealed himself in nature. But for a theist God has also revealed himself in words—in propositional, verbalized revelation to his prophets and the various biblical writers. And, theists maintain, God has also revealed himself in his Son, Jesus—"the Word became flesh" (Jn 1:14). But for deists God does not communicate with people. No special revelation is necessary, and none has occurred.

Émile Bréhier, a historian of philosophy, sums up well the difference between deism and theism:

> We see clearly that a new conception of man, wholly incompatible with the Christian faith, had been introduced: God the architect who produced and maintained a marvelous order in the universe had been discovered in nature, and there was no longer a place for the God of the Christian drama, the God who bestowed upon Adam "the power to sin and to *reverse the order.*" God was in nature and no longer in history; he was in the wonders analyzed by naturalists and biologists and no longer in the human conscience, with feelings of sin, disgrace, or grace that accompanied his presence; he had left man in charge of his own destiny.[15]

---

[14]John Locke, *An Essay Concerning Human Understanding* 4.18.10 (New York: Dover Publications, 1959), 2:425-26.
[15]Bréhier, *History of Philosophy* 5:15.

The God who was discovered by the deists was an architect, but not a lover or a judge or personal in any way. He was not one who acted in history. He simply had left the world alone. But humanity, while in one sense the maker of its own destiny, was yet locked into the closed system. Human freedom from God was not a freedom *to* anything; in fact, it was not a freedom at all.

One tension in deism is found at the opening of Alexander Pope's *Essay on Man* (1732-1734). Pope writes,

> Say first, of God above or man below,
> What can we reason but from what we know?
> Of man what see we but his station here
> From which to reason, or to which refer?
> Through worlds unnumbered though the God be known,
> 'Tis ours to trace him only in our own.[16]

These six lines state that we can know God only through studying the world around us. We learn from data and proceed from the specific to the general. Nothing is revealed to us outside that which we experience. Then Pope continues,

> He who through vast immensity can pierce,
> See worlds on worlds compose one universe,
> Observe how system into system runs,
> What other planets circle other suns,
> What varied being peoples ev'ry star,
> May tell why heav'n has made us as we are.
> But of this frame the bearings and the ties,
> The strong connections, nice dependencies,
> Gradations just, has thy pervading soul
> Looked through? or can a part contain the whole?[17]

Pope assumes here a knowledge of God and of nature that is not capable of being gained by experience. He even admits this as he challenges us as readers on whether we really have "looked through" the universe and seen its clockwork. But if we haven't seen it, then presumably neither has Pope. How then does Pope know it is a vast, all-ordered clockwork?

One can't have it both ways. Either (1) all knowledge comes from expe-

---

[16]Alexander Pope, *Essay on Man* 1.17-22.
[17]Ibid., lines 23-32; cf. lines 233-58.

rience and we, not being infinite, cannot know the system as a whole, or (2) some knowledge comes from another source—for example, from innate ideas built into us or from revelation from the outside. But Pope, like most deists, discounts revelation. So we have a tension in Pope's epistemology. And it was just such tensions that made eighteenth-century deism an unstable worldview.

6. Worldview Question 6: *Ethics is intuitive or limited to general revelation; because the universe is normal, it reveals what is right.*

Deism's ethics in general is founded on the notion that built into human nature is the capacity to sense the difference between good and evil. Human reason is not "fallen" as in Christian theism; so when it is employed by people of good will, it results in moral discernment. Of course, human beings are free not to do what they discern as good; evil then is a result of human beings not conforming to their inherent nature.[18]

So much for human good and evil. But what about natural evil? Natural events—floods, hurricanes, earthquakes—bring disaster, massive pain and suffering to so many. Deists do not consider either human reason or the universe itself to be "fallen." Rather it is in its normal state. How, then, can the normal universe in which we experience so much tragedy still be good? Isn't God, the omnipotent Creator, responsible for everything as it is? Doesn't this world reflect either what God wants or what he is like? Is God, then, really good?

While it is probably unfair to charge deism itself with the confusion illustrated by Alexander Pope, it is instructive to see what can happen when the implications of deism are exposed. Pope writes:

All nature is but art, unknown to thee;
All chance, direction which thou canst not see;
All discord, harmony not understood;
All partial evil, universal good;
And, spite of pride, in erring reason's spite,
One truth is clear, WHATEVER IS, IS RIGHT.[19]

This position ends in destroying ethics. If whatever is is right, then

---

[18]From the standpoint of Christian theism there is much to commend in this notion of *natural law*. C. S. Lewis bases his opening argument in *Mere Christianity* on the universality of the notion of good and evil.

[19]Alexander Pope, *Essay on Man* 1.289-94.

there is no evil. Good becomes indistinguishable from evil. As Charles Baudelaire (1821-1867) said, "If God exists, he must be the devil." Or, worse luck, there must not be *good* at all. For without the ability to distinguish, there can be neither one nor the other, neither good nor evil. Ethics disappears.

It is surely necessary to point out that not all deists saw (or now see) that their assumptions entail Pope's conclusions. Some felt, in fact, that Jesus' ethical teachings were really natural law expressed in words. And, of course, the Sermon on the Mount does not contain anything like the proposition "Whatever is, is right." A deeper study of the deists would, I believe, lead to the conclusion that these early deists simply were inconsistent and did not recognize it.

Alexander Pope himself is inconsistent, for while he held that whatever is is right, he also berated humanity for pride (which, if it is, must be right!).

> In pride, in reas'ning pride our error lies;
> All quit their sphere and rush into the skies.
> Pride still aiming at blessed abodes;
> Men would be angels, angels would be gods. . . .
> And who but wishes to invert the laws
> Of order sins against th' Eternal Cause.[20]

For a person to think of himself more highly than he ought was pride. Pride was wrong, even a *sin*. Yet note: a sin not against a personal God but against the "Eternal Cause," against a philosophic abstraction. Even the word *sin* takes on a new color in such a context. More important, however, the whole notion of sin must disappear if one holds on other grounds that whatever is, is right.

7. Worldview Question 7: *History is linear, for the course of the cosmos was determined at creation. Still the meaning of the events of history remains to be understood by the application of human reason to the data unearthed and made available to historians.*

If deists were to be consistent to the clockmaker/clockwork metaphor, they would be little interested in history. As Bréhier has pointed out, they sought knowledge of God primarily in nature as understood in the grow-

---

[20]Ibid., lines 123-26, 129-30.

ing content of natural science. The course of Jewish history as recorded
in the Bible was largely dismissed as legend, at least partially because it
insisted on God's direct action on and among his chosen people. The accounts of both Testaments are filled with miracles. The deists say miracles can't happen. Thomas Jefferson (1743-1826), for example, produced
The Life and Morals of Jesus, better known as The Jefferson Bible. His
popular version excluded narratives of all the miracles. By such a proce-
dure the Bible became largely discounted as giving insight into God or
human beings or, especially, the natural order. Jefferson became the
judge of what could be true or worthy of belief. At best the biblical narratives were illustrations of divine law from which ethical principles could
be derived. Then too H. S. Reimarus (1694-1768) attempted "to recon-
struct the life and preaching of Jesus with the tools of critical history."[21]
And John Toland (1670-1722) argued that Christianity was as old as creation; the gospel was a "republication" of the religion of nature. With
views like those, even the specific acts of history are not important for
true religion. The stress is on general rules. As Pope says, "The first Almighty Cause / Acts not by partial but by gen'ral laws."[22] God is quite
uninterested in individual men and women or even whole peoples. Besides, the universe is closed, not open to his reordering at all.

Nonetheless intellectuals, historians and philosophers with a basically
deistic bent were, as Synnestvedt says, "fascinated by history." He cites
major works by seven major deistic scholars, including a *History of England* by David Hume (1711-1776), *The History of the Decline and Fall of
the Roman Empire* by Edward Gibbon (1737-1794) and *Sketch for a Historical Picture of the Progress of the Human Mind* by Marie Jean Antoine
Nicolas Caritat, marquis de Condorcet (1743-1794).[23] All of these "histories" are, of course, based totally on the autonomy of human reason; none
of them appeal to perspectives derived from revelation. As a result they
display a wide variety of interpretations of the meaning and significance
of human events.

---

[21]Dulles, "The Deist Minimum," p. 29.
[22]Alexander Pope, *Essay on Man* 1.145-46.
[23]Others mentioned by Synnestvedt in private correspondence include *The New Science* by
Giovanni Battista Vico (1688-1744), *The Age of Louis XIV* and *Essay on Manners* by Voltaire,
Letters on the Study and Use of History by Henry St. John, Lord Bolingbroke (1679-1751),
and *Idea for a Universal History from a Cosmopolitan Point of View* by Immanuel Kant
(1724-1804).

8. Worldview Question 8: *Cold deists use their own autonomous reason to determine their goal in life; warm deists may reflect on their commitment to a somewhat personal God and determine their goal in accordance with what they believe their God would be pleased with.*

Because, unlike Christian theism, there is no orthodox deism, each deist is free to use reason, intuition, tradition, or whatever squares with his or her view of ultimate reality. Deists' core commitments will thus reflect their personal passions or, in common parlance, what turns them on— the flourishing of their individual personal life, their family life, public life. Early deists such as Franklin and Jefferson took public welfare as a key commitment. Others like Paine combined their commitment to public life with a passion for their own personal freedom (and the freedom of everyone in the commonwealth) from the dictates of religion. But the more a deist becomes divorced from allegiance to a personal God, the less religious mores and traditional goals characterize their core commitments. As a result, societies themselves become more pluralistic and less socially cohesive. Thus the tie between deism as a worldview and freedom as a personal and social goal inspired the bloody violence of the French Revolution and spurred on the development of democracy and eventually the vast cultural diversification of American society. Each year the Western World, especially America, becomes more pluralistic than the year before.

MODERN DEISM

As can be seen from the above description, deism has not been a stable compound. The reasons for this are not hard to see. Deism is dependent on Christian theism for its affirmations. It is dependent on what it omits for its particular character. The first and most important loss was its rejection of the full personal character of God. God, in the minds of many in the late seventeenth and eighteenth centuries, kept his omnipotence, his character as creator and, for the most part, his omniscience, but he lost his omnipresence (his intimate connection with and interest in his creation). Eventually he lost even his will, becoming a mere abstract intelligent force, providing a sufficient reason for the existence of the universe whose origin otherwise could not be explained. The spectrum from full personality to sheer abstraction is represented by a variety of deistic types. We have already noticed the differences between *warm* and *cold*

deism as represented by early deists. Now we will examine some modern
forms and introduce new labels for them: (1) *sophisticated scientific deism*, (2) *sophisticated philosophic deism* and (3) *popular deism* of which
moralistic therapeutic deism is a particular illustration.

Sophisticated scientific deism. A *cold* deism continues to thrive in
some scientists and a few humanists in academic centers across the world.
Scientists like Albert Einstein, who "see" a higher power at work in or
behind the universe and want to maintain reason in a created world, can

---

It's hard for me to believe that everything out there is just an accident.
. . . [Yet] I don't have any religious belief. I don't believe that there is
a God. I don't believe in Christianity or Judaism or anything like that,
okay? I'm not an atheist. . . . I'm not an agnostic. . . . I'm just in a simple
state. I don't know what there is or might be. . . . But on the other hand,
what I can say is that it seems likely to me that this particular universe
we have is a consequence of something which I would call intelligent.
ROBERT WRIGHT, *Three Scientists and Their Gods*

---

be considered deists at heart, though no doubt many would not wish to
claim anything sounding quite so much like a philosophy of life.[24]

Astrophysicist Stephen Hawking also leaves room for a deistic God.
The fundamental laws of the universe "may have originally been decreed
by God," he writes, "but it appears that he has since left the universe to
evolve according to them and does not now intervene in it."[25] His rejection of a theistic God is clear. Actress and New Age leader Shirley Mac-
Laine once asked Hawking if there is a God who "created the universe
and guides his creation." "No," he replied simply in his computer-gener-
ated voice.[26] After all, if the universe is "self-contained, having no boundary or edge," as Hawking suspects is true, then there is no need for a
Creator; God becomes superfluous.[27] Hawking therefore uses "the term

---

[24]Albert Einstein, *Ideas and Opinions* (New York: Bonanza, 1954). See also Robert Jastrow, *God
and the Astronomers* (New York: Warner, 1978).
[25]Stephen Hawking, *A Brief History of Time* (New York: Bantam, 1988), p. 122.
[26]Michael White and John Gribbin, *Stephen Hawking: A Life in Science* (New York: Plume,
1992), p. 3.
[27]Hawking, *Brief History*, p. 141.

God as the embodiment of the laws of physics."[28] Hawking is not alone among scientists and other intellectuals in holding such a view.[29]

Sophisticated philosophic deism. Recently Antony Flew, a long-time vocal atheist and opponent of Christian theism, has declared himself a deist. His change of mind came from his growing sense that a variety of arguments, from those of Aristotle to the fine-tuning of the universe, are really compelling. As he put it, "he simply had to go where the evidence led."[30] God, for Flew, has most of the "classical theological attributes." Though he rejects the notion of special revelation from this God, he is open to its possibility. The authenticity of this move by such a formerly convinced atheist has been questioned, but the evidence for it is rock solid.[31]

One of the clearest exponents of a more humanistic *warm* deism is Václav Havel, the playwright, public intellectual and former president of the Czech Republic. The defining characteristic of Havel's worldview is his understanding of prime reality, his answer to the first worldview question. Havel uses several terms to label his answer: *Being, mystery of being, order of existence, the hidden sphere, absolute horizon* or *final horizon.* All of these terms suggest a *cold* deism. But there is nothing cold about his experience of this sheer Being. Havel, for example, ponders why, when he boards a streetcar late at night with no conductor to observe him, he always feels guilty when he thinks of not paying the fare. Then he comments about the interior dialogue that ensues:

Who, then, is in fact conversing with me? Obviously someone I hold in

---

[28]Kitty Ferguson, *Stephen Hawking: Quest for a Theory of the Universe* (New York: Franklin Watts, 1991), p. 84.

[29]Another possibility is that scientists who see intelligence in the workings of the universe are *panentheists.* Panentheism is a sort of halfway house between theism and pantheism. In panentheism the universe is *not* God but *in* God. Or God is the *mind* of the universe, not equated with it but not separate from it. This worldview tends to be held only by highly intellectual people. Physicist Paul Davies, for example, was awarded the Templeton Prize for Progress in Religion. See his "Physics and the Mind of God: The Templeton Prize Address," *First Things* (August/September, 1995), pp. 31-35; and also *God and the New Physics* (New York: Simon and Schuster, 1983); and *The Mind of God: The Scientific Basis for a Rational World* (New York: Simon and Schuster, 1992).

[30]See Antony Flew with Abraham Varghese, *There Is a God: How the World's Most Notorious Atheist Changed His Mind* (SanFrancisco: HarperOne, 2007); and Gary Habermas, "Antony Flew's Deism Revisited," *Philosophia Christi* 9, no. 202 (2007), also on the Web at <www.epsociety.org>.

[31]See Flew's response to Richard Dawkins's suggestion in *The God Delusion* that Flew's conversion is the result of old age not rational consideration ("Documentation: A Reply to Richard Dawkins," *First Things* [December 2008], pp. 21-22).

higher regard than the transport commission, than my best friends (this would come out when the voice would take issue with their opinions), and higher, in some regards than myself, that is, myself as subject of my existence-in-the-world and the carrier of my "existential" interests (one of which is the rather natural effort to save a crown). Someone who "knows everything" (and is therefore omniscient), is everywhere (and therefore omnipresent) and remembers everything; someone who, though infinitely understanding, is entirely incorruptible; who is for me, the highest and utterly unequivocal authority in all moral questions and who is thus Law itself; someone eternal, who through himself makes me eternal as well, so that I cannot imagine the arrival of a moment when everything will come to an end, thus terminating my dependence on him as well; someone to whom I relate entirely and for whom, ultimately, I would do everything. At the same time, this "someone" addresses me directly and personally (not merely as an anonymous public passenger, as the transport commission does).[32]

These reflections are close, if not identical, to a fully theistic conception of God. Surely some Being that is omniscient, omnipresent and good, and who addresses you directly and personally, must himself (itself just doesn't fit these criteria) be personal.

Havel too sees this. And yet he draws back from the conclusion:

But who is it? God? There are many subtle reasons why I'm reluctant to use that word; one factor here is a certain sense of shame (I don't know exactly for what, why and before whom), but the main thing, I suppose, is a fear that with this all too specific designation (or rather assertion) that "God is," I would be projecting an experience that is entirely personal and vague (never mind how profound and urgent it may be), too single-mindedly "outward," onto that problem-fraught screen called "objective reality," and thus I would go too far beyond it.[33]

So, while Being manifests characteristics that seem to demand a commitment to theism, Havel avoids this conclusion by shifting his attention from Being (as an objective existent) to himself (as a reflector on his conscious experience). What Havel does draw from this experience—to very good advantage, by the way—is that Being has a moral dimension. Being, then, is the "good" ontological foundation for human moral responsibility.[34]

---

[32]Václav Havel, *Letters to Olga; June 1979-Sepotember 1982*, trans. Paul Wilson (New York: Henry Holt, 1989), p. 345-46.

[33]Ibid., p. 346.

[34]Havel has a profound understanding of his whole worldview; this has been analyzed in my

Popular deism. Popular deism is popular in two senses. It is both a simple, easy-going belief in the existence of an omnipotent, impersonal, transcendent being, a force or an intelligence, and it is a vague belief held by millions of Americans and, I suspect, millions more in the rest of the Western world.

In its *cold* versions, God is simply the abstract force that brought the world into existence and has largely left it to operate on its own. My guess, and it is only a guess, is that many well-educated people, especially academics and professionals, would acknowledge the probable existence of such a being but would largely ignore his existence in their daily lives. Their moral sensitivity would be grounded in the public memory of common Christian virtues, the mores of society, the occasional use of their own mind when dealing with specific issues, such as honesty in business, attitudes to sexual orientation and practices. They live secular lives without much thought of what God might think. Surely a good life will prepare one for life after death, if, indeed, there is such a thing.

In its *warmest* versions, God clearly is personal and even friendly. University of North Carolina sociologists Christian Smith and Melinda Lundquist Denton recently conducted a massive study of the religious beliefs of teenagers. Their conclusion was that most of these teenagers adhered to what they called *moralistic therapeutic deism.* They summed up this world view as follows.

1. A God exists who created and orders the world and watches over human life on earth.

2. God wants people to be good, nice, and fair to each other, as taught in the Bible and by most religions.

3. The central goal of life is to be happy and to feel good about oneself.

4. God does not need to be particularly involved in one's life except when God is needed to resolve a problem.

5. Good people go to heaven when they die.[35]

God, ultimate reality, in this view makes no demand on his creation to be holy, righteous or even very good. "As one 17-year-old conservative Protes-

Václav Havel: The Intellectual Conscience of International Politics (Downers Grove, Ill.: InterVarsity Press, 2001), now out of print but available from jsire@prodigy.net.
[35]Christian Smith and Melinda Lundquist Denton, *Soul Searching: The Religious and Spiritual Lives of American Teenagers* (New York: Oxford University Press, 2005), pp. 162-63.

tant girl from Florida told us [the researchers], 'God's all around you, all the time. He believes in forgiving people and whatnot and he's there to guide us, for somebody to talk to and help us through our problems. Of course, he doesn't talk back."[36] When asked what God is like, a Bryn Mawr College student drew a big smiley face and wrote, "He's one big smiley face. Big hands . . . big hands."[37] This form of deism is certainly not limited to youth; it is, I suspect, very much like that of their parents and adult neighbors.

AN UNSTABLE COMPOUND

Enlightenment deism did not prove to be a stable worldview. Historically it held sway over the intellectual world of France and England from the late seventeenth into the first half of the eighteenth century. Then its cultural significance declined. But few, if any, major shifts in worldview disappear completely. Deism is indeed still alive and well.

What made and continues to make deism so unstable? The primary reasons, I think, are these:[38]

First, autonomous human reason replaced the Bible and tradition as the authority for the way ultimate reality was understood. Everyone could decide for themselves what God was like. Once the concept of God was up for grabs, there was no stopping his being reduced from the complex Christian theistic idea of God to a minimal, simple force or abstract intelligence. The gradual slide from a full-blooded Christian theism was thus inevitable; what replaced the biblical God was a variety of gods, each with fewer and fewer features of personality.

Second, autonomous human reason replaced the Bible and tradition as the authority for morality. At first autonomous reason and traditional morality tracked well together. The human mind exposed to the surrounding culture assumed that, for the most part, those cultural values were in fact reasonable. In the early years, deists placed confidence in the universality of human nature; people who used their reason would agree

[36]Ibid., p. 164.

[37]From a survey conducted in 1992 by students before my campus lecture.

[38]To these reasons Dulles adds these internal tensions: "[1] If there is an omnipotent God, capable of designing the entire universe and launching it into existence, it seems strange to hold that this God cannot intervene in the world. . . . [2] If God was infinite in being, . . . was it not unreasonable to reject the notion of mystery? . . . [3] If God had never intervened in the world, His existence could only be, from a human perspective, superfluous" (Dulles, "The Deist Minimum," p. 28).

on what was right and wrong.[39] This eventually turned out to be a false hope. However universal human nature may be, in practice people do not agree on matters of good and evil or what constitutes "good" behavior as much as the early deists thought.

Third, deists rejected the biblical notion of the Fall and assumed that the present universe is in its normal, created state. As Pope said, "whatever is, is right." One could derive one's values from clues from the natural order. One clue was the universality of human nature. But if whatever is, is right, then no place is left for a distinctive content to ethics.

Fourth, since the universe is closed to reordering, human action is determined. What then happens to human significance? People become cogs in the clockwork mechanism of the universe. Human significance and mechanical determinism are impossible bedfellows.

Fifth, today we find even more aspects of deism to question. Scientists have largely abandoned thinking of the universe as a giant clock. Electrons (not to mention other even more baffling subatomic particles) do not behave like minute pieces of machinery. If the universe is a mechanism, it is far more complex than was then thought, and God must be quite different from a mere "architect" or "clockmaker." Furthermore, the human personality is a "fact" of the universe. If God made that, must he not be personal?

So historically, deism was a transitional worldview, and yet it is not dead in either popular or sophisticated forms. On a popular level, many people today believe that God exists, but when asked what God is like, they limit their description to words like *Energy, The Force, First Cause,* something to get the universe running and often capitalized to give it the aura of divinity. As Étienne Gilson says, "For almost two centuries . . . the ghost of the Christian God has been attended by the ghost of Christian religion: a vague feeling of religiosity, a sort of trusting familiarity with some supreme good fellow to whom other good fellows can hopefully apply when they are in trouble."[40]

In what was to follow even the ghost of the Christian God disappeared. It is to that worldview we now turn.

---

[39]Dulles says, "Although deism portrayed itself as a pure product of unaided reason, it was not what it claimed to be. Its basic tenets concerning God, the virtuous life, and rewards beyond the grave were in fact derived from Christianity, the faith in which the deists themselves had been raised" (ibid., p. 28).

[40]Étienne Gilson, *God and Philosophy* (New Haven, Conn.: Yale University Press, 1941), pp. 106-7.

Chapter 4

THE SILENCE OF FINITE SPACE

NATURALISM

Without warning, David was visited by an exact vision of death:
a long hole in the ground, no wider than your body,
down which you were drawn while the white faces recede.
You try to reach them but your arms are pinned.
Shovels pour dirt in your face.
There you will be forever, in an upright position,
blind and silent, and in time no one will remember you,
and you will never be called. As strata of rock shift, your fingers
elongate, and your teeth are distended sideways in a great
underground grimace indistinguishable from a strip of chalk.
And the earth tumbles on, and the sun expires,
an unaltering darkness reigns where once there were stars.

JOHN UPDIKE, "PIGEON FEATHERS"

Deism is the isthmus between two great continents—theism and naturalism. To get from the first to the second, deism is the natural route. Perhaps without deism, naturalism would not have come about so readily. Deism in its *warm* eighteenth-century versions has become almost an intellectual curiosity, handy for an explanation of the foundation of American democracy, but not much held today. Other than Christian theists, there are few today who explain our situation as an indication of God's providence. Deism's sophisticated twentieth-century versions are mostly *cold* and limited to a few scientists and intellectuals and to those who, while they say they believe in God, have only a vague notion of what he, she or it might be. Naturalism, on the other hand, was and is serious business.

In intellectual terms the route is this: In theism God is the infinite-personal Creator and sustainer of the cosmos. In deism God is reduced; he begins to lose his personality, though he remains Creator and (by implication) sustainer of the cosmos. In naturalism God is further reduced; he loses his very existence.

Swing figures in this shift from theism to naturalism are legion, especially between 1600 and 1750. René Descartes (1596-1650), a Christian theist by conscious confession, set the stage by conceiving of the universe as a giant mechanism of "matter" which people comprehended by "mind." He thus split reality into two kinds of being; ever since then the Western world has found it hard to see itself as an integrated whole. The naturalists, taking one route to unification, made mind a subcategory of mechanistic matter.

John Locke, a Christian theist for the most part, believed in a personal God who revealed himself to us; Locke thought, however, that our God-given reason is the judge of what can be taken as true from the "revelation" in the Bible. The naturalists removed the "God-given" from this conception and made "reason" the sole criterion for truth.

One of the most interesting figures in this shift was Julien Offray de La Mettrie (1709-1751). In his own day La Mettrie was generally considered an atheist, but he himself says, "Not that I call in question the existence of a supreme being; on the contrary it seems to me that the greatest degree of probability is in favor of this belief." Nonetheless, he continues, "it is a theoretic truth with little practical value."[1] The reason he can conclude that God's existence is of so little practical value is that the God who exists is *only* the maker of the universe. He is not personally interested in it nor in being worshiped by anyone in it. So God's existence can be effectively discounted as being of no importance.[2]

---

[1] Julien Offray de La Mettrie, *Man a Machine* (1747), in *Les Philosophes*, ed. Norman L. Torrey (New York: Capricorn, 1960), p. 176.

[2] Alfred North Whitehead, for example, says, "Of course we find in the eighteenth century Paley's famous argument that mechanism presupposes a God who is the author of nature. But even before Paley put the argument into its final form, Hume had written the retort, that the God whom you will find will be the sort of God who makes that mechanism. In other

It is precisely this feeling, this conclusion, which marks the transition to naturalism. La Mettrie was a theoretical deist but a practical naturalist. It was easy for subsequent generations to make their theory consistent with La Mettrie's practice, so that naturalism was both believed and acted on.[3]

Behavior does indeed fuel intellectual development. In fact, if we take seriously the last phrase of the definition of *worldview* in chapter one ("on which we live and move and have our being"), we could label La Mettrie a full-fledged naturalist.

BASIC NATURALISM
This brings us, then, to the first proposition defining naturalism.

1. Worldview Question 1: *Prime reality is matter. Matter exists eternally and is all there is. God does not exist.*

As in theism and deism, the prime proposition concerns the nature of basic existence. In the former two the nature of God is the key factor. In naturalism it is the nature of the cosmos that is primary, for now, with an eternal Creator God out of the picture, the cosmos itself becomes eternal—always there though not necessarily in its present form, in fact *certainly* not in its present form.[4] Carl Sagan, astrophysicist and popularizer of science, has said it as clearly as possible: "The Cosmos is all that is or ever was or ever will be."[5]

---

words, that mechanism can, at most, presuppose a mechanic, and not merely a mechanic but *its* mechanic" (Whitehead, *Science and the Modern World* [1925; reprint, New York: Mentor, 1948], p. 77).

[3]The brash, anti-Christian, anticlerical tone of La Mettrie's essay is of a piece with its antitheistic content, exalting, as it does, human reason at the expense of revelation. A sample of this from the conclusion to *Man a Machine* is instructive: "I recognize only scientists as judges of the conclusions which I draw, and I hereby challenge every prejudiced man who is not an anatomist, or acquainted with the only philosophy which is to the purpose, that of the human body. Against such a strong and solid oak, what could the weak reeds of theology, metaphysics and scholasticism, avail; childish weapons, like our foils, which may well afford the pleasure of fencing, but can never wound an adversary. Need I say that I refer to the hollow and trivial notions, to the trite and pitiable arguments that will be urged, as long as the shadow of prejudice or superstition remains on earth, for the supposed incompatibility of two substances which meet and interact unceasingly [La Mettrie is here alluding to Descartes's division of reality into mind and matter]?" (p. 177).

[4]Strictly speaking, there are naturalists who are not materialists—that is, who hold that there may be elements of the universe that are not material—but they have had little impact on Western culture. My definition of naturalism will be limited to those who are materialists.

[5]Carl Sagan, *Cosmos* (New York: Random House, 1980), p. 4. Sagan goes on to say, "Our feeblest

Nothing comes from nothing. Something is. Therefore something always was. But that something, say the naturalists, is not a transcendent Creator but the matter of the cosmos itself. In some form all the matter of the universe has always been. Or so naturalists have traditionally held. Some recent naturalist philosophers and astrophysicists, however, reject the logic that holds that something has always had to be. The universe may rather have originated out of "a *singularity* at which space-time curvature, along with temperature, pressure and density, becomes infinite."[6] Space and time (all we know of reality) come into being together. Moreover, nothing spiritual or transcendent emerged from this cosmic event. It makes no sense to say there was a *before* before the singularity. In short, matter (or mater/energy in a complex interchange) is all there is. Ours is a *natural* cosmos.

The word *matter* is to be understood in a rather general way, for since the eighteenth century, science has refined its understanding. In the eighteenth century scientists had yet to discover either the complexity of matter or its close relationship with energy. They conceived of reality as made up of irreducible "units" existing in mechanical, spatial relationship with each other, a relationship being investigated and unveiled by chemistry and physics and expressible in inexorable "laws." Later scientists were to discover that nature is not so neat, or at least so simple. There seem to be no irreducible "units" as such, and physical laws have only mathematical expression. Physicists like Stephen Hawking may search for nothing less than a "complete description of the universe" and even hope to find it.[7] But confidence about what nature is, or is likely to be discovered to be, has almost vanished.[8]

---

contemplations of the cosmos stir us—there is a tingling in the spine, a catch in the voice, a faint sensation, as if a distant memory, of falling from a height. We know we are approaching the greatest of mysteries." For Sagan, in this book and the television series of the same name, the cosmos assumes the position of God, creating the same kind of awe in Sagan, who tries to trigger in his readers and television audience the same response. So-called science thus becomes religion, some say the religion of scientism. See Jeffrey Marsh, "The Universe and Dr. Sagan," *Commentary*, May 1981, pp. 64-68.

[6]See J. P. Moreland and William Lane Craig, *Philosophical Foundations for a Christian Worldview* (Downers Grove, Ill.: InterVarsity Press, 2003), pp. 477.

[7]Stephen Hawking, *A Brief History of Time* (New York: Bantam, 1988), p. 13. Hawking's conclusion is guardedly optimistic: "If we do discover a complete theory [of the universe] . . . it would be the ultimate triumph of human reason—for then we would know the mind of God" (p. 175).

[8]For a recent update written in lay language, see Dennis Overbye, "Dark, Perhaps Forever," *The New York Times*, June 3, 2008, sec. D, pp. 1 and 4.

Still, the proposition expressed above unites naturalists. The cosmos is not composed of two things—matter and mind, or matter and spirit. As La Mettrie says, "In the whole universe there is but a single substance with various modifications."[9] The cosmos is ultimately one thing, without any relation to a Being beyond; there is no "god," no "creator."

2. Worldview Question 2: *The cosmos exists as a uniformity of cause and effect in a closed system.*

This proposition is similar to proposition 2 in deism. The difference is that the universe may or may not be conceived of as a machine or clockwork. Modern scientists have found the relations between the various elements of reality to be far more complex, if not more mysterious, than the clockwork image can account for.

Nonetheless, the universe is a *closed* system. It is not open to reordering from the outside—either by a transcendent Being (for there is none) or, as I shall discuss later at length, by self-transcendent or autonomous human beings (for they are a part of the uniformity). Emil Bréhier, describing this view, says, "Order in nature is but one rigorously necessary arrangement of its parts, founded on the essence of things; for example, the beautiful regularity of the seasons is not the effect of a divine plan but the result of gravitation."[10]

The Humanist Manifesto II (1973), which expresses the views of those who call themselves "secular humanists," puts it this way: "We find insufficient evidence for belief in the existence of a supernatural."[11] Without God or the supernatural, of course, nothing can happen except within the realm of things themselves. Writing in *The Columbia History of the World,* Rhodes W. Fairbridge says flatly, "We reject the miraculous."[12]

---

[9]La Mettrie, *Man a Machine*, p. 177. On the other hand, to define a human being as "a field of energies moving inside a larger fluctuating system of energies" is equally naturalistic. In neither case is humankind seen as transcending the cosmos. See Marilyn Ferguson, *The Brain Revolution: The Frontiers of Mind Research* (New York: Taplinger, 1973), p. 22.

[10]Émile Bréhier, *The History of Philosophy*, trans. Wade Baskin (Chicago: University of Chicago Press, 1967), 5:129.

[11]*Humanist Manifestos I and II* (Buffalo, N.Y.: Prometheus, 1973), p. 16. These two manifestos, especially the second (which was drafted by Paul Kurtz), are convenient compilations of naturalist assumptions. Paul Kurtz is a professor of philosophy at the State University of New York at Buffalo, editor of *Free Inquiry* (a quarterly journal devoted to the propagation of "secular humanism") and editor of Prometheus Books.

[12]John A. Garraty and Peter Gay, eds., *The Columbia History of the World* (New York: Harper & Row, 1972), p. 14.

Such a statement, coming as it does from a professor of geology at Columbia University, is to be expected.

What is surprising is to find a seminary professor, David Jobling, saying much the same thing: "We [that is, modern people] see the universe as a continuity of space, time, and matter, held together, as it were, from within. . . . God is not 'outside' time and space, nor does he stand apart from matter, communicating with the 'spiritual' part of man. . . . We must find some way of facing the fact that Jesus Christ is the product of the same evolutionary process as the rest of us."[13]

Jobling is attempting to understand Christianity within the naturalistic worldview. Certainly after God is put strictly inside the system—the uniform, closed system of cause and effect—he has been denied sovereignty and much else that Christians have traditionally believed to be true about him. The point here, however, is that naturalism is a pervasive worldview, to be found in the most unlikely places.

What are the central features of this closed system? It might first appear that naturalists, affirming the "continuity of space, time, and matter, held together . . . from within," would be determinists, asserting that the closed system holds together by an inexorable, unbreakable linkage of cause and effect. Most naturalists are indeed determinists, though many would argue that this does not remove our sense of free will or our responsibility for our actions. Is such a freedom really consistent with the conception of a closed system? To answer we must first look more closely at the naturalist conception of human beings.

3. Worldview Question 3: *Human beings are complex "machines"; personality is an interrelation of chemical and physical properties we do not yet fully understand.*

While Descartes recognized that human beings were part machine, he

---

[13]David Jobling, "How Does Our Twentieth-Century Concept of the Universe Affect Our Understanding of the Bible?" *Enquiry*, September-November 1972, p. 14. Ernest Nagel, in a helpful essay defining naturalism in a midtwentieth-century form, states this position in more rigorously philosophical terms: "The first [proposition central to naturalism] is the existential and causal primacy of organized matter in the executive order of nature. This is the assumption that the occurrence of events, qualities and processes, and the characteristic behaviors of various individuals, are contingent on the organization of spatiotemporally located bodies, whose internal structures and external relations determine and limit the appearance and disappearance of everything that happens" (Ernest Nagel, "Naturalism Reconsidered" [1954], in *Essays in Philosophy*, ed. Houston Peterson [New York: Pocket Library, 1959], p. 486).

also thought they were part mind; and mind was a different substance. A great majority of naturalists, however, see mind as a function of machine. La Mettrie was one of the first to put it bluntly: "Let us conclude boldly then that man is a machine, and that in the whole universe there is but a single substance with various modifications."[14] Putting it more crudely, Pierre Jean Georges Cabanis (1757-1808) wrote that "the brain secretes thought as the liver secretes bile."[15] William Barrett, in a fascinating intellectual history of the gradual loss of the notion of the soul or the self in Western thought from Descartes to the present, writes:

> Thus we get in La Mettrie . . . those quaint illustrations of the human body as a system of imaginary gears, cogs, and ratchets. Man, the microcosm, is just another machine within the universal machine that is the cosmos. We smile at these illustrations as quaint and crude, but secretly we may still nourish the notion that they are after all in the right direction, though a little premature. With the advent of the computer, however, this temptation toward mechanism becomes more irresistible, for here we no longer have an obsolete machine of wheels and pulleys but one that seems able to reproduce the processes of the human mind. Can machines think? now becomes a leading question for our time.[16]

In any case, the point is that as human beings we are simply a part of the cosmos. In the cosmos there is one substance: matter. We are that and only that. The laws applying to matter apply to us. We do not transcend the universe in any way.

Of course we are very complex machines, and our mechanism is not yet fully understood. Thus people continue to amaze us and upset our expectations. Still, any mystery that surrounds our understanding is a result not of genuine mystery but of mechanical complexity.[17]

It might be concluded that humanity is not distinct from other objects

---

[14]La Mettrie, *Man a Machine*, p. 177.

[15]Fredrick Copleston, *A History of Philosophy* (London: Burns and Oates, 1961), 6:51. Among proponents of the notion that human beings are machines is John Brierly, *The Thinking Machine* (London: Heinemann, 1973).

[16]William Barrett, *The Death of the Soul: From Descartes to the Computer* (New York: Anchor, 1987), p. 154. Sherry Turkle, who has studied the effect of computers on human self-understanding, says that "people who try to think of themselves as computers have trouble with the notion of the self" (Carl Mitcham reports on her work in "Computer Ethos, Computer Ethics," in *Research in Philosophy and Technology* [Greenwich, Conn.: JAI Press], 8:271).

[17]Humanist Manifesto II states the situation generally with reference to the whole of nature: "Nature may indeed be broader and deeper than we now know; any new discoveries, however, will but enlarge our knowledge of the natural" (p. 16).

in the universe, that it is merely one kind of object among many. But naturalists insist this is not so. Julian Huxley, for example, says we are unique among animals because we alone are capable of conceptual thought, employ speech, possess a cumulative tradition (culture) and have had a unique method of evolution.[18] To this most naturalists would add our moral capacity, a topic I will take up separately. All of these characteristics are open and generally obvious. None of them imply any transcendent power or demand any extramaterial basis, say the naturalists.

Ernest Nagel points out the necessity of not stressing the human "continuity" with the nonhuman elements of our makeup: "Without denying that even the most distinctive human traits are dependent on things which are nonhuman, a mature naturalism attempts to assess man's nature in the light of *his* actions and achievements, *his* aspirations and capacities, *his* limitations and tragic failures, and *his* splendid works of ingenuity and imagination."[19] By stressing our humanness (our distinctness from the rest of the cosmos), a naturalist finds a basis for value, for, it is held, intelligence, cultural sophistication, a sense of right and wrong not only are human distinctives but are what make us valuable. This we will see developed further under proposition 6 below.

Finally, while some naturalists are strict determinists with regard to all events in the universe, including human action, thus denying any sense of free will, many naturalists hold that we are free to fashion our own destiny, at least in part. Some, for example, hold that while a closed universe implies determinism, determinism is still compatible with human freedom, or at least a sense of freedom.[20] We can do many things that we want to do; we are not always constrained to act against our wants. I could, for example, stop preparing a new edition of this book if I wanted to. I don't want to.

This, so many naturalists hold, leaves open the possibility for significant human action, and it provides a basis for morality. For unless we are free to do other than we do, we cannot be held responsible for what we do. The co-

---

[18]Julian Huxley, "The Uniqueness of Man," in *Man in the Modern World* (New York: Mentor, 1948), pp. 7-28. George Gaylord Simpson lists humanity's "interrelated factors of intelligence, flexibility, individualization and socialization" (*The Meaning of Evolution*, rev. ed. [New York: Mentor, 1951], p. 138).

[19]Nagel, "Naturalism Reconsidered," p. 490.

[20]Physicist Edward Fredkin, for example, believes that even in a completely deterministic universe, human actions may not be predictable and there is left a place for "pseudo-free will" (Robert Wright, *Three Scientists and Their Gods* [New York: Harper & Row, 1988], p. 67).

herence of this view has been challenged, however, and is one of the soft spots in the naturalist's system of thought, as we will see in the following chapter.

4. Worldview Question 4: *Death is extinction of personality and individuality.*

This is, perhaps, the "hardest" proposition of naturalism for people to accept, yet it is absolutely demanded by the naturalists' conception of the universe. Men and women are made of matter and nothing else. When the matter that goes to make up an individual is disorganized at death, then that person disappears.

The Humanist Manifesto II states, "As far as we know, the total personality is a function of the biological organism transacting in a social

---

That man is the product of causes which had no prevision of the end they were achieving; that his origin, his growth, his hopes and fears, his loves and his beliefs, are but the outcome of accidental collocations of atoms; that no fire, no heroism, no intensity of thought and feeling, can preserve an individual life beyond the grave; that all the labors of the ages, all the devotion, all the inspiration, all the noonday brightness of human genius, are destined to extinction in the vast death of the solar system, and that the whole temple of man's achievement must inevitably be buried beneath the debris of a universe in ruins—all these things, if not quite beyond dispute, are yet so nearly certain that no philosophy which rejects them can hope to stand. Only within the scaffolding of these truths, only on the firm foundation of unyielding despair, can the soul's habitation henceforth be safely built.

BERTRAND RUSSELL, "A Free Man's Worship"

---

and cultural context. There is no credible evidence that life survives the death of the body."[21] Bertrand Russell writes, "No fire, no heroism, no intensity of thought and feeling, can preserve an individual life beyond the grave."[22] And A. J. Ayer says, "I take it . . . to be fact that one's existence

---

[21]*Humanist Manifestos I and II*, p. 17.
[22]Bertrand Russell, "A Free Man's Worship," in *Why I Am Not a Christian* (New York: Simon & Schuster, 1957), p. 107.

ends at death."[23] In a more general sense humankind is likewise seen to be transitory. "Human destiny," Nagel confesses, "[is] an episode between two oblivions."[24]

Such statements are clear and unambiguous. The concept may trigger immense psychological problems, but there is no disputing its precision. The only "immortality," as the Humanist Manifesto II puts it, is to "continue to exist in our progeny and in the way that our lives have influenced others in our culture."[25] In his short story "Pigeon Feathers" John Updike gives this notion a beautifully human dimension as he portrays the young boy David reflecting on his minister's description of heaven as being "like Abraham Lincoln's goodness living after him."[26] Like the seminary professor quoted above, David's pastor is no longer a theist but is simply trying to provide "spiritual" counsel within the framework of naturalism.

5. Worldview Question 5: *Through our innate and autonomous human reason, including the methods of science, we can know the universe. The cosmos, including this world, is understood to be in its normal state.*

Notice the similarity between the deist and the naturalist notion of how we come to know. Both accept the internal faculty of reason and the thoughts human beings come to have as givens. From a cosmic standpoint, reason developed under the contingencies of natural evolution over a very long period of time.[27] From a human standpoint, a child is born with innate faculties which merely have to develop naturally. These faculties work on their own within the framework of the languages and cultures to which they are exposed. At no time is there any information or interpretation or mental machinery added from outside the ordinary material world. As children grow, they learn which of their thoughts help them understand and enable them to deal with the world around them. The methods of modern science are especially helpful in leading us to more and more profound knowledge of our universe. Human knowledge, then, is the product of natural human reason grounded in its perceived

---

[23]A. J. Ayer, ed., *The Humanist Outlook* (London: Pemberton, 1968), p. 9.
[24]Nagel, "Naturalism Reconsidered," p. 496.
[25]*Humanist Manifestos I and II*, p. 17.
[26]John Updike, "Pigeon Feathers," in *Pigeon Feathers and Other Stories* (Greenwich, Conn.: Fawcett, 1959), p. 96.
[27]See pp. 81-84 below.

ability to reach the truth about human beings and the world.[28]

We should notice that I have used the word *truth* to describe the end result of human reason when it is successful. In the eighteenth and early nineteenth centuries few would question its propriety. As Aristotle said, "All men desire to know," meaning "All men desire to know the truth, that is, the way reality really is." Naturalists today, especially scientists and ordinarily educated people, may continue to think this way. When most people say that water is hydrogen and oxygen, two parts to one, they think they have accurately described its chemical makeup; that's what water *is*. More philosophically minded modern naturalists are content to say that we can learn to describe what we take to be reality in language that allows us to live successfully in the world, but no one can know what something *is*. There is a rift between words and things that cannot be bridged.[29] We will see how this plays out in chapter nine on postmodernism. What is important to note here is that naturalists ground human reason in human nature itself.

6. Worldview Question 6: *Ethics is related only to human beings.*

Ethical considerations did not play a central role in the rise of naturalism. Naturalism rather came as a logical extension of certain metaphysical notions—notions about the nature of the external world. Most early naturalists continued to hold ethical views similar to those in the surrounding culture, views that in general were indistinguishable from popular Christianity. There was a respect for individual dignity, an affirmation of love, a commitment to truth and basic honesty. Jesus was seen as a teacher of high ethical values.

Though it is becoming less and less so, it is still true to some measure today. With a few recent twists—for example, a permissive attitude to premarital and extramarital sex, a positive response to euthanasia, abortion and the individual's right to suicide—the ethical norms of the Humanist Manifesto II (1973) are similar to traditional morality. Theists

---

[28]See the essays in *Naturalizing Epistemology*, 2nd ed., ed. Hilary Kornblith (Cambridge, Mass.: MIT Press, 1997) for a presentation and critique of various naturalistic ways to justify our claims to knowledge.

[29]In Christian theism there is no necessary rift between words and things; this is because everything that exists except God himself has been made by the Word (the personal intelligence of God). See chapter 2, page 36. I have also discussed this aspect of theism in *Discipleship of the Mind* (Downers Grove, Ill.: InterVarsity Press, 1990), pp. 87-94.

and naturalists can often live side by side in communal harmony on ethical matters. There have always been disagreements between them; these disagreements will, I believe, increase as humanism shifts further and further from its memory of Christian ethics.[30] But whatever the disagreements (or agreements) on ethical norms, the *basis* for these norms is radically different.

For a theist, God is the foundation of values. For a naturalist, values are constructed by human beings. The naturalist's notion follows logically from the previous propositions. If there was no consciousness prior to the existence of humans, then there was no prior sense of right and wrong. And if there were no ability to do other than what one does, any sense of right and wrong would have no practical value. So for ethics to be possible, there must be both consciousness and self-determination. In short, there must be personality.

Naturalists say both consciousness and self-determination came with the appearance of human beings, and so ethics too came then. No ethical system can be derived solely from the nature of "things" outside human consciousness. In other words, no natural law is inscribed in the cosmos. Even La Mettrie, who fudged a bit when he wrote, "Nature created us all [man and beast] solely to be happy," betraying his deistic roots, was a confirmed naturalist in ethics: "You see that natural law is *nothing but* an intimate feeling which belongs to the imagination like all other feelings, thought included."[31] La Mettrie, of course, conceived of the imagination in a totally mechanistic fashion, so that ethics became for him simply people's following out a pattern embedded in them as creatures. Certainly there is nothing whatever transcendent about morality.

The Humanist Manifesto II states the locus of naturalistic ethics in no uncertain terms: "We affirm that moral values derive their source from human experience. Ethics is *autonomous* and *situational,* needing no theological or ideological sanction. Ethics stems from human need and interest. To deny this distorts the whole basis of life. Human life has meaning because we create and develop our futures."[32] Most conscious

---

[30]This shift in the content of ethical norms can be studied by comparing Humanist Manifesto I (1933) with Humanist Manifesto II (1973). Since 1973, of course, more shifts have occurred, most notably in the ascendance of a plea that homosexuality be considered a normal human condition with attendant moral rights.

[31]La Mettrie, *Man a Machine*, p. 176, emphasis mine.

[32]*Humanist Manifestos I and II*, p. 17.

naturalists would probably agree with this statement. But exactly how value is created out of the human situation is just as much up for grabs as is the way we ought to understand the origin of the universe.

The major question is this: How does *ought* derive from *is?* Traditional ethics, that is, the ethics of Christian theism, affirms the transcendent origin of ethics and locates in the infinite-personal God the measure of

---

To discover the true principles of morality, men have no need of theology, of revelation, or of gods; they need only common sense. They have only to commune with themselves, to reflect upon their own nature, to consult their visible interests, to consider the objects of society and the individuals who compose it, and they will easily perceive that virtue is advantageous, and vice disadvantageous, to such beings as themselves. Let us persuade them to be just, beneficent, moderate, sociable, not because such conduct is demanded by the gods, but because it is a pleasure to men. Let us advise them to abstain from vice and crime, not because they will be punished in the other world, but because they will suffer for it in this.

BARON D'HOLBACH (1723-89), "Common Sense"

---

the good. Good is what God is, and this has been revealed in many and diverse ways, most fully in the life, teachings and death of Jesus Christ.

Naturalists, however, have no such appeal, nor do they wish to make one. Ethics is solely a human domain. So the question: How does one get from the fact of self-consciousness and self-determination, the realm of *is* and *can,* to the realm of what *ought* to be or to be done?

One observation naturalists make is that all people have a sense of moral values. These derive, G. G. Simpson says, from intuition ("the feeling of rightness, without objective inquiry into the reasons for this feeling and without possible test as to the truth or falseness of the premises involved"[33]), from authority and from convention. No one grows up without picking up values from the environment, and while a person may reject these and pay the consequences of ostracism or martyrdom, seldom does anyone succeed in inventing values totally divorced from culture.

---

[33]Simpson, *Meaning of Evolution,* p. 145.

Of course values differ from culture to culture, and none seems absolutely universal. So Simpson argues for an ethic based on objective inquiry and finds it in a harmonious adjustment of people to each other and their environment.[34] Whatever promotes such harmony is good; what does not is bad. John Platt, in an article that attempts to construct an ethic for B. F. Skinner's behaviorism, writes,

> Happiness is having short-run reinforcers congruent with medium-run and long-run ones, and wisdom is knowing how to achieve this. And ethical behavior results when short-run personal reinforcers are congruent with long-run group reinforcers. This makes it easy to "be good," or more exactly to "behave well."[35]

The upshot of this is a definition of good action as group-approved, survival-promoting action. Both Simpson and Platt opt for the continuance of human life as the value above all values. Survival is thus basic, but it is *human survival* that is affirmed as primary.[36]

Both Simpson and Platt are scientists with a consciousness of their responsibility to be fully human and thus to integrate their scientific knowledge and their moral values. From the side of the humanities comes Walter Lippmann. In *A Preface to Morals* (1929) Lippmann assumes the naturalists' stance with regard to the origin and purposelessness of the universe. His tack is to construct an ethic on the basis of what he takes to be the central agreement of the "great religious teachers." For Lippmann, the good turns out to be something that has been recognized so far only by the elite, a "voluntary aristocracy of the spirit."[37] His argument is that this elitist ethic is now becoming mandatory for all people if they are to survive the twentieth-century crisis of values.

The good itself consists of disinterestedness—a way of alleviating the "disorders and frustrations" of the modern world, now that the "acids of modernity" have eaten away the traditional basis for ethical behavior. It is difficult to summarize the content Lippmann pours into the word *disin-*

---

[34]Ibid., p. 149.
[35]John Platt in *The Center Magazine*, March-April 1972, p. 48.
[36]Two other naturalists who attempt to build an ethic on an evolutionary foundation are Daniel Dennett, *Darwin's Dangerous Idea* (New York: Simon & Schuster, 1995), and James Q. Wilson, *The Moral Sense* (New York: Free Press, 1993). Both explain how a moral sense may have developed; neither succeeds in avoiding the naturalistic fallacy—the attempt to derive *ought* from *is*.
[37]Walter Lippmann, *A Preface to Morals* (New York: Time, 1964), p. 190.

terested. The final third of his book is addressed to doing that. But it is helpful to notice that his ethic turns out to be based on a personal commitment of each individual who would be moral, and that it is totally divorced from the world of facts—the nature of things in general:

> A religion which rests upon particular conclusions in astronomy, biology and history may be fatally injured by the discovery of new truths. But the religion of the spirit does not depend upon creeds and cosmologies; it has no vested interest in any particular truth. It is concerned not with the organization of matter, but with the quality of human desire.[38]

Lippmann's language must be carefully understood. By *religion* he means morality or moral impulse. By *spirit* he means the moral faculty in human beings, that which exalts people above animals and above others whose "religion" is merely "popular." The language of theism is being employed, but its content is purely naturalistic.

In any case, what remains of ethics is an affirmation of a high vision of right in the face of a universe that is merely there and has no value in itself. Ethics thus are personal and chosen. Lippmann is not, to my knowledge, generally associated with the existentialists, but, as we shall see in chapter six, his version of naturalistic ethics is ultimately theirs.

Naturalists have tried to construct ethical systems in a wide variety of ways. Even Christian theists must admit that many of the naturalists' ethical insights are valid. Indeed theists should not be surprised by the fact that we can learn moral truths by observing human nature and behavior, for if women and men are made in the image of God and if that image is not totally destroyed by the Fall, then they should yet reflect—even if dimly—something of the goodness of God.

7. Worldview Question 7: *History is a linear stream of events linked by cause and effect but without an overarching purpose.*

First, the word *history,* as used in this proposition, includes both natural history and human history, for naturalists see them as a continuity. The

---

[38]Ibid., p. 307. Allan Bloom's *The Closing of the American Mind* could be described as a sustained cry for the maintenance of some other basis for human values than *commitment* or human *decision.* Without seriously contending with an infinite-personal God who acts as the foundation for these values, it is difficult to see just how contemporary values will be able to be grounded in any firm absolute. See Allan Bloom, *The Closing of the American Mind* (New York: Simon & Schuster, 1987), esp. pp. 194-216. See also Alasdair MacIntyre, *After Virtue,* 2nd ed. (Notre Dame, Ind.: Notre Dame University Press, 1984).

origin of the human family is in nature. We arose out of it and most likely will return to it (not just individually but as a species).

Natural history begins with the origin of the universe. Something happened an incredibly long time ago—a big bang or sudden emergence—that ultimately resulted in the formation of the universe we now inhabit and are conscious of. But exactly how this came to be few are willing to say. Lodewijk Woltjer, astronomer at Columbia University, speaks for many: "The origin of what is—man, the earth, the universe—is shrouded in a mystery we are no closer to solving than was the chronicler of Genesis."[39] A number of theories to explain the process have been advanced, but none have really won the day.[40] Still, among naturalists the premise always is that the process was self-activating; it was not set in motion by a Prime Mover—God or otherwise.

How human beings came to be is generally held to be more certain than how the universe came to be. The theory of evolution, long toyed with by naturalists, was given a "mechanism" by Darwin and has won the day. There is hardly a public school text that does not proclaim the theory as fact. We should be careful, however, not to assume that all forms of evolutionary theory are strictly naturalist. Many theists are also evolutionists. Evolution has, in fact, become a far more vexed issue among both Christians and naturalists than when this book was first written.[41]

---

[39]Garraty and Gay, *Columbia History of the World*, p. 3.

[40]One of the most intriguing treatments of the origin of the universe is that presented by Hawking in *A Brief History of Time*.

[41]Most scientists who are naturalists accept some form of evolutionary theory. Daniel C. Dennett is probably correct when he writes that "though there are vigorous controversies swirling around in evolutionary theory," they are family squabbles. The Darwinian idea "is about as secure as any in science"; that "human beings are products of evolution" is an "undisputable fact" (*Darwin's Dangerous Idea*, pp. 19, 481). One scientist, a naturalist, who does not accept Darwinism or neo-Darwinism, however, is Michael Denton, *Evolution: A Theory in Crisis* (Bethesda, Md.: Adler and Adler, 1985). Among Christians many scientists and theologians, especially those associated with the American Scientific Affiliation, accept some form of evolution as both scientifically possible and consistent with Christian theism (see the countless articles in the *Journal of the American Scientific Affiliation* and *Perspectives on Science and Christian Faith* [the ASA's retitled journal]). Further examples are Charles Hummel, *The Galileo Connection* (Downers Grove, Ill.: InterVarsity Press, 1985); Howard J. Van Till, *The Fourth Day* (Grand Rapids: Eerdmans, 1986); Howard J. Van Till, Davis A. Young and Clarence Menninga, *Science Held Hostage* (Downers Grove, Ill.: InterVarsity Press, 1988). Three recent books are especially helpful in sorting out the status of the current variety of judgments Christian scholars are making in regard to evolution: Darrel R. Falk, *Coming to Peace with Science: Bridging the Worlds Between Faith and Biology* (Downers Grove, Ill.: InterVarsity Press, 2004); Francis S. Collins, *The Language of God: A Scientist Presents Evidence for Belief* (New York: Free Press, 2006); and Kenneth R. Miller, *Finding Darwin's God:*

A theist sees the infinite-personal God to be in charge of all natural processes. If the biological order has evolved, it has done so by conforming to God's design; it is teleological, directed toward an end personally willed by God. For a naturalist, the process is on its own. George Gaylord Simpson puts this so well he is worth quoting at some length:

> Organic evolution is a process entirely materialistic in its origin and operation. . . . Life is materialistic in nature, but it has properties unique to itself which reside in its organization, not in its materials or mechanics.

A Scientist's Search for Common Ground Between God and Evolution (San Francisco: Harper Perennial, 2007).

    While methodological naturalism is still the reigning presupposition among most scientists—both secular and Christian—it has been seriously challenged by a number of scientists, philosophers and cultural critics. W. Christopher Stewart explains the conflict between Christians in "Religion and Science," in *Reason for the Hope Within*, ed. Michael J. Murray (Grand Rapids: Eerdmans, 1999), pp. 318-44. For those opposed to methodological naturalism and arguing instead for "design" or "theistic" science, see especially the following: biologist Michael Behe, *Darwin's Black Box: The Biochemical Challenge to Evolution* (New York: Free Press, 1996); Charles B. Thaxton, Walter L. Bradley and Roger L. Olsen, *The Mystery of Life's Origin* (New York: Philosophical Library, 1984); mathematician and philosopher William A. Dembski, *The Design Inference* (New York: Cambridge University Press, 1998); *Intelligent Design: The Bridge Between Science and Theology* (Downers Grove, Ill.: InterVarsity Press, 1999); *Signs of Intelligence: Understanding Intelligent Design* (Grand Rapids: Brazos, 2001); *No Free Lunch* (Lanham, Md.: Rowman and Littlefield, 2002); *Design Revolution: Answering the Toughest Questions About Intelligent Design* (Downers Grove, Ill.: InterVarsity Press, 2004); law professor and cultural critic Phillip E. Johnson, *Darwin on Trial* (Downers Grove, Ill.: InterVarsity Press, 1993); *Reason in the Balance: The Case Against Naturalism in Science, Law and Education* (Downers Grove, Ill.: InterVarsity Press, 1995); *The Wedge of Truth* (Downers Grove, Ill.: InterVarsity Press, 2000); and *The Right Questions* (Downers Grove, Ill.: InterVarsity Press, 2002); and chemist and historian of science Charles B. Thaxton and writer Nancy Pearcey, *The Soul of Science: Christian Faith and Natural Philosophy* (Wheaton, Ill.: Crossway, 1994). Two histories of the birth, development and criticism of the "intelligent design" movement are Thomas Woodward, *Doubts About Darwin: A History of Intelligent Design* (Grand Rapids: Baker, 2003): and *Darwin Strikes Back: Defending the Science of Intelligent Design* (Grand Rapids: Baker, 2006). Critiques of Christian arguments about evolution is found in Del Ratzsch, *The Battle of Beginnings: Why Neither Side Is Winning the Creation-Evolution Debate* (Downers Grove, Ill.: InterVarsity Press, 1996); *Science and Its Limits*, 2nd ed. (Downers Grove, Ill.: InterVarsity Press, 2000); *Nature, Design, and Science: The Status of Design in Natural Science* (Albany: State University of New York Press, 2001).

    Six collections of essays by a wide variety of scholars also focus on this topic: J. P. Moreland, ed., *The Creation Hypothesis: Scientific Evidence for an Intelligent Designer* (Downers Grove, Ill.: InterVarsity Press, 1994); Jon Buell and Virginia Hearn, eds., *Darwinism: Science or Philosophy?* (Richardson, Tex.: Foundation for Thought and Ethics, 1994); William A. Dembski, ed., *Mere Creation: Science, Faith and Intelligent Design* (Downers Grove, Ill.: InterVarsity Press, 1998); J. P. Moreland and John Mark Reynolds, *Three Views on Creation and Evolution* (Grand Rapids: Zondervan, 1999); Michael Behe with others, *Science and Evidence for Design in the Universe: Papers Presented at a Conference Sponsored by the Wethersfield Institute, September 25, 1999* (San Francisco: Ignatius, 2000); and Robert T. Pennock, ed., *Intelligent Design Creationism and Its Critics* (Cambridge, Mass.: MIT Press, 2001).

Man arose as a result of the operation of organic evolution and his being and activities are also materialistic, but the human species has properties unique to itself among all forms of life, superadded to the properties unique to life among all forms of matter and of action. Man's intellectual, social, and spiritual natures are exceptional among animals in degree, but they arose by organic evolution.[42]

This passage is significant for its clear affirmation of both human continuity with the rest of the cosmos and special uniqueness. Yet lest we conclude that our uniqueness, our position as nature's highest creation, was designed by some teleological principle operative in the universe, Simpson adds, "Man was certainly not the goal of evolution, which evidently had no goal."[43]

In some ways the theory of evolution raises as many questions as it solves, for while it offers an explanation for *what* has happened over the eons of time, it does not explain *why*. The notion of a Purposer is not allowed by naturalists. Rather, as Jacques Monod says, humanity's "number came up in the Monte Carlo game," a game of pure chance.[44] And Richard Dawkins, one of the more vocal of recent neo-Darwinian evolutionists, confirms this: "Natural selection is the blind watchmaker, blind because it does not see ahead, does not plan consequences, has no purpose in view."[45] Any intentionality is ruled out as a possibility from the beginning.[46]

In any case, naturalists insist that with the dawn of humanity, evolution suddenly took on a new dimension, for human beings are self-conscious—probably the only self-conscious beings in the universe.[47] Further, as humans we are free consciously to consider, decide and act. Thus while evolution considered strictly on the biological level continues to be

---

[42]Simpson, *Meaning of Evolution*, p. 143. Why Simpson should assign human beings a spiritual nature is not clear. We must not, however, take him to mean that they have a dimension that takes them out of the closed universe.

[43]Ibid.

[44]Jacques Monod, *Chance and Necessity*, trans. Austryn Wainhouse (New York: Alfred A. Knopf, 1971), p. 146.

[45]Richard Dawkins, *The Blind Watchmaker* (New York: W. W. Norton, 1986), p. 21.

[46]See Christoph Cardinal Schönborn, *Chance or Purpose? Creation, Evolution and a Rational Faith*, trans. Henry Taylor (San Francisco: Ignatius Press, 2007) for a Christian perspective on purpose in evolution.

[47]A few naturalists like Carl Sagan believe that given the size and age of the universe, other intelligent beings must have evolved elsewhere in it. But even Sagan admits that there is no hard evidence for this view (Sagan, *Cosmos*, pp. 292, 307-15). That was 1980; the same is true in 2009.

unconscious and accidental, human actions are not. They are not just a part of the "natural" environment. They are human history.

In other words, when human beings appear, meaningful history, human history—the events of self-conscious, self-determining men and women—appears. But like evolution, which has no inherent goal, history has no inherent goal. History is what we make it to be. Human events have only the meaning people give them when they choose them or when they look back on them.

History proceeds in a straight line, as in theism (not in a cycle as in Eastern pantheism), but history has no predetermined goal. Rather than culminating in a second coming of the God-man, it is simply going to last as long as conscious human beings last. When we go, human history disappears, and natural history goes on its way alone.

8. Worldview Question 8: *Naturalism itself implies no particular core commitment on the part of any given naturalist. Rather core commitments are adopted unwittingly or chosen by individuals.*

Each individual is free to choose whatever goal or commitment he or she wishes. Most naturalists are an integral part of a particular cultural community and orient their personal lives within the norms of their commu-

---

I would like to claim that the coming of modern secularity . . . has been coterminous with the rise of a society in which for the first time in history a purely self-sufficient humanism came to be a widely available option. I mean by this a humanism accepting no final goals beyond human flourishing, nor any allegiance to anything else beyond this flourishing. Of no previous society was this true. . . . [A] secular age is one in which the eclipse of all goals beyond human flourishing becomes conceivable; or better, it falls within the range of an imaginable life for masses of people.

CHARLES TAYLOR, *A Secular Society*

---

nity. But there is nothing in the naturalist worldview to require this, and rebels to any society-given notion of the good life cannot reasonably be criticized for their rebellion to social norms. Still, while naturalism provides no rational justification to act selflessly, naturalists often choose to serve their community or promote a purely secular human flourishing. Naturalists will not, of course, choose to live in order to please any God or gods.

NATURALISM IN PRACTICE: SECULAR HUMANISM

Two forms of naturalism deserve special mention. The first is *secular humanism,* a term that has come to be both used and abused by adherents and critics alike. Some clarification of terms is in order here.

First, secular humanism is one form of humanism in general, but not the only form. Humanism itself is the overall attitude that human beings are of special value; their aspirations, their thoughts, their yearnings are significant. There is as well an emphasis on the value of the individual person.

Ever since the Renaissance, thoughtful people of various convictions have called themselves and been called humanists, among them many Christians. John Calvin (1509-1564), Desiderius Erasmus (1456?-1536), Edmund Spenser (1552?-1599), William Shakespeare (1564-1616) and John Milton (1608-1674), all of whom wrote from within a Christian theistic worldview, were humanists, what are sometimes today called Christian humanists. The reason for this designation is that they emphasized human dignity, not as over against God but as deriving from the image of God in each person. Today there are many thoughtful Christians who so want to preserve the word *humanism* from being associated with purely secular forms that they signed a Christian humanist manifesto (1982) declaring that Christians have always affirmed the value of human beings.[48]

The tenets of secular humanism are well expressed in the Humanist Manifesto II.[49] Secular humanism is a form of humanism that is completely framed within a naturalistic worldview. It is fair to say, I believe, that most who would feel comfortable with the label "secular humanist"

---

[48]A Christian humanist manifesto was published in *Eternity,* January 1982, pp. 16-18. The signers were Donald Bloesch, George Brushaber, Richard Bube, Arthur Holmes, Bruce Lockerbie, J. I. Packer, Bernard Ramm and me. Then, too, Norman Klassen and Jens Zimmerman promote a form of Christian humanism they call "incarnational humanism" as a foundation for Christian education, especially at the university level; see their *The Passionate Intellect* (Grand Rapids: Baker Academic, 2006).

[49]*Humanist Manifestos I and II.* Another, briefer compilation of secular humanist views, "The Affirmations of Humanism: A Statement of Principles and Values," appears on the back cover of *Free Inquiry,* Summer 1987.

would find their views reflected in propositions 1-6 above. Secular humanists, in other words, are simply naturalists, though not all naturalists are secular humanists.

NATURALISM IN PRACTICE: MARXISM

Since the latter part of the nineteenth century, one of the most historically significant forms of naturalism has been Marxism.[50] The fortunes of Marxism have ebbed and flowed over the years; the collapse of communism in Eastern Europe and the former Soviet Union has left only a few "officially" Marxist countries. Nevertheless, for the better part of the twentieth century a huge section of the globe was dominated by ideas that stemmed from the philosopher Karl Marx (1818-1883). At the current time, though communism as an ideology seems down and out, many ideas of Marx remain influential among social scientists and other intellectuals in the West. Even in Eastern Europe the former communists, somewhat chastened and professing a commitment to democracy, seem to be making a political comeback.

It is difficult to define or analyze Marxism briefly, for there are many different types of "Marxists."[51] Enormous differences exist between Marxist theories of various kinds, ranging from thinkers who are humanistic and committed to democracy in some form to hard-line "Stalinists" who identify Marxism with totalitarianism. There is another huge difference between Marxist *theories* of all kinds and the reality of Marxist *practice* in the Soviet Union and other places. In theory, Marxism is supposed to benefit working people and enable them to gain economic control over their own lives. In reality, the bureaucratic rigidities of life under communism led to economic stagnation as well as loss of personal freedom.

Although Marxism has generally claimed to be a *scientific* theory (as

---

[50]This section on Marxism was written by C. Stephen Evans, University Professor of Philosophy and Humanities, Baylor University.

[51]One of the best introductions to the many sides of Marxism is Richard Schmitt, *Introduction to Marx and Engels: Critical Reconstruction* (Boulder, Colo.: Westview, 1987.) A good introduction from a Christian point of view is David Lyon, *Karl Marx: A Christian Assessment of His Life and Thought* (Downers Grove, Ill.: InterVarsity Press, 1979). There is no substitute, of course, for the actual writings of Marx to really understand him, as well as the writings of Marx's close friend and collaborator Friedrich Engels. Many of the most important writings are in Richard Tucker, ed., *The Marx-Engels Reader*, 2nd ed. (New York: W. W. Norton, 1978).

in the name "scientific socialism"), this claim has not been generally accepted. It is in many ways more helpful to think of Marxism as a kind of humanism, though of course most humanists are not Marxists. While Marxist humanism has characteristic themes of its own, Marxism and secular humanism, as forms of naturalism, share many assumptions.

All forms of Marxism can of course be traced back to the writings of Karl Marx. The question of who are Marx's "true heirs" is bitterly contested, but the more humanistic Marxists can certainly point to some important themes in Marx's writings. In one of his earliest essays, he says clearly that "man is the supreme being for man."[52] It is from this humanist theme that Marx deduces his revolutionary imperative to "overthrow all those conditions in which man is an abased, enslaved, abandoned, contemptible being."[53]

Marx arrived at his humanism through an encounter with two important nineteenth-century philosophers: Georg Wilhelm Friedrich Hegel (1770-1830) and Ludwig Feuerbach (1804-1872). Hegel's philosophy was a form of idealism that taught that God or "absolute spirit" is not a being distinct from the world but a reality that is progressively realizing itself in the concrete world. For Hegel this process is *dialectical* in nature; that is, it proceeds through conflicts in which each realization of spirit calls forth its own antagonist or "negation." Out of this conflict a still higher realization of spirit emerges, which in turn calls forth its negation, and so on. This philosophy is in essence a highly speculative philosophy of history. For Hegel the highest vehicle for the expression of spirit was human society, particularly the modern societies that were coming to fruition in the capitalistic states of nineteenth-century western Europe.

Feuerbach was a materialist who was famous for asserting that human beings "are what they eat" and that religion is a human invention. As Feuerbach saw it, God is a projection of human potentiality, an expression of our unrealized ideals. Religion functions perniciously, since as soon as we invent God we devote ourselves to pleasing our imaginary construction instead of working to overcome the shortcomings that led to the invention in the first place. Feuerbach extended his critique of religion to Hegel's philosophical idealism, seeing in Hegel's concept of "spirit"

---

[52]Karl Marx, "Contribution to the Critique of Hegel's *Philosophy of Right:* Introduction," in Tucker, *Marx-Engels Reader*, p. 60.
[53]Ibid.

yet another human projection, a slightly secularized version of the Christian God.

Marx accepted Feuerbach's critique of religion wholeheartedly, and atheism remains a part of most forms of Marxism to this day. However, he was struck by the fact that if Feuerbach's criticism of Hegel was right, then Hegel's philosophy may still contain truth. If Hegel's concept of spirit is simply a misleading projection of our human reality, then the dialectical process Hegel described may be real, just as a film when projected may give an accurate picture of the reality that was filmed. It is only necessary to "turn Hegel right side up" by translating Hegel's idealistic talk of spirit into materialistic talk of concrete human beings. Once we realize that in Hegel we are seeing a projection or "film," we can interpret his view in a way that makes it true. History *has* proceeded through conflict in which the contending parties create their own antagonists, and this series of historical conflicts is "going somewhere." The goal of history is a perfect or ideal human society, but it is misleading and confusing to call such a society "spirit."

Marx does call himself a "materialist," and in some sense he certainly is one. Despite this, Marx hardly ever talks about matter. His materialism is *historical* and *dialectical;* it is primarily a doctrine about human history, and it sees that history as a series of dialectical struggles. Economic factors are the primary determinants of that history. Since human beings are material, their lives must be understood in terms of the need to work to satisfy their material needs.

Marx believed that human history began with relatively small human communities organized in familylike tribes. Private property is unknown; a kind of primitive or natural communism holds in which individuals identify with the community as a whole, though these communities are poor and unable to allow their members to flourish. As societies develop technology, gradually a division of labor occurs. Some people in a society control the tools or resources the society depends on; this gives them the power to exploit others. Thus out of division of labor and consequent control over the means of production social classes emerge.

For Marx social classes are the dialectical antagonists of history rather than Hegel's spiritual realities. History for Marx is the history of class struggle. Since the demise of primitive societies, societies have always been dominated by the class that controls the means of production. The process by which the material goods society requires are created is the key to understanding society. This process is termed by Marxists the "base" of society. A particular system for producing material goods, such as feudal agriculture or industrial capitalism, produces a particular class structure. On that class structure depends in turn what Marx calls the "superstructure" of society: art, religion, philosophy, morality and, most important, political institutions.

Social changes occur when one system of production "dialectically" gives rise to a new system. The new economic base comes into being within the womb of the old superstructure. The dominant social classes of the old order of course try to maintain their power as long as possible, relying on the state to maintain their position. Eventually, however, the new economic system and the emerging class become too powerful. The result is a revolution in which the old superstructure is swept away in favor of a new political and social order that better reflects the underlying economic order.

The history of capitalism illustrates these truths clearly, according to Marx. Medieval feudal societies created modern industrial society, which is its dialectical opposite. For a long time the feudal aristocracy tried to hold on to its power, but in the French Revolution Marx saw the triumph of the new middle class, who controlled the means of production in capitalist society. However, the same dialectical forces that led to capitalism will also destroy it. Capitalism requires a large body of propertyless workers, the proletariat, to exploit. As Marx saw it, the economic dynamics of capitalism will necessarily lead to a society in which the proletariat are more and more numerous and more and more exploited. Capitalist societies become more and more productive, but wealth is more and more narrowly distributed. Eventually the concentration of wealth leads to a society in which more is produced than can be purchased; overproduction leads to unemployment and more suffering. At last the proletariat will be forced to revolt.

For Marx the revolt of the proletariat will be different from any previous revolution. In the past, one social class overthrew a rival oppressing class and became in its turn the oppressor. The proletariat will, however, be the majority, not a minority. They have no vested interest in the old order of things, so it will be in their own best interests to abolish the whole system of class oppression. The material abundance created by modern technology makes this a real possibility for the first time in human history, since without such abundance, struggle, competition and oppression would inevitably break out in new forms.

The new classless society that will emerge will make possible what Marxists call "the new socialist individual." People will supposedly be less individualistic and competitive, more apt to find fulfillment in working for the good of others. The "alienation" of all previous societies will be overcome, and a new and higher form of human life will emerge. This vision in many ways parallels the Christian vision of the coming of the kingdom of God, and it is therefore easy to see why some have characterized Marxism as a Christian heresy.

One can also easily see why this vision of Marx was appealing to so many for so long. Marx had a deep understanding of the human need for genuine community and for fulfillment in work. He was sensitive not merely to the problem of poverty but to the loss of dignity that occurs when human beings are seen merely as cogs in a vast industrial machine. He looked for a society in which people would creatively express themselves in their work and see in their work an opportunity to help others as well as themselves.

It is by no means clear that at some point changing conditions will not rekindle interest in Marx. Some theorists, for example, worry that in the United States there is an increasing gap between an economic elite and the great mass of people who are stagnating economically, and that this increasing inequality may make Marx's theories relevant once more.

However, there are also hard questions that Marx does not convincingly answer. One crucial set of questions deals with the reality of life under communism. How could a theory that seems so committed to humanistic liberation produce the dehumanization and oppression of Stalinism? Part of the answer here surely lies in the changes that Vladimir Lenin introduced into Marxism. Marx had predicted that socialism would develop in the most economically advanced societies, such as England and the United States; and he had little faith that true socialism would be possible in a backward country such as Russia. Lenin believed that if society were rigidly controlled by a monolithic Communist party, this would compensate for economic backwardness. So many Western Marxists committed to "democratic socialism" argue that Leninist-style communism was a heretical form of Marxism and that Marx's own ideas were never given a fair chance.

Nevertheless, even if one ignores the reality of life under communism and the horrors of the Gulag, there are many respects in which Marx's ideas appear vulnerable. One crucial concern is his faith that human history is moving toward an ideal society. Having abandoned any religious belief in providence, as well as Hegel's belief in absolute spirit as underlying history, Marx has no real basis for this expectation. He bases his own hope on empirical study of history, particularly his analysis of economic forces. However, many of Marx's predictions, such as his claim that workers in advanced capitalist countries will become increasingly impoverished, have been far off the mark. Can any social scientist—Marxist or non-Marxist—accurately predict the future?

A second problem for Marx concerns our motivation for working toward the future society, especially when we recognize that this society is by no means inevitable. Why should I work for a better society and try to end social exploitation? Marx rejects any moral values as a basis for such motivation. As a naturalist, he views morality as simply a product of human culture. There are no transcendent values that can be used as a basis for critically evaluating culture. Yet Marx himself often seems full of moral indignation as he looks at the excesses of capitalism. What is the basis for Marx's condemnation of capitalism if such moral notions as "justice" and "fairness" are just ideological inventions?

Two final grave problems for Marx lie in his vision of human nature and his analysis of the fundamental human problem. For Marx human beings are fundamentally self-creating; we create ourselves through our work. When our work or life activity is alienated, we are alienated, and when our work has become truly human, we will be human as well. Greed, competition and envy all arise because of social divisions and poverty; an ideal society will eliminate these evils.

The question is whether Marx's view of human nature and analysis of the human problem go deep enough. Is it really plausible to think that selfishness and greed are solely a product of scarcity and class division? Is it really possible to make human beings fundamentally good if we have the right environment for them? Whether we look at capitalist or professedly socialist societies, the lesson of history would seem to be that humans are very inventive in finding ways to manipulate any system for their own selfish benefit. Perhaps the problem with human nature lies deeper than Marx thought. And this problem may expose a problem with his view of human beings: are we purely material beings?

Marx was certainly right to emphasize work and economic factors as crucially important in shaping human society, but there is more to human life than economics. Certainly many young people in the most economically advanced countries struggle with finding meaning and purpose for their lives. Marxism, like all forms of naturalism, has a difficult time providing such meaning and purpose for human beings.

THE PERSISTENCE OF NATURALISM

Naturalism has had great staying power. Born in the eighteenth century, it came of age in the nineteenth and grew to maturity in the twentieth. While signs of age are now appearing and postmodern trumpeters are signaling the death of Enlightenment reason, naturalism is still very much alive. It dominates the universities, colleges and high schools. It provides the framework for most scientific study. It poses the backdrop against which the humanities continue to struggle for human value, as writers, poets, painters and artists in general shudder under its implications.[54] It is seen as the great villain of the postmodern avant-garde. Nonetheless, no rival worldview has yet been able to topple it. Still, it is fair to say that the twentieth century provided some powerful options: Christian theism is experiencing a rebirth at all levels of society and Islamic theism is posing a challenge just off stage.

What makes naturalism so persistent? There are two basic answers. First, it gives the impression of being honest and objective. One is asked to accept only what appears to be based on facts and on the assured results of scientific investigation or scholarship. Second, to a vast number of people it appears to be coherent. To them the implications of its premises are largely worked out and found acceptable. Naturalism assumes no god, no spirit, no life beyond the grave. It sees human beings as the makers of value. While it disallows that we are the center of the universe by virtue of design, it allows us to place ourselves there and to make of ourselves and for ourselves something of value. As Simpson says, "Man *is* the highest animal. The fact that he alone is capable of making such a judgment is in itself part of the evidence that this decision is correct."[55] It is up

---

[54]An important Christian critique of naturalism is found in Johnson's *Reason in the Balance*.
[55]Simpson, *Meaning of Evolution*, p. 139.

to us then to work out the implications of our special place in nature, controlling and altering, as we find it possible, our own evolution.[56]

All of this is attractive. If naturalism were really as described, it should, perhaps, be called not only attractive or persistent but true. We could then proceed to tout its virtues and turn the argument of this book into a tract for our times.

But long before the twentieth century got under way, cracks began appearing in the edifice. Theistic critics always found fault with it. They could never abandon their conviction that an infinite-personal God is behind the universe. Their criticism might be discounted as unenlightened or merely conservative, as if they were afraid to launch out into the uncharted waters of new truth. But more was afoot than this. As we shall see in more detail in the following chapter and chapter nine on postmodernism, within the camp of the naturalists themselves came rumblings of discontent. The facts on which naturalism was based—the nature of the external universe, its closed continuity of cause and effect—were not at issue. The problem was coherence. Did naturalism give an adequate reason for us to consider ourselves valuable? Unique, maybe. But gorillas are unique. So is every category of nature. Value was the first troublesome issue. Could a being thrown up by chance be worthy?

Second, could a being whose origins were so "iffy" trust his or her own capacity to know? Put it personally: If my mind is conterminous with my brain, if "I" am only a thinking machine, how can I trust my thought? If consciousness is an epiphenomenon of matter, perhaps the appearance of human freedom which lays the basis for morality is an epiphenomenon of either chance or inexorable law. Perhaps chance or the nature of things only built into me the "feeling" that I am free but actually I am not.

These and similar questions do not arise from outside the naturalist worldview. They are inherent in it. The fears that these questions raised in some minds led directly to nihilism, which I am tempted to call a worldview but which is actually a denial of all worldviews.

---

[56]Ibid., pp. 166-81. From the early days of Darwin and T. H. Huxley, naturalists have placed much hope in human evolution. Some modern optimists are Arthur C. Clarke, *Profiles of the Future* (New York: Bantam, 1964), pp. 212-27; Peter Medawar, "On Effecting All Things Possible," *The Listener*, October 2, 1969, pp. 437-42; Glenn Seaborg, "The Role of Science and Technology," *Washington University Magazine*, Spring 1972, pp. 31-35; Julian Huxley, "Transhumanism," in *Knowledge, Morality and Destiny* (New York: Mentor, 1960), pp. 13-17.

Chapter 5

ZERO POINT

NIHILISM

If I should cast off this tattered coat,
And go free into the mighty sky;
If I should find nothing there
But a vast blue,
Echoless, ignorant—
What then?

STEPHEN CRANE, *THE BLACK RIDERS AND OTHER LINES*

Nihilism is more a feeling than a philosophy, more a solitary stance before the universe than a worldview. Strictly speaking, nihilism is a denial of any philosophy or worldview—a denial of the possibility of knowledge, a denial that anything is valuable. If it proceeds to the absolute denial of everything, it even denies the reality of existence itself. In other words, nihilism is the negation of everything—knowledge, ethics, beauty, reality. In nihilism no statement has validity; nothing has meaning. Everything is gratuitous, de trop, that is, just there.

Those who have been untouched by the feelings of despair, anxiety and ennui associated with nihilism may find it hard to imagine that nihilism could be a seriously held orientation of the heart. But it is, and it is well for everyone who wants to understand the twentieth and twenty-first centuries to experience, if only vicariously, something of nihilism as a stance toward human existence.

Modern art galleries are full of its products—if one can speak of something (art objects) coming from nothing (artists who, if they exist, deny the ultimate value of their existence). As we shall see later, no art is ultimately nihilistic, but some attempts to embody many of nihilism's characteristics. Marcel Duchamp's ordinary urinal purchased on the common market, signed with a fictional name, and labeled *Fountain* will do for a start. Samuel Beckett's plays, notably *End Game* and *Waiting for Godot,* are prime examples in drama. But Beckett's nihilistic art perhaps reached its climax in *Breath,* a thirty-five-second play that has no human actors. The props consist of a pile of rubbish on the stage, lit by a light that begins dim, brightens (but never fully) and then recedes to dimness. There are no words, only a "recorded" cry opening the play, an inhaled breath, an exhaled breath and an identical "recorded" cry closing the play. For Beckett life is such a "breath."

Douglas Adams in his cosmic science-fiction novels pictures the situation for those who seek in computer science an answer to human meaning. In *The Hitchhiker's Guide to the Galaxy; The Restaurant at the End of the Universe; Life, the Universe and Everything* and *So Long and Thanks for All the Fish* Adams tells the story of the universe from the point of view of four time travelers who hitchhike back and forth across intergalactic time and space, from creation in the big bang to the final destruction of the universe.[1] During the course of this history a race of hyper-intelligent pan-dimensional beings (mice, actually) build a giant computer ("the size of a small city") to answer "The Ultimate Question of Life, the Universe and Everything." This computer, which they call Deep Thought, spends seven and a half million years on the calculation.[2]

> For seven and a half million years, Deep Thought computed and calculated, and in the end announced that the answer was in fact Forty-two—and so another, even bigger, computer had to be built to find out what the actual question was.
>
> And this computer, which was called the Earth, was so large that it was frequently mistaken for a planet—especially by the strange apelike beings who roamed its surface, totally unaware that they were simply part of a gigantic computer program.

---

[1]Douglas Adams, *The Hitchhiker's Guide to the Galaxy* (New York: Pocket, 1981); *The Restaurant at the End of the Universe* (New York: Pocket, 1982); *Life, the Universe and Everything* (New York: Pocket, 1983); *So Long and Thanks for All the Fish* (London: Pan, 1984).
[2]Adams, *Hitchhiker's Guide,* p. 173.

And this is very odd, because without that fairly simple and obvious piece of knowledge, nothing that ever happened on the Earth could possibly make the slightest bit of sense. Sadly, however, just before the critical moment of read-out, the Earth was unexpectedly demolished by the Vogons to make way—so they claimed—for a new hyperspace bypass, and so all hope of discovering a meaning for life was lost for ever. Or so it would seem.[3]

By the end of the second novel, the time travelers discover that the "question itself" (the Ultimate Question of Life, the Universe and Everything) is "What is six times nine?"[4] So, they discover, both the question and the answer are inane. Not only is 42 a meaningless answer to the question on a human level (the level of purpose and meaning), it is bad mathematics. The most rational discipline in the university has been reduced to absurdity.

By the end of the third novel, we have an explanation for why the question and the answer do not seem to fit each other. Prak, the character who is supposed to know the ultimate, says this: "I'm afraid . . . that the Question and the Answer are mutually exclusive. Knowledge of one logically precludes knowledge of the other. It is impossible that both can ever be known about the same Universe."[5] (Physics students will detect here a play on Heisenberg's uncertainty principle, where the position and momentum of an electron can both be known, but not with precision at the same time.)

So we can know the Answers—like 42—which don't mean anything without the Questions. Or we can have the Questions (which give direction to our quest). But we can't have both. That is, we cannot satisfy our longing for ultimate meaning.

To read Samuel Beckett, Franz Kafka, Eugene Ionesco, Joseph Heller, Kurt Vonnegut Jr. and, more recently, Douglas Adams is to begin to feel—if one does not already in our depressing age—the pangs of human emptiness, of life that is without value, without purpose, without meaning.[6]

---

[3]Adams, *Restaurant*, p. 3.

[4]Ibid., p. 246.

[5]Adams, *Life*, p. 222. At the end of the fourth novel, which seems not nearly so poignant in its effect, we learn God's final message to us: "We apologize for the inconvenience" (*So Long*, p. 189).

[6]Adams may have the last laugh after all, for, as my mathematician friends tell me, 6 times 9 is 54 but can be written as 42 in base 13. Go figure!

But how does one get from naturalism to nihilism? Wasn't naturalism the enlightened readout of the assured results of science and open intellectual inquiry? As a worldview, did it not account for human beings, their uniqueness among the things of the cosmos? Did it not show human dignity and value? As the highest of creation, the only self-conscious, self-determined beings in the universe, men and women are rulers of all, free to value what they will, free even to control the future of their own evolution. What more could one wish?

Most naturalists are satisfied to end their inquiry right here. They do in fact wish for no more. For them there is no route to nihilism.[7]

But for a growing number of people the results of reason are not so assured, the closed universe is confining, the notion of death as extinction is psychologically disturbing, our position as the highest in creation is seen either as an alienation from the universe or as a union with it such that we are no more valuable than a pebble on the beach. In fact, pebbles "live" longer! What bridges led from a naturalism that affirms the value of human life to a naturalism that does not? Just how did nihilism come about?

Nihilism came about not because theists and deists picked away at naturalism from the outside. Nihilism is the natural child of naturalism.

THE FIRST BRIDGE: NECESSITY AND CHANCE

The first and most basic reason for nihilism is found in the direct, logical implications of naturalism's primary propositions. Notice what happens to the concept of human nature when one takes seriously the notions that (1) matter is all there is and it is eternal, and (2) the cosmos operates with a uniformity of cause and effect in a closed system. These mean that a human being is a part of the system. Though they may not understand the implications for human freedom, naturalists agree, as we saw in proposition 3 of chapter four: *Human beings are complex machines whose personality is a function of highly complex chemical and physical properties not yet understood.* Nietzsche, however, bites the bullet and recognizes the loss to human dignity. He is simply deluded about having free will.

---

[7]My scientist friend Carl Peraino is one such person; he maintains a consistent naturalism but insists that this does not lead him to nihilism. See our dialogue in our *Deepest Differences: A Christian-Atheist Dialogue* (Downers Grove, Ill.: InterVarsity Press, 2009).

Still many naturalists try to hold on to human freedom within the closed system. Their argument goes like this. Every event in the universe is caused by a previous state of affairs, including the genetic makeup, the environmental situation of each person and even the person's wants and desires. But each person is free to express those wants and desires. If I want a sand-

---

If one were omniscient, one would be able to calculate each individual [human] action in advance, each step in the progress of knowledge, each error, each act of malice. To be sure, the acting man is caught in his illusion of volition; if the wheel of the world were to stand still for a moment and an omniscient calculating mind were there to take advantage of this interruption, he would be able to tell into the farthest future of each being and describe every rut that wheel will roll upon. The acting man's delusion about himself, his assumption that free will exists, is also part of the calculating mechanism.

FRIEDRICH NIETZSCHE, *Human, All Too Human*

---

wich and a deli is around the corner, I can choose to have a sandwich. If I want to steal the sandwich when the owner isn't looking, I can do that. Nothing constrains my choice. My actions are self-determined.

Thus human beings who are obviously self-conscious and, it would appear, self-determined can act significantly and be held responsible for their actions. I can be arrested for stealing the sandwich and reasonably required to pay the penalty.

But are things so simple? Many think not. The issue of human freedom goes deeper than these naturalists see. To be sure I can do anything I want, but what I want is the result of past states of affairs over which ultimately I had no control. I did not freely select my particular genetic makeup or my original family environment. By the time I asked whether I was free to act freely, I was so molded by nature and nurture that the very fact that the question occurred to me was determined. That is, my self itself was determined by outside forces. I can indeed ask such questions, I can act according to my wants and desires, and I can appear to myself to be free, but it is appearance only. Nietzsche is right: "the acting man's delusion about himself, his assumption that free will exists, is also part of the calculating mechanism."

The problem is that if the universe is truly closed, then its activity can be governed only from within. Any force that acts to change the cosmos on whatever level (microcosmic, human, macrocosmic) is a part of the cosmos. There would thus seem to be *only* one explanation for change: the present state of affairs must govern the future state. In other words, the present must cause the future, which in turn must cause the next future, and so on.

The objection that in an Einsteinian universe of time-relativity simultaneity is impossible to define and causal links are impossible to prove is beside the point. We are not talking here about how the events are linked together, only noting that they are linked. Events occur because other events have occurred. All activity in the universe is connected this way. We cannot, perhaps, know what the links are, but the premise of a closed universe forces us to conclude that they must exist.

Moreover, there is evidence that such links exist, for patterns of events are perceivable, and some events can be predicted from the standpoint of earth time with almost absolute precision, for example, precisely when and where the next eclipse will take place. For every eclipse in the next fifteen centuries the exact shadow can be predicted and tracked in space and time across the earth. Most events cannot be so predicted, but the presumption is that that is because all the variables and their interrelations are not known. Some events are more predictable than others, but none is *uncertain*. Each event must come to be.

In a closed universe the possibility that some things need not be, that others are possible, is not possible. For the only way change can come is by a force moving to make that change, and the only way that force can come is if it is moved by another force, ad infinitum. There is no break in this chain, from eternity past to eternity future, forever and ever, amen.

To the ordinary person determinism does not appear to be the case. We generally perceive ourselves as free agents. But our perception is an illusion. We just do not know what "caused" us to decide. Something did, of course, but we feel it was our free choice. Such perceived freedom—if one does not think much about its implications—is quite sufficient, at least according to some.[8]

---

[8]John Platt, for example, thinks this is the only freedom a person really needs (*Center Magazine*, March-April 1972, p. 47).

In a closed universe, in other words, freedom must be a *determinacy unrecognized,* and for those who work out its implications, this is not enough to allow for self-determinacy or moral responsibility. For if I robbed a bank, that would ultimately be due to inexorable (though unperceived) forces triggering my decisions in such a way that I could no longer consider these decisions mine. If these decisions are not mine, I cannot be held responsible. And such would be the case for every act of every person.

A human being is thus a mere piece of machinery, a toy—complicated, very complicated, but a toy of impersonal cosmic forces. A person's self-consciousness is only an epiphenomenon; it is just part of the machinery looking at itself. But consciousness is only part of the machinery; there is no "self" apart from the machinery. There is no "ego" that can stand over against the system and manipulate it at its own will. Its "will" is the will of the cosmos. In this picture, by the way, we have a rather good description of human beings as seen by behavioral psychologist B. F. Skinner. To change people, says Skinner, change their environment, the contingencies under which they act, the forces acting on them. A person must respond in kind, for in Skinner's view every person is only a reactor: "A person does not act on the world, the world acts on him."[9]

The nihilists follow this argument, which can now be stated briefly: Human beings are conscious machines without the ability to affect their own destiny or do anything significant; therefore, human beings as valuable beings are dead. Their life is Beckett's "breath," not the life God "breathed" into the first person in the Garden (Gen 2:7).

But perhaps the course of my argument has moved too fast. Have I missed something? Some naturalists would certainly say so. They would say that I went wrong when I said that the only explanation for change is the continuity of cause and effect. Jacques Monod, for example, attributes all basic change—certainly the appearance of anything genuinely new—to chance. And naturalists admit that new things have come into being by the uncountable trillions: every step on the evolutionary scale from hydrogen, carbon, oxygen, nitrogen and so forth in free association to the formation of complex amino acids and other basic building blocks of life. At every turn—and these are beyond count—chance introduced the new

---

[9]B. F. Skinner, *Beyond Freedom and Dignity* (New York: Alfred A. Knopf, 1971), p. 211. Skinner's behaviorism, always highly criticized, is now (more than three decades later) generally considered simplistic and inadequate as an explanation for human behavior.

thing. Then necessity, or what Monod calls "the machinery of invariance," took over and duplicated the chance-produced pattern. Slowly over eons of time through the cooperation of chance and necessity, cellular life, multicellular life, the plant and animal kingdoms and human beings emerged.[10] So chance is offered as the trigger for humanity's emergence.

But what is chance? Either chance is the inexorable proclivity of reality to happen as it does, appearing to be chance because we do not know the reason for what happens (making chance another name for our ignorance of the forces of determinism), or it is absolutely irrational.[11] In the first case, chance is just unknown determinism and not freedom at all. In the second case, chance is not an explanation but the absence of an explanation.[12] An event occurs. No cause can be assigned. It is a chance event. Not only might such an event have not happened, it could never have been expected to happen. So while chance produces the appearance of freedom, it actually introduces absurdity. Chance is causeless, purposeless, directionless.[13] It is

---

[10]Jaques Monod, *Chance and Necessity*, trans. Austryn Wainhouse (New York: Alfred A. Knopf, 1971), pp. 98, 112.

[11]Some scientists are wary of basing metaphysical conclusions on scientific concepts. Richard Bube, for example, argues that chance as a scientific concept is not the same as chance as a worldview (that is, metaphysical) concept, noting that in science *chance* is the term given to a scientific description that is "able only to predict the probability of the future state of a system from the knowledge of its present state" (Richard Bube, *Putting It All Together: Seven Patterns for Relating Science and the Christian Faith* [Lanham, Md.: University Press of America, 1995], p. 23). Scientific *chance*, then, labels a limit to knowledge rather than describes a characteristic of "reality" (i.e., makes a metaphysical statement). Such scientific chance then is compatible with the notion of a rational world, as understood by Christians and naturalists alike. But it is clear that chance often functions, even in the writings of scientists (notably Monod), in a worldview (that is, metaphysical) sense.

[12]See Nancy Pearcey and Charles Thaxton, *The Soul of Science: Christian Faith and Natural Philosophy* (Wheaton, Ill.: Crossway, 1994), pp. 214-15; chap. 9, "Quantum Mysteries: Making Sense of the New Physics," pp. 187-219, is a lucid exposition of the issues involved.

[13]The scientific concept of chance is vexed. The Heisenberg principle of indeterminacy holds that one cannot determine with accuracy both the location and the momentum of any given electron. One can have precise knowledge of either, but not both at the same time. It is an epistemological principle. But many scientists, including Werner Heisenberg, drew ontological implications from the epistemological principle that are clearly not warranted. Heisenberg himself said, "Since all experiments are subjected to the laws of quantum mechanics, . . . the invalidity of the law of causality is definitely proved by quantum mechanics" (quoted by Stanley Jaki, "Chance or Reality," in *Chance or Reality and Other Essays* [Lanham, Md.: University Press of America, 1986], pp. 6-7). The implication is that not only is the universe not understandable at a fundamental level, but the universe is itself irrational or, even, unreal.

Heisenberg, along with at least some other scientists and popularizers of science, has moved from ignorance of reality to knowledge about that reality. I cannot measure X; therefore X does not exist. It is just such a movement from the limits of knowledge to the declaration that we have no justification for thinking we know anything that constitutes much of

sudden givenness—gratuity incarnated in time and space.

But as Monod says, it introduced into time and space a push in a new direction. A chance event is causeless, but it itself is a cause and is now an integral part of the closed universe. Chance opens the universe not to reason, meaning and purpose but to absurdity. Suddenly we don't know where we are. We are no longer a flower in the seamless fabric of the universe, but a chance wart on the smooth skin of the impersonal.

Chance, then, does not supply a naturalist with what is necessary for a person to be both self-conscious and free. It only allows one to be self-conscious and subject to caprice. Capricious action is not a free expression of a person with character. It is simply gratuitous, uncaused. Capricious action is by definition not a response to self-determination, and thus we are still left without a basis for morality.[14] Such action simply is.

To summarize: The first reason naturalism turns into nihilism is that naturalism does not supply a basis on which a person can act significantly. Rather, it denies the possibility of a self-determining being who can choose on the basis of an innate self-conscious character. We are machines—determined or capricious. We are not persons with self-consciousness and self-determination.

---

the postmodern pattern of thinking (see chapter nine of this book). Reality has to conform to the human mind in a theoretically completely knowable way or it does not exist. In fact, solipsism "has for long been recognized as an inevitable implication of the drastic meaning of Heisenberg's principle" (Jaki, "Chance or Reality," pp. 12-13).

One way out of the dilemma was taken by Niels Bohr, who insisted that "all statements about ontology or being must be avoided" (ibid., p. 8). As Jaki says, W. Pauli agreed "that questions about reality were as metaphysical and useless as was the concern of medieval philosophers about the number of angels that could be put on a pinhead" (ibid., p. 10).

Another way out, taken by Albert Einstein and other scientists, tried to get around the principle itself by finding ways of conceiving how measurements could be complete and accurate at the same time. Their attempt failed. All that could be said is, in Einstein's words, "God doesn't play dice with the universe" (ibid., p. 9). But this was more a pretheoretical commitment, a presupposition, than a conclusion drawn from successful theorizing from either laboratory or thought experiments. This then left the ontological conclusion to be drawn as many did: the universe is not fundamentally understandable (ibid., p. 8).

A premodern humility about the human ability to know might have prevented this rash and illogical move. Think of the apostle Paul's caution ("Now we see through a glass darkly") and then hope ("but then face to face"; 1 Cor 13:12 KJV).

The issue, Jaki concludes, boils down to a confusion of ontology and epistemology. "The science of quantum mechanics states only the impossibility of perfect accuracy in measurements. The philosophy of quantum mechanics states ultimately the impossibility of distinguishing between material and non-material, and even between being and non-being. . . . At any rate, if it is impossible to distinguish between being and non-being, then efforts to say anything about freedom and determinism become utterly meaningless" (Jaki, "Chance or Reality," p. 14).

[14]Jaki notes that knowledge too loses its foundation ("Chance or Reality," p. 17).

THE SECOND BRIDGE: THE GREAT CLOUD
OF UNKNOWING

The metaphysical presupposition that the cosmos is a closed system has implications not only for metaphysics but also for epistemology. The argument in brief is this: if any given person is the result of impersonal forces—whether working haphazardly or by inexorable law—that person has no way of knowing whether what he or she seems to know is illusion or truth. Let us see how that is so.

Naturalism holds that perception and knowledge are either identical with or a byproduct of the brain; they arise from the functioning of matter. Without matter's functioning there would be no thought. But matter functions by a nature of its own. There is no reason to think that matter has any interest in leading a conscious being to true perception or to logical (that is, correct) conclusions based on accurate observation and true presuppositions.[15] The only beings in the universe who *care* about such matters are humans. But people are bound to their bodies. Their consciousness arises from a complex interrelation of highly "ordered" matter. Why should whatever that matter is conscious of be in any way related to what actually is the case? Is there a test for distinguishing illusion from reality? Naturalists point to the methods of scientific inquiry, pragmatic tests and so forth. But all these utilize the brain they are testing. Each test could well be a futile exercise in spinning out the consistency of an illusion.

For naturalism nothing exists outside the system itself. There is no God—deceiving or nondeceiving, perfect or imperfect, personal or impersonal. There is only the cosmos, and humans are the only conscious beings. But they are latecomers. They "arose," but how far? Can they trust their mind, their reason?

Charles Darwin himself once said, "The horrid doubt always arises whether the convictions of man's mind, which has developed from the mind of the lower animals, are of any value or at all trustworthy. Would anyone trust the conviction of a monkey's mind, if there are any convic-

---

[15]Alvin Plantinga uses an argument of this type to reject Darwin's "dangerous idea" that the human mind developed by means of natural selection—the survival of the fittest. See "Dennett's Dangerous Idea," Plantinga's review of Daniel C. Dennett's *Darwin's Dangerous Idea* (New York: Simon & Schuster, 1995), in *Books and Culture*, May/June 1996, p. 35. A full version of his argument is found in his *Warrant and Proper Function* (New York: Oxford University Press, 1993), chap. 12.

tions in such a mind?"[16] In other words, if my brain is no more than that of a superior monkey, I cannot even be sure that my own theory of my origin is to be trusted.

Here is a curious case: If Darwin's naturalism is true, there is no way of even establishing its credibility, let alone proving it. Confidence in logic is ruled out. Darwin's own theory of human origins must therefore be accepted by an act of faith. One must hold that a brain, a device that came to be through natural selection and chance-sponsored mutations, can actually *know* a proposition or set of propositions to be true.

C. S. Lewis puts the case this way:

> If all that exists is Nature, the great mindless interlocking event, if our own deepest convictions are merely the by-products of an irrational process, then clearly there is not the slightest ground for supposing that our sense of fitness and our consequent faith in uniformity tell us anything about a reality external to ourselves. Our convictions are simply *a fact about us*—like the colour of our hair. If Naturalism is true we have no reason to trust our conviction that Nature is uniform.[17]

What we need for such certainty is the existence of some "Rational Spirit" outside both ourselves and nature from which our own rationality could derive. Theism assumes such a ground; naturalism does not.

Not only are we boxed in by the past—our origin in inanimate, unconscious matter—we are also boxed in by our present situation as thinkers. Let us say that I have just completed an argument on the level of "All men are mortal; Aristotle Onassis is a man; Aristotle Onassis is mortal." That's a proven conclusion. Right?

Well, how do we know it's right? Simple. I have obeyed the laws of logic. *What laws? How do we know them to be true?* They are self-evident. After all, would any thought or communication be possible without them? *No.* So aren't they true? *Not necessarily.*

---

[16]From a letter to W. Graham (July 3, 1881), quoted in *The Autobiography of Charles Darwin and Selected Letters* (1892; reprint, New York: Dover, 1958). I am indebted to Francis A. Schaeffer for this observation, which he made in a lecture on Darwin. C. S. Lewis in a parallel argument quotes J. B. S. Haldane as follows: "If my mental processes are determined wholly by the motion of atoms in my brain, I have no reason to suppose that my beliefs are true . . . and hence I have no reason for supposing my brain to be composed of atoms" (*Miracles* [London: Fontana, 1960], p. 18).

[17]Lewis, *Miracles*, p. 109. In another context Lewis remarks, "It is only when you are asked to believe in Reason coming from non-reason that you must cry Halt, for, if you don't, all thought is discredited" (p. 32).

Any argument we construct implies such laws—the classical ones of identity, noncontradiction and the excluded middle. But that fact does not guarantee the "truthfulness" of these laws in the sense that anything we think or say that obeys them necessarily relates to what is so in the objective, external universe. Moreover, any argument to check the validity of an argument is itself an argument that might be mistaken. When

---

Almost all our discoveries are due to our violences [*sic*], to the exacerbation of our instability. Even God insofar as He interests us—it is not in our inmost selves that we discern God, but at the extreme limits of our fever, at the very point where, our rage confronting His, a shock results, an encounter as ruinous for Him as for us. Blasted by the curse attached to acts, the man of violence forces his nature, rises above himself only to relapse, an aggressor, followed by his enterprises, which come to punish him for having instigated them. Every work turns against its author: the poem will crush the poet, the system the philosopher, the event the man of action. Destruction awaits anyone who, answering to his vocation and fulfilling it, exerts himself within history; only the man who sacrifices every gift and talent escapes: released from his humanity, he may lodge himself in Being. If I aspire to a metaphysical career, I cannot, at any price, retain my identity: whatever residue I retain must be liquidated; if, on the contrary, I assume a historical role it is my responsibility to exasperate my faculties until I explode along with them. One always perishes by the self one assumes: to bear a name is to claim an exact mode of collapse.

E. M. CIORAN, *The Temptation to Exist*

---

we begin to think like this, we are not far from an infinite regress; our argument chases its tail down the ever-receding corridors of the mind. Or, to change the image, we lose our bearings in a sea of infinity.

But haven't we gone astray in arguing against the possibility of knowledge? We do *seem* to be able to test our knowledge in a way that generally satisfies us. Some things we think we know can be shown to be false or at least highly unlikely—for example, that microbes are spontaneously generated from totally inorganic mud. And all of us *know* how to boil water, scratch our itches, recognize our friends and distinguish them from others in a crowd.

Virtually no one is a full-fledged epistemological nihilist. Yet naturalism does not allow a person to have any solid reason for confidence in human reason. We thus end in an ironic paradox. Naturalism, born in the Age of Enlightenment, was launched on a firm acceptance of the human ability to know. Now naturalists find that they can place no confidence in their knowing.

The whole point of this argument can be summarized briefly: Naturalism places us as human beings in a box. But for us to have any confidence that our knowledge that we are in a box is true, we need to stand outside the box or to have some other being outside the box provide us with information (theologians call this "revelation"). But there is nothing or no one outside the box to give us revelation, and we cannot ourselves transcend the box. Ergo: epistemological nihilism.

A naturalist who fails to perceive this is like the man in Stephen Crane's poem:

> I saw a man pursuing the horizon;
> Round and round they sped.
> I was disturbed at this;
> I accosted the man.
> "It is futile," I said,
> "You can never—"
> "You lie," he cried,
> And ran on.[18]

In the naturalistic framework, people pursue a knowledge that forever recedes before them. We can never *know*.

One of the worst consequences of taking epistemological nihilism seriously is that it has led some to question the very facticity of the universe.[19] To some, nothing is real, not even themselves. People who reach this state are in deep trouble, for they can no longer function as human beings. Or, as we often say, they can't cope.

We usually do not recognize this situation as metaphysical or episte-

---

[18]From Stephen Crane, *The Black Riders and Other Lines*, frequently anthologized.

[19]Stanley Jaki comments on physicists who attempt to skirt this problem yet end as antirealists after all ("Chance or Reality," pp. 8-16).

mological nihilism. Rather, we call it schizophrenia, hallucination, fantasizing, daydreaming or living in a dream world. And we treat the person as a "case," the problem as a "disease." I have no particular quarrel with doing this, for I do believe in the reality of an external world, one I hold in common with others in my space-time frame. Those who cannot recognize this are beyond coping. But while we think of such situations primarily in psychological terms and while we commit such people to institutions where someone will keep them alive and others will help them return from their inner trip and get back to waking reality, we should realize that some of these far-out cases may be perfect examples of what happens when a person no longer knows in the commonsense way of knowing. It is the "proper" state, the logical result, of epistemological nihilism. If I cannot know, then any perception or dream or image or fantasy becomes equally real or unreal. Life in the ordinary world is based on our ability to make distinctions. Ask the man who has just swallowed colorless liquid which he thought was water but which was actually wood alcohol.

Most of us never see the far-out "cases." They are quickly committed. But they exist, and I have met some people whose stories are frightening. Most full epistemological nihilists, however, fall in the class described by Robert Farrar Capon, who simply has no time for such nonsense:

> The skeptic is never for real. There he stands, cocktail in hand, left arm draped languorously on one end of the mantelpiece, telling you that he can't be sure of anything, not even of his own existence. I'll give you my secret method of demolishing universal skepticism in four words. Whisper to him: "Your fly is open." If he thinks knowledge is so all-fired impossible, why does he always look?[20]

As noted above, there is just too much evidence that knowledge is possible. What we need is a way to explain why we have it. This naturalism does not do. So the one who remains a consistent naturalist must be a closet nihilist who does not know where he is.

THE THIRD BRIDGE: IS AND OUGHT

Many naturalists—most, so far as I know—are very moral people. They are not thieves, they do not tend to be libertines. Many are faithful husbands and wives. Some are scandalized by the personal and public im-

---

[20]Robert Farrar Capon, *Hunting the Divine Fox* (New York: Seabury, 1974), pp. 17-18.

morality of our day. The problem is not that moral values are not recognized but that they have no basis. Summing up the position reached by
Nietzsche and Max Weber, Allan Bloom remarks, "Reason cannot establish values, and its belief that it can is the stupidest and most pernicious
illusion."[21]

Remember that for a naturalist the world is merely there. It does not
provide humanity with a sense of oughtness. It only *is.* Ethics, however, is
about what ought to be, whether it is or not.[22] Where, then, does one go
for a basis for morality? Where is *oughtness* found?

As I have noted, every person has moral values. There is no tribe without taboos. But these are merely facts of a social nature, and the specific
values vary widely. In fact, many of these values conflict with each other.
Thus we are forced to ask, Which values are the true values, or the higher
values?

Cultural anthropologists, recognizing that this situation prevails, answer clearly: Moral values are relative to one's culture. What the tribe,
nation, social unit says is valuable is valuable. But there is a serious flaw
here. It is only another way of saying that *is* (the fact of a specific value)
equals *ought* (what should be so). Moreover, it does not account for the
situation of cultural rebels whose moral values are not those of their
neighbors. The cultural rebel's *is* is not considered *ought.* Why? The answer of cultural relativism is that the rebel's moral values cannot be allowed if they upset social cohesiveness and jeopardize cultural survival.
So we discover that *is* is not *ought* after all. The cultural relativist has affirmed a value—the preservation of a culture in its current state—as
more valuable than its destruction or transformation by one or more rebels within it. Once more, we are forced to ask *why.*

Cultural relativism, it turns out, is not forever relative. It rests on a
primary value affirmed by cultural relativists themselves: that cultures
should be preserved. So cultural relativism does not rely only on *is* but on
what its adherents think *ought* to be the case. The trouble here is that

---

[21]Allan Bloom, *The Closing of the American Mind* (New York: Simon & Schuster, 1987), p.
194.
[22]See Antony Flew, "From Is to Ought," in *The Sociobiology Debate,* ed. Arthur L. Caplan (New
York: Harper & Row, 1978), pp. 142-62, for a rigorous explanation of why the naturalistic attempt to get *ought* from *is* is a fallacy. One scientist who saw the paucity of physics to provide
an ethical norm was Einstein, who "told one of his biographers that he never derived a single
ethical value from physics" (Jaki, "Chance or Reality," citing P. Michelmore, *Einstein: Profile
of the Man* [New York: Dodd, 1962], p. 251).

some anthropologists are not cultural relativists. Some think certain values are so important that cultures that do not recognize them *should* recognize them.[23] So cultural relativists must, if they are to convince their colleagues, show why their values are the true values.[24] Again we approach the infinite corridor down which we chase our arguments.

But let's look again. We must be sure we see what is implied by the fact that values do really vary widely. Between neighboring tribes values conflict. One tribe may conduct "religious wars" to spread its values. Such wars *are*. *Ought* they to be? Perhaps, but only if there is indeed a nonrelative standard by which to measure the values in conflict. But a naturalist has no way of determining which values among the ones in existence are the basic ones that give meaning to the specific tribal variations. A naturalist can point only to the fact of value, never to an absolute standard.

This situation is not so critical as long as sufficient space separates peoples of radically differing values. But in the global community of the twenty-first century this luxury is no longer ours. We are forced to deal with values in conflict, and naturalists have no standard, no way of knowing when peace is more important than preserving another value. We may give up our property to avoid doing violence to a robber. But what shall we say to white racists who own rental property in the city? Whose values are to govern their actions when a black person attempts to rent their property? Who shall say? How shall we decide?

The argument can again be summarized like that above: Naturalism places us as human beings in an ethically relative box. For us to know what values within that box are true values, we need a measure imposed on us from outside the box; we need a moral plumb line by which we can evaluate the conflicting moral values we observe in ourselves and others. But there is nothing outside the box; there is no moral plumb line, no ultimate, nonchanging standard of value. Ergo: ethical nihilism.[25]

---

[23]In an outrageous section of his *Darwin's Dangerous Idea*, Dennett, with no foundation at all, universalizes his own subjective ethic: "Save the Elephants! Yes, of course, but not *by all means*. Not by forcing the people of Africa to live nineteenth-century lives, for instance. . . . Save the Baptists! Yes, of course, but not *by all means*. Not if it means tolerating the deliberate misinforming of children about the natural world [that is, not if it means they get to teach their children that the book of Genesis is literally true]" (pp. 515-16).

[24]See Bloom's discussion of values (*Closing of the American Mind*, pp. 25-43, 194-215).

[25]Richard Dawkins represents a common stance among naturalists. While he makes moral judgments (he rejects the notion that the weak should be simply allowed to die), he admits that he has no rational foundation for this judgment. Here is a naturalist who refuses to accept for his own life the logical consequences of naturalism. Nihilists with greater integrity

But nihilism is a feeling, not just a philosophy. And on the level of human perception, Franz Kafka catches in a brief parable the feeling of life in a universe without a moral plumb line.

> I ran past the first watchman. Then I was horrified, ran back again and said to the watchman: "I ran through here while you were looking the other way." The watchman gazed ahead of him and said nothing. "I suppose I really oughtn't to have done it," I said. The watchman still said nothing. "Does your silence indicate permission to pass?"[26]

When people were conscious of a God whose character was moral law, when their consciences were informed by a sense of rightness, their watchmen would shout halt when they trespassed the law. Now their

---

One knows my demand of philosophers that they place themselves *beyond* good and evil—and that they have the illusion of moral judgement [*sic*] *beneath* them. This demand follows from an insight formulated by me: *that there are no moral facts whatever*. Moral judgement has this in common with religious judgement that it believes in realities which do not exist. Morality is only an interpretation of certain phenomena, more precisely a *mis*interpretation. Moral judgement belongs, as does religious judgement, to a level of ignorance at which even the concept of the real, the distinction between the real and the imaginary, is lacking: so that at such a level "truth" denotes nothing but things which we today call "imaginings." To this extent moral judgement is never to be taken literally: as such it never contains anything but nonsense. But as *semiotics* it remains of incalculable value: it reveals, to the informed man at least, the most precious realities of cultures and inner worlds which did not *know* enough to "understand" themselves. Morality is merely sign-language, merely symptomatology: one must already know *what* it is about to derive profit form it.

FRIEDRICH NIETZSCHE, "The 'Improvers' of Mankind"

---

bite the bullet (see Nick Pollard's interview with Dawkins in the *Space/Time Gazette*, Autumn 1995, as reported in the *Newsletter of the ASA and CSCA*, July/August 1996, p. 4).
[26]Franz Kafka, "The Watchman," in *Parables and Paradoxes* (New York: Schocken, 1961), p. 81.

watchmen are silent. They serve no king and protect no kingdom. The wall is a fact without a meaning. One scales it, crosses it, breaches it, and no watchman ever complains. One is left not with the fact but with the feeling of guilt.[27]

In a haunting dream sequence in Ingmar Bergman's film *Wild Strawberries,* an old professor is arraigned before the bar of justice. When he asks the charge, the judge replies, "You are guilty of guilt."

"Is that serious?" the professor asks.

"Very serious," says the judge.

But that is all that is said on the subject of guilt. In a universe where God is dead, people are not guilty of violating a moral law; they are only guilty of guilt, and that is very serious, for nothing can be done about it. If one had sinned, there might be atonement. If one had broken a law, the lawmaker might forgive the criminal. But if one is only guilty of guilt, there is no way to solve the very personal problem.[28]

And that states the case for a nihilist, for no one can avoid acting as if moral values exist and as if there is some bar of justice that measures guilt by objective standards. But there is no bar of justice, and we are left not in sin, but in guilt. Very serious, indeed.

THE LOSS OF MEANING

The strands of epistemological, metaphysical and ethical nihilism weave together to make a rope long enough and strong enough to hang a whole culture. The name of the rope is Loss of Meaning. We end in a total despair of ever seeing ourselves, the world and others as in any way significant. Nothing has meaning.

Kurt Vonnegut Jr., in a parody of Genesis 1, captures this modern dilemma:

> In the beginning God created the earth, and he looked upon it in His cosmic loneliness.

---

[27]One of Nietzsche's epigrams in *The Gay Science* echoes Kafka's parable: *"Guilt.* Although the most acute judges of the witches, and even the witches themselves, were convinced of the guilt of witchery, the guilt nevertheless was nonexistent. It is thus with all guilt" (*The Portable Nietzsche,* trans. Walter Kaufmann [New York: Viking, 1954], pp. 96-97).

[28]One could reply that such guilt (that is, guilt feelings) can be removed by Freudian psychoanalysis or other psychotherapy and thus there is something that can be done. But this merely emphasizes the amorality of human beings. It solves a person's problem of feeling guilty by not allowing one any way at all to act morally.

And God said, "Let Us make creatures out of mud, so mud can see what We have done." And God created every living creature that now moveth, and one was man. Mud as man alone could speak. God leaned close as mud as man sat up, looked around and spoke. Man blinked. "What is the purpose of all this?" he asked politely.

"Everything must have a purpose?" asked God.

"Certainly," said man.

"Then I leave it to you to think of one for all this," said God. And he went away.[29]

This may first appear to be a satire on theism's notion of the origin of the universe and human beings, but it is quite the contrary. It is a satire on the naturalist's view, for it shows our human dilemma. We have been thrown up by an impersonal universe. The moment a self-conscious, self-determining being appears on the scene, that person asks the big question: What is the meaning of all this? What is the purpose of the cosmos? But the person's creator—the impersonal forces of bedrock matter—cannot respond. If the cosmos is to have meaning, we must manufacture it for ourselves.

As Stephen Crane put it in the poem quoted in the opening of the first chapter, the existence of people has not created in the universe "a sense of obligation." Precisely: We exist. Period. Our maker has no sense of value, no sense of obligation. We alone make values. Are our values valuable? By what standard? Only our own. Whose own? Each person's own. Each of us is king and bishop of our own realm, but our realm is pointland. For the moment we meet another person, we meet another king and bishop. There is no way to arbitrate between two free value makers. There is no king to whom both give obeisance. There are values, but no Value. Society is only a bunch of windowless monads, a collection of points, not an organic body obeying a superior, all-encompassing form that arbitrates the values of its separate arms, legs, warts and wrinkles. Society is not a body at all. It is only a bunch.

Thus does naturalism lead to nihilism. If we take seriously the implications of the death of God, the disappearance of the transcendent, the closedness of the universe, we end right there.

Why, then, aren't most naturalists nihilists? The obvious answer is the best one: Most naturalists do not take their naturalism seriously. They

[29]Kurt Vonnegut Jr., *Cat's Cradle* (New York: Dell, 1970), p. 177.

are inconsistent. They affirm a set of values. They have friends who affirm a similar set. They appear to know and don't ask how they know they know. They seem to be able to choose and don't ask themselves whether their apparent freedom is really caprice or determinism. Socrates said that the unexamined life is not worth living, but for a naturalist he is wrong. For a naturalist it is the examined life that is not worth living.

INNER TENSIONS IN NIHILISM

The trouble is that no one can live the examined life if examination leads to nihilism, for nobody can live a life consistent with nihilism. At every step, at every moment, nihilists think, and think their thinking has substance, and thus they cheat on their philosophy. There are, I believe, at least five reasons that nihilism is unlivable.

First, from meaninglessness nothing at all follows, or rather, anything follows. If the universe is meaningless and a person cannot know and nothing is immoral, any course of action is open. One can respond to meaninglessness by any act whatsoever, for none is more or less appropriate. Suicide is one act, but it does not "follow" as any more appropriate than going to a Walt Disney movie.

Yet whenever we set ourselves on a course of action, putting one foot in front of the other in other than a haphazard way, we are affirming a goal. We are affirming the value of a course of action, even if to no one other than ourselves. Thus we are not living by nihilism. We are creating value by choice. From this type of argument comes Albert Camus's attempt to go beyond nihilism to existentialism, which we will consider in the following chapter.[30]

Second, every time nihilists think and trust their thinking, they are inconsistent, for they have denied that thinking is of value or that it can lead to knowledge. But at the heart of a nihilist's one affirmation lies a self-contradiction. *There is no meaning in the universe,* nihilists scream. That means that their only affirmation is meaningless, for if it were to mean anything it would be false.[31] Nihilists are indeed boxed in. They

---

[30]I am indebted to Helmut Thielicke, *Nihilism*, trans. John W. Doberstein (London: Routledge and Kegan Paul, 1962), pp. 148-66, esp. 163-66, for this observation about nihilism.

[31]Another way to put this argument is to point out that constructing sentences is such a fundamental act, such a paradigmatic affirmation of meaning, that to construct sentences to deny meaning is self-contradictory. Keith Yandell in "Religious Experience and Rational Appraisal," *Religious Studies*, June 1974, p. 185, expresses the argument as follows: "If a con-

can get absolutely nowhere. They merely are; they merely think; and none of this has any significance whatsoever. Except for those whose actions place them in institutions, no one seems to act out their nihilism. Those who do we treat as patients.

Third, while a limited sort of practical nihilism is possible for a while, eventually a limit is reached. The comedy of *Catch-22* rests on just this premise. Captain Yossarian is having a knock-down theological argument with Lt. Scheisskopf's wife, and God is coming in for a good deal of hassling. Yossarian is speaking:

> [God] is not working at all. He's playing. Or else He's forgotten all about us. That's the kind of God you people talk about—a country bumpkin, a clumsy, bungling, brainless, conceited, uncouth hayseed.
>
> Good God, how much reverence can you have for a Supreme Being who finds it necessary to include such phenomena as phlegm and tooth decay in His system of creation?[32]

After several unsuccessful attempts to handle Yossarian's verbal attack, Lt. Scheisskopf's wife turns to violence.

> "Stop it! Stop it!" Lieutenant Scheisskopf's wife screamed suddenly, and began beating him ineffectually about the head with both fists. "Stop it!" . . .
>
> "What the hell are you getting so upset about?" he asked her bewilderedly in a tone of contrite amusement. "I thought you didn't believe in God."
>
> "I don't," she sobbed, bursting violently into tears. "But the God I don't believe in is a good God, a just God, a merciful God. He's not the mean and stupid God you make Him out to be."[33]

Here is another paradox: In order to deny God one must have a God to deny. In order to be a *practicing* nihilist, there must be something against which to do battle. A practicing nihilist is a parasite on meaning. She runs out of energy when there is nothing left to deny. The cynic is out of business when she is the last one around.

Fourth, nihilism means the death of art. Here too we find a paradox, for much modern art—literature, painting, drama, film—has nihilism for

ceptual system *F* is such that it can be shown that (a) *F is true* and (b) *F is known to be true*, are incompatible, then this fact provides a good (though perhaps not conclusive) reason for supposing that *F is false.*"

[32]Joseph Heller, *Catch-22* (New York: Dell, 1962), p. 184.
[33]Ibid., p. 185.

its ideological core. And much of this literature is excellent by the traditional canons of art. Ernest Hemingway's "A Clean Well-Lighted Place," Samuel Beckett's *End Game,* Ingmar Bergman's *Winter Light,* Franz Kafka's *The Trial,* Francis Bacon's various heads of popes spring immediately to mind. The twist is this: to the extent that these artworks display the

---

A younger and an older waiter are closing a "clean well-lighted" bar for the night. When the young waiter leaves, the older lonely waiter thinks to himself. What did he fear? It was not fear or dread. It was nothing that he knew too well. It was all a nothing and a man was nothing too. It was only that and light was all it needed and a certain cleanness and order. Some lived in it and never felt it but he knew it all was nada y pues nada y nada y pues nada. Our nada who art in nada, nada be thy name thy kingdom nada thy will be nada in nada as it is in nada. Give us this nada our daily nada and nada us our nada as we nada our nadas and nada us not into nada but deliver us from nada; pues nada. Hail nothing full of nothing, nothing is with thee. He smiled and stood before a bar with a shining steam pressure coffee machine.

ERNEST HEMINGWAY, "A Clean Well-Lighted Place"

---

human implication of a nihilistic worldview, they are not nihilistic; to the extent that they themselves are meaningless, they are not artworks.

Art is nothing if not formal, that is, endowed with structure by the artist. But structure itself implies meaning. So to the extent that an artwork has structure, it has meaning and thus is not nihilistic. Even Beckett's *Breath* has structure. A junkyard, the garbage in a trash heap, a pile of rocks just blasted from a quarry have no structure. They are not art.

Some contemporary art attempts to be anti-art by being random. Much of John Cage's music is predicated on sheer chance, randomness. But it is both dull and grating, and very few people can listen to it. It's not art. Then there is Kafka's "Hunger Artist," a brilliant though painful story about an artist who tries to make art out of public fasting, that is, out of nothing. But no one looks at him; everyone passes by his display at the circus to see a young leopard pacing in his cage. Even the "nature" of the leopard is more interesting than the "art" of the nihilist. *Breath* too, as minimal as it is, is structured and means something. Even if it means only that human beings are meaningless, it participates in the paradox I examined above. In short, art implies meaning and is ultimately nonnihilistic, despite the ironic attempt of nihilists to display their wares by means of it.

Fifth, and finally, nihilism poses severe psychological problems for a nihilist. People cannot live with it because it denies what every fiber of their waking being calls for—meaning, value, significance, dignity, worth. "Nietzsche," Bloom writes, "replaces easygoing or self-satisfied atheism with agonized atheism, suffering its human consequences. Longing to believe, along with intransigent refusal to satisfy that longing, is, according to him, the profound response to our entire spiritual condition."[34]

Nietzsche ended in an asylum. Ernest Hemingway affirmed a "lifestyle" and eventually committed suicide. Beckett writes black comedy. Vonnegut and Adams revel in whimsy. And Kafka—perhaps the greatest artist of them all—lived an almost impossible life of tedium, writing novels and stories that boil down to a sustained cry: "God is dead! God is dead! Isn't he? I mean, surely he is, isn't he? God is dead. Oh, I wish, I wish, I wish he weren't."

It is thus that nihilism forms the hinge for modern people. No one who has not plumbed the despair of the nihilists, heard them out, felt as they felt—if only vicariously through their art—can understand the past century. Nihilism is the foggy bottomland through which we modern people must pass if we are to build a life in Western culture. There are no easy answers to our questions, and none of these answers is worth anything unless it takes seriously the problems raised by the possibility that nothing whatever of value exists.

[34]Bloom, *Closing of the American Mind*, p. 196.

Chapter 6

BEYOND NIHILISM

Every existing thing is born without reason,
prolongs itself out of weakness and dies by chance.
I leaned back and closed my eyes.
The images, forewarned, immediately leaped up
and filled my closed eyes with existences: existence is a fullness
which man can never abandon. . . . I knew it was the World,
the naked World suddenly revealing itself, and I choked
with rage at this gross absurd being.

ROQUENTIN IN JEAN-PAUL SARTRE, *NAUSEA*

In an essay published in 1950, Albert Camus wrote, "A literature of despair is a contradiction in terms. . . . In the darkest depths of our nihilism I have sought only for the means to transcend nihilism."[1] Here the essence of existentialism's most important goal is summed up in one phrase: *to transcend nihilism.* In fact, every important worldview that has emerged since the beginning of the twentieth century has had that as a major goal. For nihilism, coming as it does directly from a culturally pervasive worldview, is the problem of our age. A worldview that ignores this fact has little chance of proving relevant to modern thinking people.

---

[1]Albert Camus, *L'Été,* quoted in John Cruickshank, *Albert Camus and the Literature of Revolt* (New York: Oxford University Press, 1960), p. 3.

Existentialism, especially in its secular form, not only takes nihilism seriously, it is an answer to it.

From the outset it is important to recognize that existentialism takes two basic forms, depending on its relation to previous worldviews, because existentialism is not a full-fledged worldview. Atheistic existentialism is a parasite on naturalism; theistic existentialism is a parasite on theism.[2]

Historically, we have an odd situation. On the one hand, atheistic existentialism developed to solve the problem of a naturalism that led to nihilism, but it did not appear in any fullness till well into the twentieth century, unless we count a major theme in Nietzsche that quickly became distorted.[3] On the other hand, theistic existentialism was born in the middle of the nineteenth century as Søren Kierkegaard responded to the dead orthodoxy of Danish Lutheranism. Yet it was not until after World War I that either form of existentialism became culturally significant, for it was only then that nihilism finally gripped the intellectual world and began affecting the lives and attitudes of ordinary men and women.[4]

World War I had not made the world safe for democracy. The generation of flappers and bathtub gin, the rampant violation of an absurd antiliquor law, the quixotic stock market that promised so much—these prefaced in the United States the Dust Bowl 1930s. With the rise of National Socialism in Germany and its incredible travesty of human dignity, students and intellectuals the world over were ready to conclude that life is absurd and human beings are meaningless. In the soil of such frustration and cultural discontent, existentialism in its atheistic form sank its cultural roots. It was to flower into a significant worldview by the 1950s.

To some extent all worldviews have subtle variations. Existentialism is no exception. Camus and Sartre, both existentialists and once friends, had a falling-out over important differences, and Martin Heidegger's existentialism is quite different from Sartre's. But as with other worldviews, we will focus on major features and general tendencies. The language of most of the propositions listed below derives from either Sartre or Ca-

---

[2]I am indebted to C. Stephen Board for this observation.

[3]The theme to which I refer is the "will to power" ending in the notion of the *Übermensch* (the "Overman" or "Superman"), all that is left after the total loss of any transcendent standard for either ethics or epistemology. I will discuss this in the section on postmodernism (chapter nine).

[4]Thus fulfilling Nietzsche's "prophecy" in the parable of the madman. See p. 214 below.

mus. That is quite intentional, because that is the form in which it has been most digested by today's intelligentsia, and through their literary works even more than their philosophic treatises, Sartre and Camus are still wielding enormous influence. To many modern people the propositions of existentialism appear so obvious that people "do not know what they are assuming because no other way of putting things has ever occurred to them."[5]

BASIC ATHEISTIC EXISTENTIALISM

Atheistic existentialism begins by accepting naturalism's answers to worldview questions 1, 4, 5, 6 and 7. In short: *Matter exists eternally; God does not exist. Death is extinction of personality and individuality. Through our innate and autonomous human reason, including the methods of science, we can know the universe. The cosmos, including this world, is understood to be in its normal state. Ethics is related only to human beings. History is a linear stream of events linked by cause and effect but without an overarching purpose.*

In other words, atheistic existentialism affirms most of the propositions of naturalism except those relating to human nature and our relationship to the cosmos. Indeed, existentialism's major interest is in our humanity and how we can be significant in an otherwise insignificant world.

1. Worldview Question 2: *The cosmos is composed solely of matter, but to human beings reality appears in two forms—subjective and objective.*

The world, it is assumed, existed long before human beings came on the scene. It is structured or chaotic, determined by inexorable law or subject to chance. Whichever it is makes no difference. The world merely is.

Then came a new thing, conscious beings—ones who distinguished *he* and *she* from *it*, ones who seemed determined to determine their own destiny, to ask questions, to ponder, to wonder, to seek meaning, to endow the external world with special value, to create gods. In short, then came human beings. Now we have—for no one knows what reason—two kinds of being in the universe, the one seemingly having kicked the other out of itself and into separate existence.

The first sort of being is the objective world—the world of material, of

[5]A. N. Whitehead, *Science and the Modern World* (1925; reprint, New York: Mentor, 1948), p. 49.

inexorable law, of cause and effect, of chronological, clock-ticking time, of flux, of mechanism. The machinery of the universe, spinning electrons, whirling galaxies, falling bodies and rising gases and flowing waters—each is doing its thing, forever unconscious, forever just being where it is when it is. Here, say the existentialists, science and logic have their day. People know the external, objective world by virtue of careful observation, recording, hypothesizing, checking hypotheses by experiment, ever refining theories and proving guesses about the lay of the cosmos we live in.

The second sort of being is the subjective world—the world of mind, of consciousness, of awareness, of freedom, of stability. Here the inner awareness of the mind is a conscious present, a constant now. Time has no meaning, for the subject is always present to itself, never past, never future. Science and logic do not penetrate this realm; they have nothing to say about subjectivity. Subjectivity is the self's apprehension of the not-

---

Existence is not something which lets itself be thought of from a distance: it must invade you suddenly, master you, weigh heavily on your heart like a great motionless beast—or else there is nothing more at all.
REQUENTIN IN JEAN-PAUL SARTRE, *Nausea*

---

self; subjectivity is making that not-self part of itself. The subject takes in knowledge not as a bottle takes in liquid but as an organism takes in food. Knowledge turns into the knower.

Naturalism had emphasized the unity of the two worlds by seeing the objective world as the real and the subjective as its shadow. "The brain secretes thought," said Pierre Jean Georges Cabanis, "as the liver secretes bile." The real is the objective. Sartre says, "The effect of all materialism is to treat all men, including the one philosophizing, as objects, that is, as an ensemble of determined reactions in no way distinguished from the ensemble of qualities and phenomena which constitute a table or a chair or a stone."[6] By that route, as we saw, lies nihilism. The existentialists take another path.

Existentialism emphasizes the disunity of the two worlds and opts

---

[6]Jean-Paul Sartre, "Existentialism," reprinted in *A Casebook on Existentialism,* ed. William V. Spanos (New York: Thomas Y. Crowell, 1966), p. 289.

strongly in favor of the subjective world, what Sartre calls "an ensemble of values distinct from the material realm."[7] For people are *the* subjective beings. Unless there are extraterrestrial beings, a possibility most existentialists do not even consider, we are the only beings in the universe who are self-conscious and self-determinate. The reason we have become that way is past finding out. But we perceive ourselves to be self-conscious and self-determinate, and so we work from these givens.

Science and logic do not penetrate our subjectivity, but that is all right because value and meaning and significance are not tied to science and logic. We *can mean;* we *can be valuable;* or better, *we* can mean and be valuable. Our significance is not up to the facts of the objective world over which we have no control, but up to the consciousness of the subjective world over which we have complete control.

2. Worldview Question 3: *Human beings are complex "machines"; personality is an interrelation of chemical and physical properties we do not yet fully understand. For human beings alone existence precedes essence; people make themselves who they are.*

Atheistic existentialism is at one with naturalism's basic view of human nature; there is indeed no genuinely transcendent element in human beings, but they do display one important unique feature. To put it in Sartre's words, "If God does not exist, there is at least one being in whom existence precedes essence, a being who exists before he can be defined by any concept, and . . . this being is man." This sentence is the most famous definition of the core of existentialism. Sartre continues, "First of all, man exists, turns up, appears on the scene, and, only afterwards, defines himself."[8]

Note again the distinction between the objective and subjective worlds. The objective world is a world of essences. Everything comes bearing its nature. Salt is salt; trees are tree; ants are ant. Only human beings are not human before they make themselves so. Each of us makes himself or herself human by what we do with our self-consciousness and our self-determinacy. Back to Sartre: "At first he [any human being] is nothing. Only afterwards will he be something, and he himself will have made

<hr>

[7]Ibid.
[8]Ibid., p. 278.

him what he will be."[9] The subjective world is completely at the beck and call of every subjective being, that is, of every person.

How does this work out in practice? Let us say that John, a soldier, fears he is a coward. Is he a coward? Only if he acts like a coward, and his action will proceed not from a nature defined beforehand but from the choices he makes when the bullets start to fly. We can call John a coward if and only if he does cowardly deeds, and these will be deeds he chooses to do. So if John fears he is a coward but does not want to be, let him do brave deeds when they are called for.[10]

3. Worldview Question 3, continued: *Each person is totally free as regards his or her nature and destiny.*

From proposition 2 it follows that each person is totally free. Each of us is uncoerced, radically capable of doing anything imaginable with our subjectivity. We can think, will, imagine, dream, project visions, consider, ponder, invent. Each of us is king of our own subjective world.

We run into just such an understanding of human freedom in John Platt's existential defense of B. F. Skinner's naturalistic behaviorism:

> The objective world, the world of isolated and controlled experiments, is the world of physics; the subjective world, the world of knowledge, values, decisions, and acts—of purposes which these experiments are in fact designed to serve—is the world of cybernetics, of our own goal-seeking behavior. Determinism or indeterminism lies on *that* side of the boundary, while the usual idea of "free will" lies on *this* side of the boundary. They belong to different universes, and no statement about one has any bearing on the other.[11]

So we are free within. And thus we can create our own value by affirming worth. We are not bound by the objective world of ticking clocks and falling water and spinning electrons. Value is inner, and the inner is each person's own.

4. Worldview Questions 2 , 3 and 4: *The highly wrought and tightly organized objective world stands over against human beings and appears absurd.*

---

[9]Ibid.
[10]This illustration derives from Sartre, "Existentialism," pp. 283-84.
[11]John Platt in *Center Magazine*, March-April 1972, p. 47.

The objective world considered in and of itself is as the naturalist has said: a world of order and law, perhaps triggered into new structures by chance. It is the world of *thereness*.

To us, however, the facticity, the hard, cold thereness of the world, appears alien. As we make ourselves to be by fashioning our subjectivity, we see the objective world as absurd. It does not fit us. Our dreams and visions, our desires, all our inner world of value runs smack up against a universe that is impervious to our wishes. Think all day that you can step off a ten-story building and float safely to the ground. Then try it.

The objective world is orderly; bodies fall if not supported. The subjective world knows no order. What is present to it, what is here and now, *is*.

So we are all strangers in a foreign land. And the sooner we learn to accept that, the sooner we transcend our alienation and pass through the despair.

The toughest fact to transcend is the ultimate absurdity—death. We are free so long as we remain subjects. When we die, each of us is just an object among other objects. So, says Camus, we must ever live in the face of the absurd. We must not forget our bent toward nonexistence, but live out the tension between the love of life and the certainty of death.

5. Worldview Questions 5: *In full recognition of and against the absurdity of the objective world, the authentic person must revolt and create value.*

Here is how an existentialist goes beyond nihilism. Nothing is of value in the objective world in which we become conscious, but while we are conscious we create value. The person who lives an authentic existence is the one who keeps ever aware of the absurdity of the cosmos but who rebels against that absurdity and creates meaning.

Fyodor Dostoyevsky's "underground man" is a paradigm of the rebel without a seemingly reasonable cause. In the story the underground man is challenged:

> Two and two do make four. Nature doesn't ask your advice. She isn't interested in your preferences or whether or not you approve of her laws. You must accept nature as she is with all the consequences that that implies. So a wall is a wall, etc., etc.

The walls referred to here are the "laws of nature," "the conclusions of the natural sciences, of mathematics." But the underground man is equal to the challenge:

> But, Good Lord, what do I care about the laws of nature and arithmetic if I have my reasons for disliking them, including the one about two and two making four! Of course, I won't be able to breach this wall with my head if I'm not strong enough. But I don't have to accept a stone wall just because it's there and I don't have the strength to breach it.[12]

It is thus insufficient to pit the objective world against the subjective and point to its ultimate weapon, death. The person who would be authentic is not impressed. Being a cog in the cosmic machinery is much worse than death. As the underground man says, "The meaning of a man's life consists in proving to himself every minute that he is a man and not a piano key."[13]

Ethics, that is, a system of understanding what is the good, is solved simply for an existentialist. The good action is the consciously chosen action. Sartre writes, "To choose to be this or that is to affirm at the same time the value of what we choose, because we can never choose evil. We

---

If I've discarded God the Father, there has to be someone to invent values. You've got to take things as they are. Moreover, to say that we invent values means nothing else than this: life has no meaning *a priori*. Before you come alive, life is nothing; it's up to you to give it meaning, and value is nothing else but the meaning you choose. In that way, you see, there is a possibility of creating human community.

JEAN-PAUL SARTRE, *Existentialism and Human Emotions*

---

always choose the good."[14] So the good is whatever a person chooses; the good is part of subjectivity; it is not measured by a standard outside the individual human dimension.

The problem with this position is twofold. First, subjectivity leads to solipsism, the affirmation that each person alone is the determiner of values and that there are thus as many centers of value as there are persons

---

[12]Fyodor Dostoyevsky, *Notes from Underground*, trans. Andrew R. MacAndrew (New York: New American Library, 1961), p. 99.
[13]Ibid., p. 115.
[14]Sartre, "Existentialism," p. 279.

in the cosmos at any one time. Sartre recognizes this objection and counters by insisting that every person in meeting other persons encounters a recognizable center of subjectivity.[15] Thus we see that others like us must be involved in making meaning for themselves. We are all in this absurd world together, and our actions affect each other in such a way that "nothing can be good for us without being good for all."[16] Moreover, as I act and think and effect my subjectivity, I am engaged in a social activity: "I am creating a certain image of man of my own choosing. In choosing myself, I choose man."[17] According to Sartre, therefore, people living authentic lives create value not only for themselves but for others too.

The second objection Sartre does not address, and it seems more telling. If, as Sartre says, we create value simply by choosing it and thus "can never choose evil," does good have any meaning? The first answer is yes, for evil is "not-choosing." In other words, evil is passivity, living at the direction of others, being blown around by one's society, not recognizing the absurdity of the universe, that is, not keeping the absurd alive. If the good is in choosing, then choose. Sartre once advised a young man who sought his counsel, "You're free, choose, that is, invent."[18]

Does this definition satisfy our human moral sensitivity? Is the good merely any action passionately chosen? Too many of us can think of actions seemingly chosen with eyes open that were dead wrong. In what frame of mind have the Russian pogroms against the Jews been ordered and executed? And the bombing of Vietnamese villages or the Federal Building in Oklahoma City or the targets of the Unabomber? What about the terrorist leveling of the World Trade Center on September 11, 2001? Sartre himself has sided with causes that appear quite moral on grounds many traditional moralists accept. But not every existentialist has acted like Sartre, and the system seems to leave open the possibility for the Unabomber to claim ethical immunity for his murders, or for the perpetrators of the events of 9/11 to glory in the nobility of their cause.

Placing the locus of morality in each individual's subjectivity leads to the inability to distinguish a moral from an immoral act on grounds that satisfy our innate sense of right, a sense that says others have the same

---

[15]Ibid., p. 289.
[16]Ibid., p. 279.
[17]Ibid., p. 280.
[18]Ibid., p. 285.

rights as I do. My choice may not be the desired choice of others though in my choosing I choose for others, as Sartre says. Some standard external to the "subjects" involved is necessary to shape truly the proper actions and relationships between "subjects."

6. Worldview Question 8: *The core commitment of every full-blown atheistic existentialist is to himself or herself.*

Ordinary naturalists can choose to commit themselves to their families or neighbors, their communities or country, the environment or the world. They need not display overarching egotism or selfishness. But full-blown atheistic existentialists have already committed themselves to themselves. If they are indeed committed to this Sartrean notion of human selves making themselves whom they will come to be, they are the emperors and bishops of their own pointland. Since they themselves make themselves who they are, they are responsible only to themselves. They admit they are finite beings in an absurd world, subject to death without exception. The authenticity of their value comes solely by virtue of their own conscious choices.

Before we abandon existentialism to the charge of solipsism and a relativism that fails to provide a basis for ethics, we should give more than passing recognition to Albert Camus's noble attempt to show how a good life can be defined and lived. This, it seems to me, is the task Camus sets for himself in *The Plague.*

A SAINT WITHOUT GOD

In *The Brothers Karamazov* (1880) Dostoevsky has Ivan Karamazov say that if God is dead everything is permitted. In other words, if there is no transcendent standard of the good, then there can ultimately be no way to distinguish right from wrong, good from evil, and there can be no saints or sinners, no good or bad people. If God is dead, ethics is impossible.

Albert Camus picks up that challenge in *The Plague* (1947), which tells the story of Oran, a city in North Africa, in which a deadly strain of infectious disease breaks out. The city closes its gates to traffic and thus becomes a symbol of the closed universe, a universe without God. The disease, on the other hand, comes to symbolize the absurdity of this universe. The plague is arbitrary; one cannot predict who will and who will not contract it. It is not "a thing made to man's measure."[19] It is terrible in its effects—painful physically and mentally. Its origins are not known, and yet it becomes as familiar as daily bread. There is no way to avoid it. Thus the plague comes to stand for death itself, for like death it is unavoidable and its effects are terminal. The plague helps make everyone in Oran live an authentic existence, because it makes everyone aware of the absurdity of the world they inhabit. It points up the fact that people are born with a love of life but live in the framework of the certainty of death.

The story begins as rats start to come out from their haunts and die in the streets; it ends a year later as the plague lifts and life in the city returns to normal. During the intervening months, life in Oran becomes life in the face of total absurdity. Camus's genius is to use that as a setting against which to show the reactions of a cast of characters, each of whom represents in some way a philosophic attitude.

M. Michel, for example, is a concierge in an apartment house. He is outraged at the way the rats are coming out of their holes and dying in his apartment building. At first he denies they exist in his building, but eventually he is forced to admit it. Early in the novel he dies cursing the rats. M. Michel represents the man who refuses to acknowledge the absurdity of the universe. When he is forced to admit it, he dies. He cannot live in the face of the absurd. He represents those who are able to live only inauthentic lives.

The old Spaniard has a very different reaction. He had retired at age fifty and gone immediately to bed. Then he measured time, day in and day out, by moving peas from one pan to another. "'Every fifteen peas,' he said, 'it's feeding time. What could be simpler?'"[20] The old Spaniard never leaves his bed, but he takes a sadistic pleasure in the rats, the heat and the plague, which he calls "life."[21] He is Camus's nihilist. Nothing in his life— inside or out, objective world or subjective world—has value. So he lives it with a complete absence of meaning.

M. Cottard represents a third stance. Before the plague grips the city, he is nervous, for he is a criminal and is subject to arrest if detected. But as the plague becomes severe, all city employees are committed to alleviating the distress, and Cottard is left free to do as he will. And what he

---

[19]Albert Camus, *The Plague*, trans. Stuart Gilbert (New York: Random House, 1948), p. 35.
[20]Ibid. p. 108.
[21]Ibid., pp. 9, 29, 277.

wills to do is live off the plague. The worse conditions get, the richer, happier and friendlier he becomes. "Getting worse every day isn't it? Well, anyhow, everyone's in the same boat," he says.[22] Jean Tarrou, one of the chief characters in the novel, explains Cottard's happiness this way: "He's in the same peril of death as everyone else, but that's just the point; he's in it *with the others*."[23]

When the plague begins to lift, Cottard loses his feeling of community because he again becomes a wanted man. He loses control of himself, shoots up a street and is taken by force into custody. Throughout the plague his actions were criminal. Instead of alleviating the suffering of others, he feasted on it. He is Camus's sinner in a universe without God—proof, if you will, in novelistic form that evil is possible in a closed cosmos.

If evil is possible in a closed cosmos, then perhaps good is too. In two major characters, Jean Tarrou and Dr. Rieux, Camus develops this theme. Jean Tarrou was baptized into the fellowship of nihilists when he visited his father at work, heard him argue as a prosecuting attorney for the death of a criminal, and then saw an execution. This had a profound effect on him. As he puts it, "I learned that I had had an indirect hand in the deaths of thousands of people. . . . We all have the plague."[24] And thus he lost his peace.

From then on, Jean Tarrou has made his whole life a search for some way to become "a saint without God."[25] Camus implies that Tarrou succeeds. His method lies in comprehension and sympathy and ultimately issues in action.[26] He is the one who suggests a volunteer corps of workers to fight the plague and comfort its victims. Tarrou works ceaselessly in this capacity. Yet there remains a streak of despair in his lifestyle: "winning the match" for him means living "only with what one knows and what one remembers, cut off from what one hopes for!" So, writes Dr. Rieux, the narrator of the novel, Tarrou "realized the bleak sterility of a life without illusions."[27]

Dr. Rieux himself is another case study of the good man in an absurd world. From the very beginning he sets himself with all his strength to

[22]Ibid., p. 174.
[23]Ibid., p. 175.
[24]Ibid., pp. 227-28.
[25]Ibid., p. 230.
[26]Ibid., pp. 120, 230.
[27]Ibid., pp. 262-63.

fight the plague—to revolt against the absurd. At first his attitude is passionless, detached, aloof. Later, as his life is deeply touched by the lives and deaths of others, he softens and becomes compassionate. Philosophically, he comes to understand what he is doing. He is totally unable to accept the idea that a good God could be in charge of things. As Baudelaire said, that would make God the devil. Rather, Dr. Rieux takes as his task "fighting against creation as he found it."[28] He says, "Since the order of the world is shaped by death, mightn't it be better for God if we refuse to believe in Him and struggle with all our might against death, without raising our eyes toward the heaven where He sits in silence."[29]

Dr. Rieux does exactly that: he struggles against death. And the story he tells is a record of "what had had to be done, and what assuredly would have to be done again in the never ending fight against terror and its relentless onslaughts, despite their personal afflictions, by all who, while unable to be saints but refusing to bow down to pestilences, strive their utmost to be healers."[30]

I have dwelt at length on *The Plague* (though by no means exhausting its riches either as art or as a lesson in life)[31] because I know of no novel or work of existential philosophy that makes so appealing a case for the possibility of living a good life in a world where God is dead and values are ungrounded in a moral framework outside the human frame. *The Plague* is to me almost convincing. Almost, but not quite. For the same questions occur within the intellectual framework of *The Plague* as within the system of Sartre's "Existentialism."

Why should the affirmation of life as Dr. Rieux and Jean Tarrou see it be good and Cottard's living off the plague be bad? Why should the old Spaniard's nihilistic response be any less right than Dr. Rieux's positive action? True, our human sensibility sides with Rieux and Tarrou. But we recognize that the old Spaniard is not alone in his judgment. Who then is right? Those who side with the old Spaniard will not be convinced by Camus or by any reader who sides with Rieux, for without an external moral referent there is no common ground for discussion. There is but one conviction versus another. *The Plague* is attractive to those whose

---

[28]Ibid., p. 116.
[29]Ibid., pp. 117-18.
[30]Ibid., p. 278.
[31]The novel can and probably should also be read as a commentary on the Nazi regime, a plague on all of Europe and North Africa, not just Oran.

moral values are traditional, not because Camus offers a base for those values but because he continues to affirm them even though they have no base. Unfortunately, affirmation is not enough. It can be countered by an opposite affirmation.

It may be that in the last two years of his life Camus recognized his failure to go beyond nihilism. Howard Mumma, the summer pastor of the American Church in Paris, recounts private talks with Camus during these two years in which Camus gradually came to feel that the Christian explanation was true. He asked Mumma what it meant to be "born again" and whether Mumma would baptize him. The baptism did not take place,

---

Since I have been coming to church, I have been thinking a great deal about the idea of a transcendent, something that is other than this world. . . . And since I have been reading the Bible, I sense that there is something—I don't know if it is personal or if it is a great idea or powerful influence—but there is something that can bring meaning to my life.
CAMUS IN DIALOGUE WITH MUMMA, HOWARD MUMMA, *Albert Camus and the Minister*

---

first, because Mumma considered Camus's childhood baptism valid and, second, because Camus was not yet ready for a public display of his conversion. The issue was not resolved when Mumma left Paris at the end of summer, expecting to see Camus again the following year. Camus died in an automobile accident the following February.[32]

HOW FAR BEYOND NIHILISM?

Does atheistic existentialism transcend nihilism? It certainly tries to—with passion and conviction. Yet it fails to provide a referent for a morality that goes beyond each individual. By grounding human significance in subjectivity, it places it in a realm divorced from reality. The objective world keeps intruding: death, the ever present possibility and the ultimate certainty, puts a halt to whatever meaning might otherwise be possible. It forces an existentialist forever to affirm and affirm and affirm; when affirmation ceases, so does authentic existence.

Considering precisely this objection to the possibility of human value,

---

[32]Howard Mumma, *Albert Camus and the Minister* (Brewster, Mass.: Paraclete, 2000).

H. J. Blackham agrees to the terms of the argument. Death indeed does end all. But every human life is more than itself, for it stems from a past humanity and it affects humanity's future. Moreover, "there is heaven and there is hell in the economy of every human imagination."[33] That is, says Blackham, "I am the author of my own experience."[34] After all the objections have been raised, Blackham retreats to solipsism. And that seems to me the end of all attempts at ethics from the standpoint of atheistic existentialism.

Atheistic existentialism goes beyond nihilism only to reach solipsism, the lonely self that exists for fourscore and seven (if it doesn't contract the plague earlier), then ceases to exist. Many would say that that is not to go beyond nihilism at all; it is only to don a mask called value, a mask stripped clean away by death.

BASIC THEISTIC EXISTENTIALISM

As was pointed out above, theistic existentialism arose from philosophic and theological roots quite different from those of its atheistic counterpart. It was Søren Kierkegaard's answer to the challenge of a theological nihilism—the dead orthodoxy of a dead church. As Kierkegaard's themes were picked up two generations after his death, they were the response to a Christianity that had lost its theology completely and had settled for a watered-down gospel of morality and good works. God had been reduced to Jesus, who had been reduced to a good man pure and simple. The death of God in liberal theology did not produce among liberals the despair of Kafka but the optimism of one English bishop in 1905 who, when asked what he thought would prevent humankind from achieving a perfect social union, could think of nothing.

Late in the second decade of the twentieth century, however, Karl Barth in Germany saw what ought to happen when theology became anthropology, and he responded by refurbishing Christianity along existential lines. What he and subsequent theologians such as Emil Brunner and Reinhold Niebuhr affirmed came to be called neo-orthodoxy, for while it was significantly different from orthodoxy, it put God very much back in the picture.[35] It is not my goal to look specifically at any one form of neo-

---

[33]H. J. Blackham, "The Pointlessness of It All," in *Objections to Humanism*, ed. H. J. Blackham (Harmondsworth, U.K.: Penguin, 1965), p. 123.
[34]Ibid., p. 124.
[35]Edward John Carnell gives an excellent introduction to neo-orthodoxy and how it arose in

orthodoxy. Rather, I will seek to identify propositions that are common to the theistic existential stance.

Theistic existentialism begins by accepting theism's answers to worldview questions 1, 2, 3, 4, 6 and 8. In short: *God is infinite and personal (triune), transcendent and immanent, omniscient, sovereign and good. God created the cosmos ex nihilo to operate with a uniformity of cause and effect in an open system. Human beings are created in the image of God and thus possess personality, self-transcendence, intelligence, morality, gregariousness and creativity. Human beings were created good, but through the Fall the image of God became defaced, though not so ruined as not to be capable of restoration; through the work of Christ, God redeemed humanity and began the process of restoring people to goodness, though any given person may choose to reject that redemption. For each person death is either the gate to life with God and his people or the gate to eternal separation from the only thing that will ultimately fulfill human aspirations. Ethics is transcendent and is based on the character of God as good (holy and loving). As a core commitment Christian theists live to seek first the kingdom of God, that is, to glorify God and enjoy him forever.*

This list of propositions, identical to that of theism, suggests that theistic existentialism is just Christian theism. I am tempted to say that is in fact what we have, but this would do an injustice to the special existential variations and emphases. The existential version of theism is much more a particular set of emphases within theism than it is a separate worldview. Still, because of its impact on twentieth-century theology and its confusing relation to atheistic existentialism, it deserves a special treatment. Moreover, some tendencies within the existential version of theism place it at odds with traditional theism. These tendencies will be highlighted as they arise in the discussion.

As with atheistic existentialism, theistic existentialism's most characteristic elements are concerned not with the nature of the cosmos or God, but with human nature and our relation to the cosmos and God.

1. Worldview Questions 3 and 5: *Human beings are personal beings who, when they come to full consciousness, find themselves in an alien universe; whether or not God exists is a tough question to be solved not by reason but by faith.*

The Theology of Reinhold Niebuhr, rev. ed. (Grand Rapids: Eerdmans, 1960), pp. 13-39.

Theistic existentialism does not start with God. This is its most important variation from theism. With theism God is assumed certainly to be there and of a given character; then people are defined in relationship to God. Theistic existentialism arrives at the same conclusion, but it starts elsewhere.

Theistic existentialism emphasizes the place in which human beings find themselves when they first come to self-awareness. Self-reflect for a moment. Your certainty of your own existence, your own consciousness, your own self-determinacy—these are your starting points. When you look around, check your desires against the reality you find, look for a meaning to your existence, you are not blessed with certain answers. You find a universe that does not fit you, a social order that scratches where you don't itch and fails to scratch where you do. And, worse luck, you do not immediately perceive God.

The human situation is ambivalent, for evidence of order in the universe is ambiguous. Some things seem explicable by laws that seem to govern events; other things do not. The fact of human love and compassion gives evidence for a benevolent deity; the fact of hatred and violence and the fact of an impersonal universe point in the other direction.

It is here that Father Paneloux in *The Plague* images for us an existential Christian stance. Dr. Rieux, you will recall, refused to accept the "created order" because it was "a scheme of things in which children are put to torture."[36] Father Paneloux, on the other hand, says, "But perhaps we should love that which we cannot understand."[37] Father Paneloux has "leaped" to faith in and love for the existence of a good God, even though the immediate evidence is all in the other direction. Rather than accounting for the absurdity of the universe on the basis of the Fall, as a Christian theist would do, Father Paneloux assumes God is immediately responsible for this absurd universe; therefore he concludes that he must believe in God in spite of the absurdity.

Camus elsewhere calls such faith "intellectual suicide," and I am inclined to agree with him. But the point is that while reason may lead us to atheism, we can always refuse to accept reason's conclusions and take a leap toward faith.

To be sure, if the Judeo-Christian God exists, we had better acknowl-

---

[36]Camus, *Plague*, p. 197.
[37]Ibid., p. 196.

edge it because in that case our eternal destiny depends on it. But, say the
existentialists, the data is not all in and never will be, and so every person
who would be a theist must step forth and choose to believe. God will
never reveal himself unambiguously. Consequently each person, in the
loneliness of his or her own subjectivity, surrounded by a great deal more
darkness than light, must choose. And that choice must be a radical act
of faith. When a person does choose to believe, a whole panorama opens.
Most of the propositions of traditional theism flood in. Yet the subjective,
choice-centered basis for the worldview colors the style of each Christian
existentialist's stance within theism.

2. Worldview Questions 3 and 6: *The personal is the valuable.*

As in atheistic existentialism, theistic existentialism emphasizes the
disjunction between the objective and the subjective worlds. Martin
Buber, a Jewish existentialist whose views have greatly influenced
Christians, uses the terms *I-Thou* and *I-It* to distinguish between the
two ways a person relates to reality. In the *I-It* relationship a human being is an objectifier:

> Now with the magnifying glass of peering observation he bends over par-
> ticulars and objectifies them, or with the field-glass of remote inspection
> he objectifies them and arranges them as scenery, he isolates them in ob-
> servation without any feeling of their exclusiveness, or he knits them into
> a scheme of observation without any feeling of universality.[38]

This is the realm of science and logic, of space and time, of measurability.
As Buber says, "Without *It* man cannot live. But he who lives by *It* alone
is not man."[39] The *Thou* is necessary.

In the *I-Thou* relationship, a subject encounters a subject: "When
Thou is spoken [Buber means experienced], the speaker has nothing
for his object."[40] Rather, such speakers have a subject like themselves
with whom to share a mutual life. In Buber's words, "All real living is
meeting."[41]

Buber's statement about the primacy of *I-Thou,* person-to-person rela-

[38]Martin Buber, *I and Thou,* trans. Ronald Gregor Smith (New York: Charles Scribner, 1958),
    pp. 29-30.
[39]Ibid., p. 34.
[40]Ibid., p. 4.
[41]Ibid., p. 11.

tionships is now recognized as a classic. No simple summary can do it justice, and I encourage readers to treat themselves to the book itself. Here we must content ourselves with one more quotation about the personal relationship Buber sees possible between God and people:

> Men do not find God if they stay in the world. They do not find Him if they leave the world. He who goes out with his whole being to meet his *Thou* and carries to it all being that is in the world, finds Him who cannot be sought. Of course God is the "wholly Other"; but He is also the wholly Same, the Wholly Present. Of course He is the *Mysterium Tremendum* that appears and overthrows; but He is also the mystery of the self-evident, nearer to me than my *I*.[42]

So theistic existentialists emphasize the personal as of primary value. The impersonal is there; it is important; but it is to be lifted up to God, lifted up to the *Thou* of all *Thous*. To do so satisfies the *I* and serves to eradicate the alienation so strongly felt by people when they concentrate on *I-It* relations with nature and, sadly, with other people as well.

This discussion may seem rather abstract to Christians whose faith in God is a daily reality that they live out rather than reflect on. Perhaps the chart in figure 6.1 comparing two ways of looking at some basic elements of Christianity will make the issues clearer. It is adapted from a lecture given by theologian Harold Englund at the University of Wisconsin in the early 1960s. Think of the column on the left as describing a dead orthodoxy contrasted with the column on the right describing a live theistic existentialism.

	Depersonalized	**Personalized**
Sin	Breaking a rule	Betraying a relationship
Repentance	Admitting guilt	Sorrowing over personal betrayal
Forgiveness	Canceling a penalty	Renewing fellowship
Faith	Believing a set of propositions	Committing oneself to a person
Christian life	Obeying rules	Pleasing the Lord, a Person

Figure 6.1. Comparison of depersonalized and personalized views of Christian faith.

[42]Ibid., p. 7.

When put this way, the existential version is obviously more attractive. Of course, traditional theists may well respond in two ways: first, the second column demands or implies the existence of the first column and, second, theism has always included the second column in its system. Both responses are well founded. The problem has been that theism's total worldview has not always been well understood and churches have tended to stick with column one. It has taken existentialism to restore many theists to a full recognition of the richness of their own system.

3. Worldview Question 6: *Knowledge is subjectivity; the whole truth is often paradoxical.*

An existentialist's stress on personality and wholeness leads to an equal emphasis on the subjectivity of genuine human knowledge. Knowledge about objects involves *I-It* relationships; they are necessary but not sufficient. Full knowledge is intimate interrelatedness; it involves the *I-Thou* and is linked firmly to the authentic life of the knower. In 1835 when Kierkegaard was faced with deciding what should be his life's work, he wrote,

> What I really need is to become clear in my own mind what I must do, not what I must know—except in so far as a knowing must precede every action. The important thing is to understand what I am destined for, to perceive what the Deity wants me to do; the point is to find the truth for me, to find that idea for which I am ready to live and die. What good would it do me to discover a so-called objective truth, though I were to work my way through the systems of the philosophers and were able, if need be, to pass them in review?[43]

Some readers of Kierkegaard have understood him to abandon the concept of objective truth altogether; certainly some existentialists have done precisely that, disjoining the objective and subjective so completely that the one has no relation to the other.[44] This has been especially true

---

[43]Søren Kierkegaard, from a letter quoted by Walter Lowrie in *A Short Life of Kierkegaard* (Princeton, N.J.: Princeton University Press, 1942), p. 82.

[44]Kierkegaard's own stance regarding this is a matter of scholarly debate. Those emphasizing his rejection of the value of objective truth include Marjorie Grene, *Introduction to Existentialism* (Chicago: University of Chicago Press, 1948), pp. 21-22, 35-39, and Francis A. Schaeffer, *The God Who Is There* (Downers Grove, Ill: InterVarsity Press, 1968), pp. 51-54. On the other side are C. Stephen Evans, *Subjectivity and Religious Beliefs* (Grand Rapids: Christian University Press, 1978), and John Macquarrie, *Existentialism* (Philadelphia: Westminster Press, 1972), pp. 74-123.

of atheistic existentialists like John Platt.[45] It is not that the facts are unimportant but that they must be facts for someone, facts for me. And that changes their character and makes knowledge become the knower. Truth in its personal dimension is subjectivity; it is truth digested and lived out on the nerve endings of a human life.

When knowledge becomes so closely related to the knower, it has an edge of passion, of sympathy, and it tends to be hard to divide logically from the knower himself. Buber describes the situation of a person standing before God: "Man's religious situation, his being there in the Presence, is characterized by its essential and indissoluble antinomy." What is one's relation to God as regards freedom or necessity? Kant, says Buber, resolved the problem by assigning necessity to the realm of appearances and freedom to the realm of being.

> But if I consider necessity and freedom not in worlds of thought but in the reality of standing before God, if I know that "I am given over for disposal" and know at the same time that "It depends on myself," then I cannot try to escape the paradox that has to be lived by assigning irreconcilable propositions to two separate realms of validity; nor can I be helped to an ideal reconciliation by any theological device: but I am compelled to take both to myself, to be lived together, and in being lived they are one.[46]

The full truth is in the paradox, not in an assertion of only one side of the issue. Presumably this paradox is resolved in the mind of God, but it is not resolved in the human mind. It is to be lived out: "God, I rely completely on you; do your will. I am stepping out to act."

The strength of stating our understanding of our stance before God in such a paradox is at least in part a result of the inability most of us have had in stating our stance nonparadoxically. Most nonparadoxical statements end by denying either God's sovereignty or human significance. That is, they tend either to Pelagianism or to hyper-Calvinism.

The weakness of resting in paradox is the difficulty of knowing where to stop. What sets of seemingly contradictory statements are to be lived out as truth? Surely not every set. "Love your neighbor; hate your neighbor." "Do good to those who persecute you. Call your friends together and do in your enemies." "Don't commit adultery. Have every sexual liaison you can pull off."

---

[45]See pp. 136-37 above.
[46]Buber, *I and Thou*, p. 96.

So beyond the paradoxical it would seem that there must be some noncontradictory proposition governing which paradoxes we will try to live out. In the Christian form of existentialism the Bible taken as God's special revelation has set the bounds. It forbids many paradoxes, and it seems to encourage others. The doctrine of the Trinity, for example, may be an unresolvable paradox, but it does justice to the biblical data.[47]

What logic does is to articulate and to make explicit those rules which are in fact embodied in actual discourse and which, being so embodied, enable men both to construct valid arguments and to avoid the penalties of inconsistency. . . . A pupil of Duns Scotus demonstrated that . . . from a contradiction any statement whatsoever can be derived. It follows that to commit ourselves to asserting a contradiction is to commit ourselves to asserting anything whatsoever, to asserting anything whatsoever that it is possible to assert—and of course also to its denial. The man who asserts a contradiction thus succeeds in saying nothing and also in committing himself to everything; both are failures to assert anything determinate, to say that this is the case and not this other. We therefore depend upon our ability to utilize and to accord with the laws of logic in order to speak at all, and a large part of formal logic clarifies for us what we have been doing all along.

Alasdair MacIntyre, *Herbert Marcuse: An Exposition and a Polemic*

Among those who have no external objective authority to set the bounds, paradox tends to run rampant. Marjorie Grene comments about Kierkegaard, "Much of Kierkegaard's writing seems to be motivated not so much by an insight into the philosophical or religious appropriateness of paradox to a peculiar problem as by the sheer intellectual delight in the absurd for its own sake."[48] Thus this aspect of theistic existentialism has come in for a great deal of criticism from those holding a traditional theistic worldview. The human mind is made in the image of God's mind, and thus though our mind is finite and incapable of encompassing the

---

[47]See Donald Bloesch, *God the Almighty* (Downers Grove, Ill.: InterVarsity Press, 1995), pp. 166-67.

[48]Grene, *Introduction*, p. 36.

whole of knowledge, it is yet able to discern some truth. As Francis Schaeffer puts it, we can have substantial truth but not exhaustive truth, and we can discern truth from foolishness by the use of the principle of noncontradiction.[49]

4. Worldview Question 7: *History as a record of events is uncertain and unimportant, but history as a model or type or myth to be made present and lived is of supreme importance.*

Theistic existentialism took two steps away from traditional theism. The first step was to begin to distrust the accuracy of recorded history. The second step was to lose interest in its facticity and to emphasize its religious implication or meaning.

The first step is associated with the higher criticism of the mid-nineteenth century. Rather than taking the biblical accounts at face value, accepting miracles and all, the higher critics, such as D. F. Strauss (1808-1874) and Ernest Renan (1823-1892), started from the naturalistic assumption that miracles cannot happen. Accounts of them must therefore be false, not necessarily fabricated by writers who wished to deceive but propounded by credulous people of primitive mindset.

This, of course, tended to undermine the authority of the biblical accounts even where they were not riddled with the miraculous. Other higher critics, most notably Julius Wellhausen (1844-1918), also turned their attention to the inner unity of the Old Testament and discovered, so they were sure, that the Pentateuch was not written by Moses at all. In fact, the texts showed that several hands over several centuries had been at work. This undermined what the Bible says about itself and thus called into question the truth of its whole message.[50]

Rather than change their naturalistic presuppositions to match the

---

[49]Francis A. Schaeffer, *He Is There and He Is Not Silent* (Wheaton, Ill.: Tyndale House, 1972), pp. 37-88, esp. p. 79.

[50]For a consideration of the current state of scholarship on the subjects treated by higher criticism, see Stephen Neill and Tom Wright, *The Interpretation of the New Testament 1861-1986* (New York: Oxford University Press, 1988); Gerald Bray, *Biblical Interpretation: Past and Present* (Downers Grove, Ill.: InterVarsity Press, 1996); Donald Carson et al., *An Introduction to the New Testament* (Grand Rapids: Zondervan, 1992); Raymond B. Dillard and Tremper Longman III, *An Introduction to the Old Testament* (Grand Rapids: Zondervan, 1994); Craig Blomberg, *The Historical Reliability of the Gospels* (Downers Grove, Ill.: InterVarsity Press, 1987); and N. T. Wright, Christian Origins and the Question of God, 3 vols. (Minneapolis: Fortress Press): *The New Testament and the People of God* (1992); *Jesus and the Victory of God* (1996); and *The Resurrection and the Son of God* (2003).

data of the Bible, they concluded that the Bible was historically untrustworthy. This could have led to an abandonment of Christian faith in its
entirety. Instead it led to a second step—a radical shift in emphasis. The
facts the Bible recorded were not important; what was important were its
examples of the good life and its timeless truths of morality.

Matthew Arnold wrote in 1875 that Christianity "will live, because it
depends upon a true and inexhaustible fruitful idea, the idea of death and
resurrection as conceived and worked out by Jesus. . . . The importance of
the disciples' belief in their Master's resurrection lay in their believing
what was true, although they materialized it. Jesus had died and risen
again, but in his own sense not theirs."[51] History—that is, space-time
events—was not important; belief was important. And the doctrine of
death and resurrection came to stand not for the atonement of humankind by the God-man Jesus Christ but for a "new life" of human service
and sacrifice for others. The great mystery of God's entrance into time
and space was changed from fact to myth, a powerful myth, of course,
one that could transform ordinary people into moral giants.

These steps took place long before the nihilism of Nietzsche or the
despair of Kafka. They were responses to the "assured results of scholarship" (which as those who pursue the matter will find are now not so assured). If objective truth could not be found, no matter. Real truth is poetically contained in the "story," the narrative.

It is interesting to note what soon happened to Matthew Arnold. In
1875 he was saying that we should read the Bible as poetry; if we did it
would teach us the good life. In 1880 he had taken the next step and was
advocating that we treat poetry in general in the same way we used to
treat the Bible: "More and more mankind will discover that we have to
turn to poetry to interpret life for us, to console us, to sustain us. . . . Most
of what now passes with us for religion and philosophy will be replaced
by poetry."[52] For Arnold, poetry in general had become Scripture.

In any case, when theistic existentialists (Reinhold Niebuhr, Rudolf
Bultmann and the like) began appearing on the theological scene, they
had a ready-made solution to the problem posed for orthodoxy by the
higher critics. So the Bible's history was suspect. What matter? The ac-

[51]Matthew Arnold, *God and the Bible*, in *English Prose of the Victorian Era*, ed. Charles Frederick Harrold and William D. Templeman (New York: Oxford University Press, 1938), p. 1211.
[52]Matthew Arnold, "The Study of Poetry," in *English Prose of the Victorian Era*, p. 1248.

counts are "religiously" (that is, poetically) true. So while the doctrine of
the neo-orthodox theologians looks more like the orthodoxy of Calvin
than like the liberalism of Matthew Arnold, the historical basis for the
doctrines was discounted, and the doctrines themselves began to be
lifted out of history.

The Fall was said not to have taken place back there and then in space
and time. Rather, each person reenacts in their own life this story. Each
enters the world like Adam, sinless; each one rebels against God. The Fall
is existential—a here-and-now proposition. Edward John Carnell sum-
marizes the existential view of the Fall as "a mythological description of
a universal experience of the race."[53]

Likewise the resurrection of Jesus may or may not have occurred in
space and time. Barth believes it did; Bultmann, on the other hand, says,
"An historical fact that involves a resurrection from the dead is utterly
inconceivable!"[54] Again, no matter. The reality behind the resurrection is
the new life in Christ experienced by the disciples. The "spirit" of Jesus
was living in them; their lives were transformed. They were indeed living
the "cruciform life style."[55]

Other supernatural doctrines are similarly "demythologized," among
them creation, redemption, the resurrection of the body, the second coming, the antichrist. Each is said to be a symbol of "religious" import. Either
they are not to be taken literally or, if they are, their meaning is not in
their facticity but in what they indicate about human nature and our relationship to God.[56]

---

[53]Carnell, *Theology of Reinhold Niebuhr*, p. 168.

[54]Rudolf Bultmann, *Kerygma and Myth* (New York: Harper & Brothers, 1961), p. 39.

[55]Luke Timothy Johnson, after a blistering criticism of modern attempts to malign the historical reliability of the Gospels (on the one hand) and to place too much emphasis on the facticity of the Gospel narratives (on the other hand), says, "The *real* Jesus for Christian faith is not
simply a figure of the past but very much and above all a figure of the present, a figure, indeed,
who defines believers present by his presence" (*The Real Jesus* [San Francisco: HarperCollins,
1996], p. 142). This is existentialist Christianity in contemporary dress; it is not necessarily
in conflict with orthodox Christian theism, but it puts the emphasis on the living relational
present at the expense of concern for historical fact.

[56]The history of scholarly studies of Jesus parallels the intellectual history I have been tracing
in this book. First there was the uncritical acceptance of the Gospels as reliable history. Then
with the deists and naturalists (e.g., Ernest Renan) came the denial of the historicity of any
supernatural events in Jesus' life. This was followed by the neo-orthodox emphasis on the religious and existential significance of the story of Jesus, which was itself thought to be largely
mythical (e.g., Rudolf Bultmann), and then by the radical reshapers, using an imaginative
blend of naturalistic skepticism and speculative fantasy (e.g., John Dominic Crossan). Reactions to these naturalistic quests for the historical Jesus by both traditional theistic scholars

It is here—in the understanding of history and of doctrine—that theists most find fault with their existential counterparts. The charge is twofold. First, theists say that the existentialists start with two false, or certainly highly suspect, presuppositions: (1) that miracles are impossible (Bultmann here, but not Barth) and (2) that the Bible is historically untrustworthy. On the level of presuppositions Bultmann simply buys the naturalist notion of the closed universe; Bultmann, although usually associated with the neo-orthodox theologians, is thus not really a "theistic" existentialist at all. Much recent scholarship has gone a long way toward restoring confidence in the Old Testament as an accurate record of events, but existential theologians ignore this scholarship or discount the importance of its results. And that brings us to the second major theistic critique.

Theists charge the existentialists with building theology on the shifting sand of myth and symbol. As a reviewer said about Lloyd Geering's *Resurrection: A Symbol of Hope,* an existential work, "How can a non-event [a resurrection which did not occur] be regarded as a symbol of hope or indeed of anything else? If something has happened we try to see what it means. If it has not happened the question cannot arise. We are driven back on the need for an Easter event."[57]

There must be an event if there is to be meaning. If Jesus arose from the dead in the traditional way of understanding this, then we have an event to mean something. If he stayed in the tomb or if his body was taken elsewhere, we have another event and it must mean something else. So a theist refuses to give up the historical basis for faith and challenges the existentialist to take more seriously the implications of abandoning historical facticity as religiously important. Such abandonment should lead to doubt and loss of faith. Instead it has led to a leap of faith. Meaning is created in the subjective world, but it has no objective referent.

In this area theistic existentialism comes very close to atheistic existentialism. Perhaps when existentialists abandon facticity as a ground of meaning, they should be encouraged to take the next step and abandon meaning altogether. This would place them back in the trackless wastes of nihilism, and they would have to search for another way out.

(e.g., Ben Witherington and N. T. Wright) and modestly neo-orthodox scholars (e.g., Luke Timothy Johnson) are playing an important role in putting the historical study of Jesus on more solid ground.

[57]Review of *Resurrection: A Symbol of Hope,* by Lloyd Geering, *Times Literary Supplement,* November 26, 1971, p. 148.

THE PERSISTENCE OF EXISTENTIALISM

The two forms of existentialism are interesting to study, for they are a pair of worldviews that bear a brotherly relationship but are children of two different fathers. Theistic existentialism arose with Kierkegaard as a response to dead theism, dead orthodoxy, and with Karl Barth as a response to the reduction of Christianity to sheer morality. It took a subjectivist turn, lifted religion from history and focused its attention on inner meaning. Atheistic existentialism came to the fore with Jean-Paul Sartre and Albert Camus as a response to nihilism and the reduction of people to meaningless cogs in the cosmic machinery. It took a subjectivist turn, lifted philosophy from objectivity and created meaning from human affirmation.

Brothers in style though not in content, these two forms of existentialism are still commanding attention and vying for adherents. So long as those who would be believers in God yearn for a faith that does not demand too much belief in the supernatural or the accuracy of the Bible, theistic existentialism will be a live option. So long as naturalists who cannot (or refuse to) believe in God are searching for a way to find meaning in their lives, atheistic existentialism will be of service. I would predict that both forms—in probably ever-new and changing versions—will be with us for a long time.

Chapter 7

JOURNEY TO THE EAST

EASTERN PANTHEISTIC MONISM

And all the voices, all the goals,
all the yearnings, all the sorrows,
all the pleasures, all the good and evil,
all of them together was the world. . . .
The great song with thousand voices
consisted of one word: OM—perfection.

HERMANN HESSE, *SIDDHARTHA*

In the course of Western thought eventually we reach an impasse. Naturalism leads to nihilism, and nihilism is hard to transcend on the terms that the Western world, permeated by naturalism, wishes to accept. Atheistic existentialism, as we have seen, is one attempt, but it has some rather serious problems. Theism is an option, but for a naturalist it is uninviting. How can one accept the existence of an infinite-personal, transcendent God? For over a century that question has posed a serious barrier. Many people today would rather stick with their naturalism, for it still seems to be a decided improvement on the fabulous religion it rejected. Moreover, modern Christendom, with its hypocritical churches and its lack of compassion, is a poor testimony to the viability of theism. No, it is thought, that way will not do.

Perhaps we should look again at naturalism. Where did we go wrong? Well, for one thing we discover that by following reason our naturalism leads to nihilism. But we need not necessarily abandon our naturalism; we can simply say reason is not to be trusted. Existentialism went partway down this route; perhaps we should now go all the way. Second, since we in the West tend to quarrel over "doctrines," ideas and so forth, let us call a moratorium not only on quarreling but on distinguishing intellectually at all. Perhaps any "useful" doctrine should be considered true. Third, if all our activism to produce change by manipulating the system of the universe produces pollution and our efforts at social betterment go unrewarded, why not abandon our activism? Let's stop doing and raise our quality of life by simply being. Finally, if Western quarrels turn into armed conflicts, why not retreat completely? Let go and let happen: can that be any worse than what we have now? Has, perhaps, the East a better way?

On a sociological level, we can trace the interest in the East to the rejection of middle-class values by the young generation of the 1960s. First, Western technology (that is, reason in its practical application) made possible modern warfare. The Vietnam War (young Americans had not personally experienced earlier conflicts) is a result of reason. So let us abandon reason. Second, Western economics has led to gross inequity and economic oppression of masses of people. So let us reject the presuppositions from which such a system developed. Third, Western religion has seemed largely to support those in control of technology and the economic system. So let us not fall into that trap.

The swing to Eastern thought since the 1960s is, therefore, primarily a retreat from Western thought. The West ends in a maze of contradictions, acts of intellectual suicide and a specter of nihilism that haunts the dark edges of all our thought. Is there not another way?

Indeed, there is—a very different way. With its antirationalism, its syncretism, its quietism, till recently its lack of technology, its uncomplicated lifestyle, and most significantly, its exotic and radically different religious framework, the East is extremely attractive. Moreover, the East has an even longer tradition than the West. Sitting, as it were, next door to us for centuries have been modes of conceiving and viewing the world that are poles apart from ours. Maybe the East, that quiet land of meditating gurus and simple life, has the answer to our longing for meaning and significance.

For over a century Eastern thought has been flowing west. The Hindu and Buddhist scriptures have been translated and now circulate in inex-pensive paperback editions. As early as 1893 at the first Parliament of World Religions in Chicago, Swami Vivekananda began introducing the teachings of his own Indian guru, Sri Ramakrishna Paramahamsa. D. T. Suzuki from Japan poured Zen into Western publications. And Alan Watts from the West imbibed Zen and returned to teach his fellow West-

---

Tibetan Buddhism has attracted devotees in the West. Its teachers offer insights into suffering and methods for cultivating mental equanimity and compassion. It appeals to Westerners' utilitarian pursuit of self-betterment because it seems, at first anyway, to set aside the neces-sity of faith and to ask the inquirer only to try its methods and see the results. It says that one can become a Buddha, an "awakened" one, by one's own efforts. Its goal is enlightenment about a truth beyond the limits of contingent reality. It is as dubious about objective reality as certain currents of Western philosophy have become. It proclaims im-permanence and emptiness, and so fits our experience of upheaval. It questions the reality of the "self." Nowadays the West does too, and of-ten conceives the Gospel as a manual not for the personal development of holiness, but for the impersonal engineering of social justice.

JOHN B. BUESCHER, "Everything Is on Fire: Tibetan Buddhism Inside Out"

---

erners. By the 1960s Eastern studies had filtered down to the undergrad-uate level. Indian gurus have been crossing and recrossing the United States and Europe for several decades. In the last couple decades the Ti-betan Dalai Lama with his quiet, sensitive demeanor and his quest for a peaceful solution to our international conflicts has made a mark as well. Knowledge of the East is now easy to obtain, and more and more its view of reality is becoming a live option in the West.[1]

---

[1]The present account of the recent swing to Eastern thought is painfully superficial. For more detail see the following: R. C. Zaehner, *Zen, Drugs and Mysticism* (New York: Vintage, 1974). A more expansive and scholarly examination is found in the essays collected in Irving I. Za-retsky and Mark P. Leone, eds., *Religious Movements in Contemporary America* (Princeton, N.J.: Princeton University Press, 1974). Stephen Neill in *Christian Faith and Other Faiths* (Downers Grove, Ill.: InterVarsity Press, 1984) surveys and evaluates several religions, includ-ing Hinduism and Buddhism. A Christian critique of the Western trend toward the East is found in Os Guinness, *The Dust of Death* (Wheaton, Ill.: Crossway, 1994), pp. 195-234. In

BASIC EASTERN PANTHEISTIC MONISM

The East is, of course, as rich and as hard to label and categorize as the West, as will be obvious to anyone who simply scans the table of contents of a study such as Surendranath Dasgupta's five-volume *History of Indian Philosophy.*[2] The following description is limited to the Eastern world-view most popular in the West: pantheistic monism. This is the root worldview that underlies the Hindu Advaita Vedanta system of Shankara, the Transcendental Meditation of Maharishi Mahesh Yogi, and much of the Upanishads. There are especially the views so beautifully captured by the German writer Hermann Hesse in his *Siddhartha,* a novel that became popular with college students in the 1970s and thus served as a transmitter of a generic pantheistic monism. Buddhism, which developed from Hinduism, shares many of its features but differs with it at a key point: the nature of ultimate reality.

Pantheistic monism is distinguished from other related Eastern worldviews by its monism, the notion that only one impersonal element constitutes reality. Hare Krishna does not fit in this worldview, for while it shares many of the characteristics of Eastern pantheistic monism, it declares that reality is ultimately personal (and thus shares a similarity to theism totally absent in Advaita Vedanta).

Hopefully these cryptic remarks will become clearer as we proceed. But before we do, we need to address two difficulties in doing worldview analysis. First, we must realize that the eight worldview questions imply a set of categories that do not neatly fit the categories (or lack of them)

---

chap. 11 of *Miracles* (London: Fontana, 1960), pp. 85-98, C. S. Lewis argues that even in the West pantheism is humankind's natural religion, and his critique of this form of pantheism is helpful. See also Ernest Becker's highly critical analysis of Zen Buddhism from the standpoint of modern psychoanalysis and psychotherapy theory in *Zen: A Rational Critique* (New York: W. W. Norton, 1961).

[2]Surendranath Dasgupta, *A History of Indian Philosophy,* 5 vols. (Cambridge: Cambridge University Press, 1922-1969). For texts of Eastern philosophy and religion see Sarvapalli Radhakrishnan and Charles A. Moore, eds., *A Source Book in Indian Philosophy* (Princeton, N.J.: Princeton University Press, 1957); Wing-tsit Chan, ed., *A Source Book in Chinese Philosophy* (Princeton, N.J.: Princeton University Press, 1963); and Lucien Stryk, ed., *World of the Buddha* (New York: Grove, 1968). For general studies of Eastern religions, philosopher Keith Yandell recommends Stuart Hackett, *Oriental Philosophy* (Madison: University of Wisconsin Press, 1979); David L. Johnson, *A Reasoned Look at Asian Religions* (Minneapolis: Bethany House, 1985); Julius Lipner, *The Face of Truth* (London: Macmillan, 1986); Eric Lott, *God and the Universe in the Vedantic Theology of Ramanuja* (Madras: Ramanuja Research Society, 1976); and Lott, *Vedantic Approaches to God* (London: Macmillan, 1980).

that characterize Eastern thought.[3] The East does not readily accept the
distinctions we so readily assume between God and the cosmos (his creation); human beings and the rest of the cosmos; good and evil and illusion and reality. We may use these terms, but we must be aware of their
somewhat different meanings.

Second, we must be aware of the vast differences among religious
and cultural embodiments of Eastern pantheism. Worldview analysis is
neither a description nor an analysis of religions. For that, readers

---

Buddhism includes an enormous range of diversity in belief and practice. Learning that someone is a Buddhist does not tell you about that
person's beliefs. Knowing his or her geographical origin may or may not
be helpful. For example, knowing that a Buddhist is from Sri Lanka,
Myanmar or Thailand can be helpful because these countries are dominated by Theraveda Buddhism. On the other hand, knowing that a Buddhist is from China or Japan leaves matters completely open. Asking
Buddhists from China or Japan what school of Buddhism they adhere
to may not be of much help either. Many people think of the Buddhism
they practice as Buddhism—plain and simple. They are not necessarily
attuned to the Western practice of differentiating one specific group
from all others and believing that it is right and all others are false. For
them they are Buddhists, and that's all they are concerned with. And
what they actually practice may have very little to do with any "official"
school of Buddhism.

WINFRIED CORDUAN, *Neighboring Faiths: A Christian Introduction to World
Religions*

---

should consult books on comparative religion. Win Corduan's *Neighboring Faiths* is a good place to start.[4] He focuses on the diversity of
beliefs and practices among adherents to each religion (see sidebar).
When we try to grasp the worldview of any given writer or individual
person, we need to pay careful attention to his or her understanding of

---

[3]See chapter 9, pp. 218-20 below.
[4]Winfried Corduan, *Neighboring Faiths: A Christian Introduction to World Religions* (Downers
Grove, Ill.: InterVarsity Press, 1998).

their basic intellectual commitments. We must not conclude that, because people identify themselves as a Buddhist or Hindu, they hold any of the propositions identified here as Eastern pantheistic monism. Still, to introduce those of us with basically Western intellectual roots to the various mindsets of our Eastern counterparts, understanding these worldview notions will be helpful.

1. Worldview Questions 1, 2 and 3: *Atman is Brahman; that is, the soul of each and every human being is the Soul of the cosmos (ultimate reality).*

"Atman is Brahman," a phrase from the Hindu *Upanishads*, is the pantheistic counterpart and contrast to the opening declaration of the biblical book of Genesis: "In the beginning God created the heavens and the earth" (Gen 1:1). Instead of drawing a bold line between God and his creation, however, the Hindu text declares them to be one and the same. Atman (the essence, the soul, of any person) is Brahman (the essence, the Soul of the whole cosmos). What is a human being? That is, what is at the very core of each of us? Each person is the whole shooting match. Each person is (to put it boldly but accurately in Eastern terms) God.

But we must define God in pantheistic terms. God is the one, infinite-impersonal, ultimate reality. That is, God is the cosmos. God is all that exists; nothing exists that is not God.[5] If anything that is not God appears to exist, it is *maya,* illusion, and does not truly exist. In other words, anything that exists as a separate and distinct object—this chair, not that one; this rock, not that tree; me, not you—is an illusion. It is not our separateness that gives us reality, it is our oneness, the fact that we are Brahman and Brahman is One. Yes, Brahman is *the* One.

Ultimate reality is beyond distinction; it just *is.* In fact, as we shall see in the discussion of epistemology, we cannot express in language the nature of this oneness. We can only "realize" it by becoming it, by seizing our unity, our "godhead," and resting there beyond any distinction whatsoever.

In the West we are not used to this kind of system. To distinguish is to

---

[5]Sri Ramakrishna (1836-1886) once touched his disciple Naren (who later became Swami Vivekananda and traveled to Chicago for the first Parliament of World Religions, becoming as a result a major figure in the introduction of Eastern thought to the West); he fell into a trance and saw in a flash "that everything actually *is* God, that nothing whatsoever exists but the Divine, that the entire universe is His body, and all things are His forms" (Richard Schiffman, *Sri Ramakrishna: A Prophet for a New Age* [New York: Paragon House, 1989], p. 153).

think. The laws of thought demand distinction: *A* is *A*; but *A* is not non-*A*.
To know reality is to distinguish one thing from another, label it, catalog it,
recognize its subtle relation to other objects in the cosmos. In the East to
"know" reality is to pass beyond distinction, to "realize" the oneness of all
by being one with the all. This sort of conception—insofar as it can be understood by the mind—is best expressed indirectly. *The Upanishads*
abound in attempts to express the inexpressible indirectly in parables.

> "Bring me a fruit from this banyan tree."
>
> "Here it is, father."
>
> "Break it."
>
> "It is broken, Sir."
>
> "What do you see in it?"
>
> "Very small seeds, Sir."
>
> "Break one of them, my son."
>
> "It is broken, Sir."
>
> "What do you see in it?"
>
> "Nothing at all, Sir."
>
> Then his father spoke to him: "My son, from the very essence in the
> seed which you cannot see comes in truth this vast banyan tree.
>
> "Believe me, my son, an invisible and subtle essence is the spirit of the
> whole universe. That is Reality. That is Atman. THOU ART THAT."[6]

So the father, a guru, teaches his son, a novice, that even a novice is
ultimate reality. Yet all of us, Eastern and Western alike, perceive distinctions. We do not "realize" our oneness. And that leads us to the second
proposition.

2. Worldview Questions 1, 2 and 3, continued: *Some things are more
one than others.*

Here we seem to be multiplying cryptic remarks and getting nowhere.
But we ought not despair. Eastern "thought" is like that.

"Some things are more one than others" is another way of saying that
reality is a hierarchy of appearances. Some "things," some appearances or
illusions, are closer than others to being at one with the One. The ordinary Eastern hierarchy looks rather like one Westerners might construct
but for a different reason. Matter pure and simple (that is, mineral) is the

---

[6]From the Chandogya Upanishad, in *The Upanishads*, trans. Juan Mascaró (Harmondsworth,
U.K.: Penguin, 1965), p. 117.

least real; then vegetable life, then animal and finally humanity. But humanity too is hierarchical; some people are closer to unity than others. The Perfect Master, the Enlightened One, the guru are the human beings nearest to pure being.

Partly, consciousness seems to be the principle of hierarchy here. To "realize" oneness would seem to imply consciousness. But as we shall see, when one is one with the One, consciousness completely disappears and one merely *is* infinite-impersonal Being. Consciousness, like techniques of meditation, is just one more thing to be discarded when its usefulness is past. Still, pure matter is further from realization of its oneness than is humanity, and that is what counts.

At the furthest reaches of illusion, then, is matter. While its essence is Atman, it is not. Yet it should so *be.* We must be careful here not to attach any notion of morality to our understanding of the requirement that all things be at one with the One. Here it means simply that being itself requires unity with the One. The One is ultimate reality, and all that is not the One is not really anything. True, it is not anything of value either, but more important, it has no being at all.

So we are back to the original proposition: Some things are more one, that is, more real, than others. The next question is obvious: how does an individual, separate being get to be one with the One?

3. Worldview Questions 1, 2 and 3: *Many (if not all) roads lead to the One.*

Getting to oneness with the One is not a matter of finding the one true path. There are many paths from maya to reality. I may take one, you another, a friend a third, ad infinitum. The goal is not to be with one another on the same path but to be headed in the right direction on our own path. That is, we must be oriented correctly.

Orientation is not so much a matter of doctrine as of technique. On this the East is adamant. Ideas are not finally important. As Sri Ramakrishna said, "Do not argue about doctrines and religions. There is only one. All rivers flow to the Ocean. Flow and let others flow too!"[7]

On a doctrinal level, you and I may only occasionally agree on what is true about anything—ourselves, the external world, religion. No matter.

---

[7]Schiffman, *Sri Ramakrishna*, p. 214, quoting from Rolland Romain, *The Life of Ramakrishna* (Calcutta: Advaita Ashrama, 1931), p. 197.

Eventually religions lead to the same end. Realizing oneness with the One is not a matter of belief but of technique, and even techniques vary.

Some gurus, such as the Maharishi Mahesh Yogi, stress chanting a mantra, a seemingly meaningless Sanskrit word sometimes selected by a spiritual master and given in secret to an initiate. Others recommend meditation on a mandala, a highly structured, often fascinatingly ornate and beautiful circular image, symbol of the totality of reality. Others require endless repetition of prayers or acts of obeisance.

Almost all of these techniques, however, require quiet and solitude. They are methods of intellectually contentless meditation. One attempts to get on the vibe level with reality, to turn one's soul to the harmony of the cosmos and ultimately to the one solid, nonharmonic, nondual, Ultimate vibration—Brahman, the One. To achieve this is the Eastern monistic way of achieving salvation.

Of all the "paths," one of the most common, especially with Western practitioners, involves chanting the word *Om* or a phrase with that word in it, for example, "Om Mane Padme Hum." Both the word *Om* and the phrase are essentially untranslatable because they are intellectually contentless. Some have suggested for *Om* the following: *yes, perfection, ultimate reality, all, the eternal word.* Maharishi Mahesh Yogi says that *Om* is the "sustainer of life," "the beginning and end of all creation," "that hum, which is the first silent sound, first silent wave that starts from that silent ocean of unmanifested life."[8]

It is obvious that the word *meaning* is not used in this Eastern system in the same way it is used in theism or naturalism. We are not talking here about rational content but metaphysical union. We can truly "pronounce" *Om* and "understand" its meaning only when we are at one with the One, when "Atman is Brahman" is not an epistemological statement but an ontological realization, that is, a "becoming real."

The Mandukya Upanishad says it this way:

OM. This eternal Word is all: what was, what is and what shall be, and what beyond is in eternity. All is OM.

Brahman is all and Atman is Brahman. Atman, the Self, has four conditions.

The first condition is the waking life of outward-moving consciousness, enjoying the seven outer gross elements.

---

[8]*Meditations of Maharishi Mahesh Yogi* (New York: Bantam, 1968), p. 18.

The second condition is the dreaming life of inner-moving consciousness, enjoying the seven subtle inner elements in its own light and solitude.

The third condition is the sleeping life of silent consciousness when a person has no desires and beholds no dreams. That condition of deep sleep is one of oneness, a mass of silent consciousness made of peace and enjoying peace.

This silent consciousness is all-powerful, all-knowing, the inner ruler, the source of all, the beginning and end of all beings.

The fourth condition is Atman in his own pure state: the awakened life of supreme consciousness. It is neither outer nor inner consciousness, neither semi-consciousness, nor sleeping-consciousness, neither consciousness nor unconsciousness. He is Atman, the Spirit himself, that cannot be seen or touched, that is above all distinction, beyond thought and ineffable. In the union with him is the supreme proof of his reality. He is the end of evolution and non-duality. He is peace and love.

This Atman is the eternal Word OM. Its three sounds, A, U, and M, are the first three states of consciousness, and these three states are the three sounds.

The first sound A is the first state of waking consciousness, common to all men. It is found in the words *Apti*, "attaining," and *Adimatvam*, "being first." Who knows this attains in truth all his desires, and in all things becomes first.

The second sound U is the second state of dreaming consciousness. It is found in the words *Utkarsha*, "uprising," and *Ubhayatvam*, "bothness." Who knows this raises the tradition of knowledge and attains equilibrium. In his family is never born any one who knows not Brahman.

The third sound M is the third state of sleeping consciousness. It is found in the words *Miti*, "measure," and in the root *Mi*, "to end," that gives *Apti*, "final end." Who knows this measures all with his mind and attains the final End.

The word OM as one sound is the fourth state of supreme consciousness. It is beyond the senses and is the end of evolution. It is non-duality and love. He goes with his self to the supreme Self who knows this, who knows this.[9]

I have quoted this Upanishad at length because it contains several key ideas in a relatively short passage. At the moment I am most concerned with the word *Om* and how it represents ultimate reality. To say *Om* is not to convey intellectual content. *Om* means anything and everything and there-

---

[9]Mascaró, *Upanishads*, pp. 83-84.

fore, being beyond distinction, can just as well be said to *mean* nothing. To say *Om* is rather to become or attempt to become what *Om* symbolizes.

4. Worldview Questions 1, 2 and 3: *To realize one's oneness with the cosmos is to pass beyond personality.*

Let us go back for a moment to the first proposition and see where it leads us when we turn our attention to human beings in this world. Atman is Brahman. Brahman is one and impersonal. Therefore, Atman is impersonal. Note the conclusion again: Human beings in their essence—their truest, fullest being—are impersonal.

This notion in pantheistic monism is at diametrical odds with theism. In theism, personality is the chief thing about God and the chief thing about people. It means an individual has complexity at the core of his or her being. Personality demands self-consciousness and self-determinacy, and these involve duality—a thinker and a thing thought. Both God and humanity in theism are complex.

In pantheism the chief thing about God is Oneness, a sheer abstract, undifferentiated, nondual unity. This puts God beyond personality. And since Atman is Brahman, human beings are beyond personality too. For any of us to "realize" our being is for us to abandon our complex personhood and enter the undifferentiated One.

Let us return for a moment to a section of the Mandukya Upanishad quoted above. Atman, it proclaims, has "four conditions": waking life, dreaming life, deep sleep and "the awakened life of pure consciousness." The progression is important; the higher state is the state most approaching total oblivion, for one goes from the activity of ordinary life in the external world to the activity of dreaming to the nonactivity, the nonconsciousness, of deep sleep and ends in a condition that in its designation sounds like the reversal of the first three, "pure consciousness."

Then we note that "pure consciousness" has nothing to do with any kind of consciousness with which we are familiar. "Pure consciousness" is, rather, sheer union with the One and not "consciousness" at all, for that demands duality—a subject to be conscious and an object for it to be conscious of. Even self-consciousness demands duality in the self. But this "pure consciousness" is not consciousness; it is pure being.

This explanation may help us understand why Eastern thought often leads to quietism and inaction. To be is not to do. Meditation is the main route to being, and meditation—whatever the style—is a case study in quietude. A symbol of this is the Hindu guru sitting cross-legged on a lonely ledge of a Himalayan peak in rapt contemplation.

5. Worldview Question 5: *To realize one's oneness with the cosmos is to pass beyond knowledge. The principle of noncontradiction does not apply where ultimate reality is concerned.*

From the statement Atman is Brahman, it also follows that human beings in their essence are beyond knowledge. Knowledge, like personality, demands duality—a knower and a known. But the One is beyond duality; it is sheer unity. Again as the Mandukya Upanishad says, "He is Atman, the Spirit himself, . . . above all distinction, beyond thought and ineffable." In other words, to *be* is not to know.

In *Siddhartha*, perhaps the most Eastern novel ever written by a Westerner, Hesse has the illumined Siddhartha say:

> Knowledge can be communicated, but not wisdom. . . . In every truth the opposite is equally true. For example, a truth can only be expressed and enveloped in words if it is one-sided. Everything that is thought and expressed in words is one-sided, only half the truth; it lacks totality, completeness, unity.[10]

The argument is simple. Reality is one; language requires duality, several dualities in fact (speaker and listener, subject and predicate); ergo, language cannot convey the truth about reality. Juan Mascaró explains what this means for the doctrine of God:

> When the sage of the *Upanishads* is pressed for a definition of God, he remains silent, meaning God is silence. When asked again to express God in words, he says: "Neti, neti," "Not this, not this"; but when pressed for a positive explanation he utters the sublime words: "TAT TVAM ASI," "Thou art That."[11]

Of course! We have already seen this under proposition 3. Now we see more clearly why Eastern pantheistic monism is nondoctrinal. No doctrine can be true. Perhaps some can be more useful than others in getting a subject to achieve unity with the cosmos, but that is different. In fact, a lie or a myth might even be more useful.

---

[10]Hermann Hesse, *Siddhartha,* trans. Hilda Rosner (New York: New Directions, 1951), p. 115.
[11]Mascaró, *Upanishads,* p. 12.

But again we go astray. We are back to thinking like a Westerner. If there can be no true statement, neither can there be a lie. In other words, truth disappears as a category, and the only relevant distinction is usefulness.[12] In short, we are back to technique—the substance of much Eastern concern.

6. Worldview Questions 1, 2, 3 and 6: *To realize one's oneness with the cosmos is to pass beyond good and evil; the cosmos is perfect at every moment.*

We come to a rather touchy subject here. It is one of the softest spots in Eastern pantheism, because people refuse to deny morality. They continue to act as if some actions were right and others wrong. Moreover, the concept of karma is almost universal in Eastern thought.

Karma is the notion that one's present fate, one's pleasure or pain, one's being a king or a slave or a gnat, is the result of past action, especially in a former existence. It is, then, tied to the notion of reincarnation, which follows from the general principle that nothing that is real (that is, no soul) ever passes out of existence. It may take centuries upon centuries to find its way back to the One, but no soul will ever not be. All soul is eternal, for all soul is essentially Soul and thus forever the One.

On its way back to the One, however, it goes through whatever series of illusory forms its past action requires. Karma is the Eastern version of "you reap what you sow." But karma implies strict necessity. If you have "sinned," there is no God to cancel the debt and to forgive. Confession is of no avail. The sin must and will be worked out. Of course a person can choose his future acts; thus karma does not imply determinism or fatalism.[13]

This sounds very much like the description of a moral universe. People should do the good. If they do not, they will reap the consequences, if not in this life, in the next, perhaps even by coming back as a being lower in the hierarchy. As popularly conceived, a moral universe is what the East in fact has.

---

[12]Sri Ramakrishna, who yielded to the Hindu god Kali the categories of knowledge and ignorance, purity and impurity, good and evil, confesses to the difficulty of living beyond the duality of truth and untruth. But he does so for the love of Kali (implying a duality with hate), and he tells his disciples, "I could not bring myself to give up truth" (which implies a duality with falsehoods) (quoted by Schiffman, *Sri Ramakrishna,* p. 135).

[13]In *Siddhartha,* for example, Siddhartha hurts many people as he goes on the path to unity with the One. But he never apologizes or confesses. Neither has meaning in his system.

But two things should be noted about this system. First, the basis for doing good is not so that the good will be done or so that you benefit another person. Karma demands that every soul suffer for its past "sins," so there is no value in alleviating suffering. The soul so helped will have to suffer later. So there is no agape love, giving love, nor would any such love benefit the recipient. One does good deeds in order to attain unity with the One. Doing good is first and foremost a self-helping way of life.

The world, Govinda, is not imperfect or slowly evolving along a long path to perfection. No, it is perfect at every moment; every sin already carries grace within it, all small children are potential old men, all sucklings have death within them, all dying people—eternal life. . . . Therefore, it seems to me that everything that exists is good—death as well as life, sin as well as holiness, wisdom as well as folly.

Siddhartha in Herman Hesse, *Siddhartha*

Second, all actions are merely part of the whole world of illusion. The only "real" reality is ultimate reality, and that is beyond differentiation, beyond good and evil. Brahman is beyond good and evil.

Like true and false, ultimately the distinction between good and evil fades away. Everything is good (which, of course, is identical to saying, "Nothing is good" or "Everything is evil"). The thief is the saint is the thief is the saint . . .

What then shall we say about all of the evidence that people of the East act as if their actions could be considered right or wrong? First, the East has no fewer naive and inconsistent adherents than the West. Second, theists would say, human beings are human beings; they must act as if they were moral beings, for they are moral beings. Third, their moral-looking actions may be done for purely selfish reasons: who wants to return as a gnat or a stone? Of course, in a nonmoral system selfishness would not be considered immoral.

Hesse tips his hand, however, in *Siddhartha* and has his hero seemingly say with ordinary meaning that "love is the most important thing in the world."[14] And Hesse introduces value distinction when he says that it

---

[14]Hesse, *Siddhartha*, p. 119.

is better to be illumined or enlightened than to be an ordinary person.[15] It would seem, therefore, that even many of the illumined have a tendency to act morally rather than to live out the implications of their own system. Perhaps this is a way of saying that some people are "better" than their conscious worldview would allow.

7. Worldview Question 4: *Death is the end of individual, personal existence, but it changes nothing essential in an individual's nature.*

I have already discussed death as it relates to karma and reincarnation. But it deserves, as in every worldview, a separate treatment. Human death signals the end of an individual embodiment of Atman; it signals as well the end of a person. But the soul, Atman, is indestructible.

But note: no human being in the sense of individual or person survives death. Atman survives, but Atman is impersonal. When Atman is reincarnated, it becomes another person. So does Hinduism teach the immortality of the soul? Yes, but not personal and individual immortality.

Of course, through Eastern eyes the personal and individual are illusory anyway. Only Atman is valuable. So death is no big deal. Nothing of value perishes; everything of value is eternal. This may help explain the remark Westerners often make about the cheapness of life in the East. Individual embodiments of life—this man, that woman, you, me—are of no value. But in essence they are all of infinite value; for in essence they are infinite.

The ramifications of this for Westerners who search the East for meaning and significance should not be ignored. For a Westerner who places value on individuality and personality—the unique value of an individual human life—Eastern pantheistic monism will prove a grave disappointment.

8. Worldview Question 7: *To realize one's oneness with the One is to pass beyond time. Time is unreal. History is cyclical.*

One of the central images in *Siddhartha* is the river. From the river Siddhartha learns more than from all the teachings of the Buddha or from all the contact with his spiritual father, Vasudeva. At the climax of the novel Siddhartha bends down and listens intently to the river:

---

[15]Ibid., p. 106.

Siddhartha tried to listen better. The picture of his father, his own picture, and the picture of his son all flowed into each other. Kamala's picture also appeared and flowed on, and the picture of Govinda and others emerged and passed on. They all became part of the river. It was the goal of all of them, yearning, desiring, suffering; and the river's voice was full of longing, full of smarting woe, full of insatiable desire. The river flowed on towards its goal. Siddhartha saw the river hasten, made up of himself and his relatives and all the people he had ever seen. All the waves and water hastened, suffering, towards goals, many goals, to the waterfall, to the sea, to the current, to the ocean and all goals were reached and each one was succeeded by another. The water changed to vapor and rose, became rain and came down again, became spring, brook and river, changed anew, flowed anew. But the yearning voice had altered. It still echoed sorrowfully, searchingly, but other voices accompanied it, voices of pleasure and sorrow, good and evil voices, laughing and lamenting voices, hundreds of voices, thousands of voices.[16]

Finally all the voices, images and faces intertwine: "And all the voices, all the goals, all the yearnings, all the sorrows, all the pleasures, all the good and evil, all of them together was the world. . . . The great song of a thousand voices consisted of one word: Om—perfection."[17] It is at this point that Siddhartha achieves an inner unity with the One, and "the serenity of knowledge" shines in his face.

The river in this long passage, and throughout the book, becomes an image for the cosmos. When looked at from the standpoint of a place along the bank, the river flows (time exists). But when looked at in its entirety—from spring to brook to river to ocean to vapor to rain to spring—the river does not flow (time does not exist). It is an illusion produced by one's sitting on the bank rather than seeing the river from the heavens. Time likewise is cyclical; history is what is produced by the flow of water past a point on the shore. It is illusory. History then has no meaning where reality is concerned. In fact, our task as people who would realize their godhead is to transcend history.

This should help explain why Western Christians, who place great emphasis on history, find their presentation of the historical basis of Christianity almost completely ignored in the East. To the Western mind, whether or not Jesus existed, performed miracles, healed the sick, died and rose

---

[16]Ibid., p. 110.
[17]Ibid., pp. 110-11.

from the dead is important. If it happened, there must be a vital meaning to these strange, unnatural events. Perhaps there is a God after all.

To the Eastern mind, the whole argument is superfluous. Yesterday's facts are not meaningful in themselves. They do not bear on me today unless they have a here-and-now meaning; and if they have a here-and-now meaning, then their facticity as history is of no concern. The Eastern scriptures are filled with epigrams, parables, fables, stories, myths, songs, haiku, hymns, epics, but almost no history in the sense of events recorded because they took place in an unrepeatable space-time context.

To be concerned with such stuff would be to invert the whole hierarchical order. The unique is not the real; only the absolute and all-encompassing is real. If history is valuable, it will be so as myth and myth only, for myth takes us out of particularity and lifts us to essence.

One of the images of human life and the quest for unity with the One is closely tied to the images of the cycle, the wheel, the great mandala. Siddhartha says, "Whither will my path lead me? This path is stupid, it goes in spirals, perhaps in circles, but whichever way it goes, I will follow it."[18] Mascaró echoes, "The path of Truth may not be a path of parallel lines but a path that follows one circle: by going to the right and climbing the circle, or by going to the left and climbing the circle we are bound to meet at the top, although we started in apparently contradictory directions."[19]

This symbol is worked out in the novel *Siddhartha;* the paths of the Buddha, Vasudeva, Siddhartha and Govinda meet and cross several times, but all of them arrive at the same place. To change the image, Hesse shows this in the exact identity of the smiles on the face of the radiant Buddha, Vasudeva and Siddhartha.[20] All the Enlightened Ones are one in the All.

THE BUDDHIST DIFFERENCE

From the outside Buddhism may seem much like Hinduism. The worldview behind both emphasizes, for example, the singularity of primal reality. But there is a key difference nonetheless. To get a sense of what is involved more generally, note the contrast between advaita vedanta (nondualist Hinduism) and Buddhism.

[18]Ibid., p. 78.
[19]Mascaró, *Upanishads*, p. 23.
[20]Hesse, *Siddhartha*, p. 122.

Hindu monism holds that final reality is Brahman, the One. The One has or, better, *is* Being itself—the single undifferentiated final "whatever." It makes sense to name this Brahman or to speak of the One. Like a light bulb shining photons of light farther and farther into the darkness, dispersing its photons more and more from each other, from Brahman (the One) emanates the cosmos (the many).

Buddhist monism holds that final reality is the Void.[21] Final reality is nothing that can be named or grasped. To say it is nothing is incorrect, but to say that it is something is equally incorrect. That would degrade its essence by reducing it to a thing among things. The Hindu One is still a thing among things, though it is the chief among things. The Void is not a thing at all. It is instead the origin of every thing.

This distinction leads to a different understanding of human beings too. For a Hindu, an individual person is a soul (Atman) and thus has substantial (spiritual, not material) reality because it is an emanation of Brahman (reality itself). In death an individual soul loses its bodily residence but is reincarnated in another individual—a sort of transmigration of the soul.

For a Buddhist, an individual person is a not-soul. There is no namable nature at the core of each person. In fact, each person is an aggregate of previous persons. There is not so much the transmigration of the soul as the disappearance of a person at death and the reconstitution of another person from the five aggregates or "existence factors": "body, feeling, perception, mental formations, and consciousness."[22]

Religious practice, techniques of meditation, differ too. Hindus will commonly repeat a mantra, like *Om,* and thus induce a trance or trance-like state that is taken to be an ascent toward godhood. Buddhists may likewise repeat a mantra, but their goal is to reach a state of realizing their root in nonbeing—the nonentity of their "face before they were born," for example.[23] A Zen master may challenge a novice with koans, puzzling questions like "What is the sound of one hand?"[24] or "What is the dharma

---

[21]Robert Linssen, *Zen: The Art of Life* (New York: Pyramid, 1962), pp. 142-43.

[22]Sigmund Kvaloy, "Norwegian Ecophilosophy and Ecopolitics and Their Influence from Buddhism," in *Buddhist Perspectives on the Ecocrisis*, The Wheel Publication 346/348 (Kandy, Sri Lanka: Buddhist Publication Society, 1987), p. 69.

[23]Zen master Myocho (1281-1337), "The Original Face," in *A First Zen Reader* (Rutland, Vt.: Charles E. Tuttle, 1960), p. 21.

[24]This koan is often translated as "What is the sound of one hand clapping?" but the word *clapping* does not occur in the Japanese.

body of the Buddha [i.e., what is reality]?"[25] Or the master may direct the
novice to do *zazen* ("just sit"). In any case, the attempt is made to empty
the mind of all analytical thought, for ultimate reality is not only nonbeing, it is also "no-mind," that is, a *mind* that does not analyze what it is

---

*Kitta, the son of an elephant trainer, inquired of The Enlightened One
(the Buddah) whether any of the three modes of personality—the past
you, the present you and the future you—are real. The Enlightened One
replied:*

> Just, Kitta, as from a cow comes milk, and from the milk curds,
> and from the curds butter, and from the butter ghee and from the
> ghee junket; but when it is milk it is not called curds, or butter, or
> ghee, or junket; and when it is curds it is not called by any of the
> other names; and so on—Just so, Kitta, when any one of the three
> modes of personality is going on, it is not called by the name of
> the other. For these, Kitta, are merely names, expressions, turns
> of speech, designations in common use in the world. And of these
> a Tathâgata (one who has won the truth) makes use indeed, but is
> not led astray by them.*

POTTHAPADA SUTTA

*A note follows this text: "The point is, of course, that just as there is *no substratum* in the
products of the cow, so there is no *ego*, no constant unity, no 'soul' (in the animistic sense
of the word, as used by savages). There are a number of qualities that, when united, make
up a personality—always changing. When the change has reached a certain point, it is
convenient to change the designation, the name, by which the personality is known—just
as in the case of the cow. But the abstract term is only a convenient *form of expression.*
There never was any personality, *as a separate reality,* all the time (from *Potthapada
Sutta*, [201], 51-53 <www.sacred-texts.com/bud/dob/dob-09tx.htm>).

---

grasping but grasps what is only as what it *is.* The answer, therefore, to
"What is the sound of one hand?" is simply "the sound of one hand."

Still, with these and other differences, the effect of both nondualist
Hinduism and Buddhism is to put a person in a state where all distinc-

---

[25]Isshu Miura and Ruth Fuller Sasaki, *The Zen Koan* (New York: Harcourt Brace and World,
1956), p. 44; D. T. Suzuki, *An Introduction to Zen Buddhism* (New York: Grove, 1964), pp.
59, 99-117.

tions disappear—here and there, now and then, illusion and reality, truth and falsity, good and evil. Despite the noble attempt of Buddhist masters like D. T. Suzuki to insist that Buddhism is not nihilistic, it will usually seem so to Western readers.[26]

9. Worldview Question 8: *Core commitments among individual Eastern pantheistic monists may vary widely, but one consistent commitment is, by the elimination of desire, to achieve salvation, that is, to realize one's union with the One (Hinduism) or the Void, pure consciousness (Buddhism).*

Hinduism and Buddhism both locate the problem with human beings in their separateness from the really real, the One or the Void.[27] Human beings live an illusory material existence in an illusory material world, desiring illusory goals. The result is suffering. To avoid suffering, one should eliminate this desire. There are, of course, as noted above, multiple techniques for eliminating desire. Hinduism focuses on a variety of meditation practices. Buddhism presents an eightfold path: right view, right intention, right speech, right action, right livelihood, right effort, right mindfulness and right consciousness.

Of course, just like Christian theists who often get caught up in beliefs and practices that do not bring glory to God or witness to the presence of the kingdom of God, so Eastern pantheists often are diverted into seeking the illusory goals of wealth, fame and endless hedonistic pleasures. For the Eastern pantheist, salvation sought is not necessarily salvation gained. Unlike a Christian who receives salvation as a gift of God's grace, the pantheist is on his or her own.

EAST AND WEST: A PROBLEM IN COMMUNICATION

Cyclical history, paths that cross, doctrines that disagree, evil that is good, knowledge that is ignorance, time that is eternal, reality that is

---

[26]Suzuki, *Introduction*, p. 39, writes, for example, "Zen wants to rise above logic, Zen wants to find a higher affirmation where there are no antitheses. Therefore, in Zen, God is neither denied nor insisted upon; only there is in Zen no such God as has been conceived by Jewish and Christian minds." See also pp. 48-57.

[27]Charles Taylor notes the radical difference between what Buddhists and Christians count as "human flourishing." The Buddhist notion requires individuals to "detach themselves from their own flourishing, to the extinction of self," while Christians aim at "renunciation of human fulfillment to serve God" (*A Secular Age* [Cambridge, Mass.: Belknap, 2007], p. 17).

unreal: all these are the shifting, paradoxical, even contradictory masks
that veil the One. What can Westerners say? If they point to its irration-
ality, the Easterner rejects reason as a category. If they point to the disappearance of morality, the Easterner scorns the duality that is required
for the distinction. If they point to the inconsistency between the Easterner's moral action and amoral theory, the Easterner says, "Well, consistency is no virtue except by reason, which I have already rejected,
and furthermore I'm not yet perfect. When I am rid of this load of
karma, I'll cease acting as if I were moral. In fact, I'll cease acting at all
and just meditate." If the Westerner says, "But if you don't eat, you'll
die," the Easterner responds, "So what? Atman is Brahman. Brahman is
eternal. A death to be wished!"

It is, I think, no wonder Western missionaries have made little
headway with committed Hindus and Buddhists. They don't speak
the same language, for they hold almost nothing in common. It is
painfully difficult to grasp the Eastern worldview even when one has
some idea that it demands a mode of thought different from the West.
It seems to many who would like Easterners to become Christians
(and thus to become theists) that Easterners have an even more difficult time understanding that Christianity is somehow unique, that
the space-time resurrection of Jesus the Christ is at the heart of the
good news of God.

In both cases, it seems to me, an understanding that the East and the
West operate on two very different sets of assumptions is the place to
start. To begin the dialogue, at least one party must know how different
their basic assumptions may turn out to be, but for true human communication, both parties must know this before the dialogue proceeds very
far. Perhaps the difficulties in Eastern thought that seem so obvious to
Westerners will at least begin to be recognized by Easterners. If an Easterner can see what knowledge, morality and reality are like as seen from,
say, the point of view of Western theism, the attractiveness of the Western way may be obvious.

Generally, however, what the East sees of the West is more ugly than
Shiva, the great god of destruction himself. Those who would communi-
cate the beauty of truth in Christ have a tough job, for the mists of ugly
Western imperialism, war, violence, greed and gluttony are thick indeed.

Where, then, does all this leave the Westerner who has gone East to search for meaning and significance?[28] Many, of course, drop out along the way, try to take a shortcut to Nirvana through drugs, or drop out, return to their former faith or come home and take over their family's corporation, leaving the East behind with little more than a beard left to show for it. (That gets trimmed before the first board meeting and removed before the second.) Others stay on the path for life. Still others perhaps find Nirvana and remain caught up in contemplation. But many simply die—by starvation, dysentery, skullduggery and who knows what else. Some shipwreck on the shores of Western communities and are slowly made seaworthy by friends.

For several decades, young and old have been flocking to various gurus. Bookstores are filled with books pointing East, their spines to the West, of course. Transcendental Meditation and other Eastern spiritual techniques are common, as commuters meditate on the way to work and classes are offered in business corporations.

Going East now has lost some of its attraction, for the Eastern world is becoming more and more Western in appearance and tone. Cities that once held an exotic attraction look more and more like downtown San Francisco. Western styles of dress and life are replacing those of the traditional East. Yet while the number of Westerners who are trekking East has seemed to decline in recent years, for some the East still holds promise. And so long as it seems to offer peace, personal meaning and significance, people are likely to respond. What will they receive? Not just an Eastern Band-Aid for a Western scratch but a whole new worldview and lifestyle.

---

[28]In "Everything Is on Fire: Tibetan Buddhism Inside Out" John B. Buescher (who was raised a Catholic, pursued Buddhism for most of his life, then returned to his Christian roots) reviews ten recent books; his reflections dramatically portray both the parallels and the eventual vast differences between Tibetan Buddhism and the Christian worldview (*Books and Culture* [January/February, 2008], pp. 40-43).

Chapter 8

A SEPARATE UNIVERSE

THE NEW AGE—SPIRITUALITY WITHOUT RELIGION

We are Creating energy, matter and life
at the interface between the void and all known creation.
We are facing into the known universe, creating it, filling it. . . .
I am "one of the boys in the engine room pumping Creation
from the void into the known universe;
from the unknown to the known I am pumping."

John Lilly, *The Center of the Cyclone*

Eastern mysticism poses one way out for Western people caught in naturalism's nihilistic bind. But Eastern mysticism is foreign. Even a watered-down version like Transcendental Meditation requires an immediate and radical reorientation from the West's normal mode of grasping reality. Such reorientation leads to new states of consciousness and feelings of meaning, as we saw, but the intellectual cost is high. One must die to the West to be born in the East.

Is there a less painful, less costly way to achieve meaning and significance? Why not conduct a search for a new consciousness along more Western lines?

This has been done by a host of scholars, medical doctors, psychologists and religious explorers, and ordinary people looking to make sense out of a confusing world. There has been an avant-garde in a number of academic disciplines from the humanities to the hard sciences, and the spillover into culture at large is at flood stage. To change the image, we are experiencing a worldview in its late adolescence.[1] Not yet completely formed, the New Age worldview contains many rough edges and inner tensions, and even flat-out contradictions. Because of its inherently eclectic character, it may now be as mature as it will ever get. Still, it has taken shape, and we can visualize it in a series of propositions as we have done with other worldviews.

When this book was first published, there were very few attempts to bring all these New Age notions together in one place. The schemata that follows was at that time almost unique.[2] Since then there have been many attempts, most notably those of Marilyn Ferguson in *The Aquarian Conspiracy*, Fritjof Capra in *The Turning Point* and Ken Wilber in *A Brief History of Everything*. The first is the more enthusiastic and popular, the latter two the more guarded and scholarly.[3] All three writers have made an impact on the New Age movement itself, giving it a sense of coherence and focus it had formerly lacked. Moreover, Douglas Groothuis in *Unmasking the New Age* and *Confronting the New Age* has contributed to a clearer and more comprehensive definition.[4] James A. Herrick has dug

---

[1]In 1976 and even in 1988 I said "infancy"; in 1997 I said "adolescence."

[2]Perhaps Sam Keen came as close as any in his brief article "The Cosmic Versus the Rational," *Psychology Today*, July 1974, pp. 56-59.

[3]Marilyn Ferguson, *The Aquarian Conspiracy: Personal and Social Transformation in the 1980s* (Los Angeles: Jeremy P. Tarcher, 1980), and Fritjof Capra, *The Turning Point: Science, Society and the Rising Culture* (New York: Bantam, 1982). See also Capra's *The Tao of Physics* (New York: Bantam, 1977). Ken Wilber has written many books, beginning with *Spectrum of Consciousness* (Wheaton, Ill.: Quest, 1977; 2nd ed. 1993); and, more recently, *A Brief History of Everything* (Boston: Shambhala, 1996); *A Theory of Everything* (Boston: Shambhala, 2000); the novel *Boomeritis* (Boston: Shambhala, 2002). These have been followed by a series of "integrating" books, the most recent of which is *Integral Life Practice: A 21st Ccentury Blueprint for Physical Health, Emotional Balance, Mental Clarity and Spiritual Awakening* (Boston: Integral Books, 2008). For a summary and analysis of Wilber's system, see Douglas Groothuis, "Ken Wilber," in *Baker Dictionary of Cults* (Grand Rapids: Baker, forthcoming), and Tyler Johnston's review of *A Brief History of Everything* in *Denver Journal* 5 (2002) <www.denverseminary.edu/dj/articles02/0400/0404.php>.

[4]See especially three books by Douglas R. Groothuis: *Unmasking the New Age* (Downers Grove, Ill.: InterVarsity Press, 1986); *Confronting the New Age* (Downers Grove, Ill.: InterVarsity Press, 1988) and *Jesus in an Age of Controversy* (Eugene, Ore.: Harvest House, 1996); the latter deals with New Age concepts of Jesus. Various specialist organizations have been watching the development; among them are the Spiritual Counterfeits Project, P.O. Box 4308, Berkeley, CA 94704; and Christian Research Institute, 6295 Blakeney Park Drive, Charlotte, NC 28277. Both publish literature evaluating the New Age movement. See too Ted Peters, *The Cosmic Self* (San Francisco: HarperSanFrancisco, 1991), and a book whose title seems a bit premature: Vishal Mangalwadi, *When the New Age Gets Old* (Downers Grove, Ill.: InterVarsity Press, 1992).

even deeper into the roots of the New Age movement, arguing persua-
sively that these roots originate in ancient Gnosticism and can be seen in
subsequent stages of Western civilization, emerging into what he calls a
New Religious Synthesis. His *The Making of the New Spirituality* is, at
least for now, the definitive history of New Age spirituality.[5]

By the mid-1970s articles and cover stories in *Time* magazine and
other major popular magazines touted the growing interest in the weird
and the wonderful.[6] By the mid-1980s interest in psychic phenomena had
become so widespread as barely to raise an eyebrow. Many magazines,
such as *Body and Soul* and *Yoga Journal*, propagate New Age ideas and
are readily available on newsstands.[7] According to the Mayan Calendar a

---

[5]James A. Herrick, *The Making of the New Spirituality* (Downers Grove, Ill.: InterVarsity Press,
2003). See also Carl A. Raschke, *The Interruption of Eternity: Modern Gnosticism and the
Origins of the New Religious Consciousness* (Chicago: Nelson-Hall, 1980).

[6]See "Boom Times on the Psychic Frontier," *Time* magazine's cover story, March 4, 1974, which
charted the interest in psychic phenomena—ESP, psychokinesis (the mental ability to influence physical objects), Kirlian photography (which supposedly shows the "aura" of living
things), psychic healing, acupuncture, clairvoyance, "out-of-body" experiences, precognition
(foreknowledge of events). A year later *Saturday Review*, February 22, 1975, paralleled *Time*'s
coverage on a more sophisticated plane, suggesting that the popularity of the new consciousness ran deeper then than mere cultural fads such as the God-is-dead theology. News of New
Age celebrations at the time of the supposed Harmonic Convergence (August 1987) were
carried in many American newspapers and newsmagazines, some written with considerable
tongue-in-cheek. The New Age generates public interest but not always public respect.

[7]*New Age Journal* has gone through an interesting metamorphosis since its inception in 1974,
when it began as a magazine published by self-confessed idealistic New Agers. Suffering the
threat of extinction in 1983, its longtime editor has written (September 1983, p. 5), it got an
infusion of funds and began to take on not only a new look—more professional design, slick
paper and four-color interior printing—but also a new editorial direction, focusing less on
the more extreme exponents of New Age thought and more on the borders between the New
Age and mainstream American culture. By June 1984 the change was signaled by new names
on its masthead at key editorial positions. The magazine then reflected much more the established ground of the New Age than the cutting edge. One might interpret this change as
signaling a coming of age of the New Age movement itself, an attempt to reach the average
newsstand magazine buyer with the more palatable New Age ideas, or a commercializing of
the New Age by middle-class management. Still, as a new editor (Joan Duncan Oliver) took
the helm of the slick journal in August 1996, she reviewed the early issues and commented
that the "focus has remained constant"; in the words of an earlier editor, "We are really talking
about healing the spirit" (August 1996, p. 6). In 2002 the journal changed its name to *Body &
Soul*, perhaps admitting that the New Age was no longer new, retaining the slick pop magazine format and its by now health-oriented content. Editor comments: "For 28 years, *New
Age* reported on the new elements of an emerging holistic movement—a movement that has
now become a lifestyle for thousands, if not millions of Americans. Now as *Body & Soul*, we
promise to continue this tradition, bringing you the best in holistic ideas, trends and news"
(*Body & Soul* [March/April 2002], p. 6); in 2008 the magazine had continued in this pop-
psych-spiritual vein. The history of the magazine is a study in commercialization: spirit has
become dollars and flesh.

Harmonic Convergence was scheduled to take place in August 1987. The date came with much attention in the media, but no evidence ever surfaced that the Age of Aquarius, a time of great peace, had arrived.

At the end of 1987 *Time* magazine again focused on the New Age, with a cover featuring Shirley MacLaine and a story surveying "faith healers, channelers, space travelers and crystals galore."[8] MacLaine had become for the 1980s perhaps the most visible proponent of New Age thought and practice. After writing a host of autobiographies and instruction on the new consciousness, she eventually dropped out as a major New Age leader.[9] And by the mid-1990s, New Age stories disappeared from the media, not because it had vanished but because it had become no longer odd, no longer newsworthy.[10] Still, the popularity of New Age thinking continues: some twenty popular New Age journals are, for example, carried in my local Borders bookstore.

THE RADICAL TRANSFORMATION OF HUMAN NATURE

Basing much of their hope on the evolutionary model—a leftover from

---

[8]*Time*, December 7, 1987, pp. 62-72.

[9]MacLaine's attempt, after leading many weekend seminars, to build her own New Age center in New Mexico had to be abandoned when "locals protested that the site was too environmentally fragile to accommodate the star's building plans" (*Time*, January 10, 1994). Much later she recalls a Belgian hiker wanting to talk with her about "God and the universe and the meaning of life" and to have her "bless him." She declines because "she didn't like being seen as a New Age guru. That was the reason I quit conducting my traveling seminars. Too many people gave away their power to me" (*The Camino* [New York: Pocket, 2000]), p. 140). Still, MacLaine has continued her autobiographies. *My Lucky Stars: A Hollywood Memoir* (New York: Bantam, 1995) focuses on her professional career; *The Camino* (2000) recounts the fantastic and fantastical events of a Spanish pilgrimage and the spiritual teachings of John the Scot, one of her spirit guides. Then MacLaine along with her dog has written *Out on a Leash: Exploring the Nature of Reality and Love* (New York: Atria Books, 2003). Finally in *Sage-ing and Age-ing* (New York: Atria Books, 2007), she recaps her life, speaks of living in ancient Atlantis, repeats her views on synchronicity, UFOs, and aliens, and predicts a massive transformation of human consciousness on December 21, 2012 (p. 231).

[10]Bob Woodward's revelation that First Lady Hillary Rodham Clinton has sought the advice of Jean Houston, a well-known New Age counselor, caused a news bubble for a few weeks in the summer of 1996, but by December it had largely been forgotten. See Bob Woodward, *The Choice* (New York: Simon & Schuster, 1996), pp. 55-57, 129-35, 271-72, 412-13. Advertisers have made use of the connection: Jean Houston's photo and an announcement of a November 1996 seminar appeared with the note "friend/advisor to Hillary Clinton" in *The Chicago Tribune*, July 28, 1996, sec. 14, p. 11. Houston has taught philosophy, psychology and religion at Columbia University, Hunter College, the New School for Social Research and Marymount College, and is a past president of the Association for Humanistic Psychology. Some of her publications are listed in note 13 below.

Western naturalism—a number of avant-garde thinkers have been proph-
esying the coming of a New Man and a New Age. In 1973 Jean Houston
of the Foundation for Mind Research in Pomona, New York, said that
what this world needs is a "psychenaut program to put the first man on
earth." But if we don't get a psychic counterpart to NASA, our psychenaut

---

An authentically empowered person is one who is so strong, so empowered, that the idea of using force against another is not a part of his or
her consciousness.

No understanding of evolution is adequate that does not have at its
core that we are on a journey toward authentic power, and that authentic empowerment is the goal of our evolutionary process and the
purpose of our being. We are evolving from a species that pursues external power into a species that pursues authentic power. We are leaving behind exploration of the physical world as our sole means of evolution. This means of evolution, and the consciousness that results from
an awareness that is limited to the five-sensory modality, are no longer
adequate to what we must become.

GARY ZUKAV, *The Seat of the Soul*

---

is coming: "It's almost as if the species [humanity] were taking a quantum
leap into a whole new way of being."[11] She concludes that if we learn "to
play upon the vast spectrum of consciousness, . . . we would have access
to a humanity of such depth and richness as the world has not yet known,
so that our great-great grandchildren may look back upon us as Neander-
thals, so different will they be."[12]

For thirty years Houston has spoken the same message: human beings
evolve toward higher consciousness; societies and cultures evolve toward
greater comprehensiveness. In the 1990s, she said we may already be in
the first few years of a "Type I High-Level Civilization," during which "our
great-great-great-great grandchildren" are going to be on other planets or

---

[11]Jerry Avorn interview with Robert Masters and Jean Houston, "The Varieties of Postpsyche-
delic Experience," *Intellectual Digest*, March 1973, p. 16.
[12]Ibid., p. 18.

space colonies "creating paradise, creating a viable ecology and a world which we mutually nourish and which nourishes us to the fullest of our capacities." After that will come "Type II-Level Civilizations in which we become responsible on the sensory level for the orchestration of the resources of the solar system. . . . We will mythically probably also be coming close to in some way incarnating the archetypes. We will become the gods that we have invoked." Later still, in Type III-Level Civilizations "we will join the galactic milieu and become the creators of worlds, capable of Genesis." And as the third millennium was beginning, she offered counsel on how to live in and promote "jump time," those times of transition to higher states of being.[13]

In 2003 Ken Wilber and Andrew Cohen outlined an even more elaborate scale of evolution (eight levels) from 100,000 years ago (the instinctive/survival stage) to thirty years ago, when a few people first entered the holistic stage. More than half of the world's population, though, is less than halfway up this evolutionary ladder. Yet when a person discovers that "it's up to me," evolution proceeds. As Wilber says, reflecting on the transition, "Yes, it's co-creation because right at that frothy, foaming, chaotic emerging edge of spirit's unfolding is where *lela*, the creative play, is."[14] The evolution of humanity (body and soul) is up to each and every person. But it's coming. "A thousand years from now," says Wilber, people will "look back on all this as 'that kindergarten stuff' that we were pushing back then."[15]

Though the theme of personal and cultural evolution has been present

---

[13]Jean Houston, "Toward Higher-Level Civilizations," *The Quest*, Spring 1990, p. 42. This general move has been the central theme in her several books, including *Life Force: The Psycho-historical Recovery of the Self* (New York: Dell, 1980); *Godseed: The Journey of Christ* (Wheaton, Ill.: Quest, 1992); *The Search for the Beloved: Journeys in Sacred Psychology* (Los Angeles: Jeremy P. Tarcher, 1987); *A Mythic Life* (San Francisco: HarperSanFrancisco, 1996); *Jump Time* (New York: Jeremy P. Tarcher, 2000); and *Mystical Dogs* (Makawao, Hawaii: Inner Ocean, 2002). Popular sociologist George Leonard, editor of *Look* magazine before it folded, predicted the same radical transformation and looked forward to "the emergence of a new human nature." His faith is unshakable: "This new species *will* evolve" (George Leonard, "Notes on the Transformation," *Intellectual Digest*, September 1972, pp. 25, 32). Shirley MacLaine echoes this: both ordinary technology and "inner technology" have advanced, attesting to the "evolution of the human mind" and "a quantum leap in the progress of mankind" (Shirley MacLaine, *It's All in the Playing* [New York: Bantam, 1987], pp. 334-35; and *Sage-ing While Age-ing*, pp. 191-92 and 254).
[14]"The Guru and the Paudit: Andrew Cohen and Ken Wilber in Dialogue," *What Is Enlightenment?* Spring/Summer 2003, p. 86.
[15]Ibid., p. 93.

from the 1970s into the 2000s, its ubiquitous emphasis by New Age teachers seems more important to me now than ever before. And well it might be, for nothing has happened in the past twenty years to improve our human lot. Apart from a radical transformation, humankind continues to go from one bloody tragedy to another. So New Age hopefuls read modern accounts of those who claim to have made a breakthrough to another dimension. They read (or, better, misread) the ancient religious teachers—Jesus, the Buddha, Zoroaster—who still have some credibility, see in them a hint of the progress that awaits all humankind, and conclude that there is a New Age coming.[16]

One major strain of optimism about the New Age has, however, become more muted than transformed. In the early 1970s Andrew Weil, M.D., a drug researcher and theoretician, argued for a new, more relaxed approach to psychedelic drug use and to alternate ways of achieving new states of consciousness. The drug revolution, he thought, was the harbinger of a New Age, an age in which humankind—because it wisely utilizes drugs and mystical techniques—will finally achieve full health. Weil wrote, "One day, when the change has occurred, we will no doubt look back on our drug problem of the 1970s as something to laugh about and shake our heads over: how could we not have seen what it was really all about?"[17] Today this optimism is linked with what Douglas Groothuis

---

[16]Reading ancient texts in the light of contemporary interests without noting that these texts are being lifted from their intellectual and worldview contexts is a minor industry among modern pundits. In *Godseed*, for example, Houston reads Jesus in light of second-century Gnostic texts rather than the first-century New Testament documents. The apostle Paul would never confuse his own identity with that of Christ, but Wilber has him doing so: he turns "Christ liveth in me" (Gal 2:20) into "the ultimate I [of each person] *is* Christ" (*Brief History of Everything*, p. 132). I have discussed such misreadings, giving many illustrations in *Scripture Twisting* (Downers Grove, Ill.: InterVarsity Press, 1980), though not by drawing primarily on New Age sources. See also the discussion of Deepak Chopra, pp. 205-7 below.

[17]Andrew Weil, *The Natural Mind: A New Way of Looking at Drugs and the Higher Consciousness* (Boston: Houghton Mifflin, 1972), p. 205; abridged in *Psychology Today*, October 1972. In 1983 (rev. 1993) Weil addressed a book on mind-altering drugs to teenagers and their parents. See his *From Chocolate to Morphine: Everything You Need to Know About Mind-Altering Drugs*, coauthored with Winifred Rosen, rev. ed. (Boston: Houghton Mifflin, 1993). Here the authors distinguish between drug use (of which they approve) and drug abuse (which they warn against); most chapters on individual types of drugs end with "suggestions and precautions" for the use of such drugs. The chapter on mind-altering drugs, for example, details what one should and should not do to get the feeling of enhanced sensation that the drugs often evoke. Weil and Rosen note in the preface to the second edition that the first edition was banned from some libraries, though I found the book in our local suburban library.

calls "technoshamanism." Advanced by followers of the late Timothy Leary, the great hope now is to lose one's normal self and take on godlike powers in the virtual reality of cyberspace.[18]

Weil himself has turned from emphasizing the safe use of mind-altering drugs to promoting "integrative medicine," which Brad Lemley describes as "a medical model that pulls the best from therapeutic systems ranging from allopathy (the drugs-and-surgery regimen of American M.D.s) to homeopathy, acupuncture, herbalism, nutritional science, hypnotherapy and many others."[19]

THE PANORAMIC SWEEP OF NEW AGE THOUGHT

From what I've said so far it should be obvious that the New Age worldview is not confined to one narrow band of humanity. We have here more than the current fad of New York intellectuals or West Coast gurus. The following list of disciplines and representatives within those disciplines emphasizes this fact. For the people listed here, New Age thought is as natural as theism is to Christians.

In *psychology* the first theorizer to recognize the validity of altered

---

[18]Douglas Groothuis remarks that Timothy Leary, the most well-known drug guru of the 1960s and 1970s, "modified his famous credo of the 1960s, 'Tune in, turn on, and drop out,' to 'Turn on, boot up, and jack in,' commenting that personal computing is 'the LSD of the 1990s.'" Nonetheless Leary still, at least occasionally, took LSD till near the end of his life. See Douglas Groothuis, "Technoshamanism: Digital Deities," in *The Soul in Cyberspace* (Grand Rapids: Baker, 1997), pp. 105-20. Then too Eugene Taylor reported in 1996 that mind-altering drug use had been making a comeback ("Psychedelics: The Second Coming," *Psychology Today,* July/August 1996, pp. 56-59, 84). It is not clear whether this resurgence in drug use was connected with a New Age mindset or was primarily recreational.

[19]Brad Lemley, "My Dinner with Andy," *New Age Journal,* December 1995, p. 66. Weil's books emphasizing health include *Health and Healing: Understanding Conventional and Alternative Medicine* (Boston: Houghton Mifflin, 1983); *Natural Health, Natural Medicine: A Comprehensive Manual for Wellness and Self-Care* (Boston: Houghton Mifflin, 1990); and *Spontaneous Healing: How to Discover and Embrace Your Body's Natural Ability to Maintain and Heal Itself* (New York: Alfred A. Knopf, 1995). *Spontaneous Healing* spent four months on the *New York Times* bestseller list, with expected sales of 400,000 within a few months (Lemley, "My Dinner with Andy," p. 66). Though he continues to give instructions for mild forms of meditation (e.g., *Spontaneous Healing,* pp. 194-209), in his books on healing Weil seems to claim far less for alternate states of consciousness than he has in earlier books. Other Weil books include *Marriage of the Son and Moon: A Quest for Unity in Consciousness* (Boston: Houghton Mifflin, 1998); *Eight Weeks to Optimum Health* (New York: Alfred A. Knopf, 1997); *Healthy Kitchen: Recipes for a Better Body, Life and Spirit* (New York: Alfred A. Knopf, 2002); and *Healthy Ageing: A Lifelong Guide to Physical and Spiritual Wellbeing* (New York: Alfred A. Knopf, 2005). For an analysis of Weil's work, see Paul C. Reisser, M.D., Dale Mabe, D.O., and Robert Velarde, *Examining Alternative Medicine: An Inside Look at the Benefits & Risks* (Downers Grove, Ill.: InterVarsity Press, 2001), pp. 140-61.

states of consciousness was William James. Later he was to be followed by Carl Jung and Abraham Maslow. Now there were or are Aldous Huxley, novelist and drug experimenter; Robert Masters and Jean Houston of the Foundation for Mind Research; Stanislav Grof at the Maryland Psychiatric Research Center, who gives dying patients LSD to help them gain a feeling of cosmic unity and thus prepare them for death; and John Lilly, whose early work was with dolphins but who progressed beyond that to drug experimentation with himself as prime subject.[20] Ken Wilber's "transpersonal synthesis of various schools of psychology and philosophy makes his work intellectually appealing and places him on the cutting edge of the New Age intelligentsia." Finally, psychologist Jon Klimo has issued an extensive study of channeling (a New Age term for mediumship).[21]

In *sociology* and *cultural history* are Theodore Roszak, especially in *Where the Wasteland Ends* and *Unfinished Animal,* and William Irwin Thompson, whose *At the Edge of History* and *Passages About Earth* trace his own intellectual journey from Catholicism through naturalism and on into an occult version of the New Age. Thompson's work is notable because as a former history teacher at MIT and York University and as a recipient of Woodrow Wilson and Old Dominion fellowships he was recognized and approved by establishment intellectuals. *Passages About Earth* shows how completely he has moved out of establishment circles.[22]

---

[20]To investigate further the work of these psychologists and brain scientists without getting bogged down in details, see Marilyn Ferguson, *The Brain Revolution: The Frontiers of Mind Research* (New York: Taplinger, 1973), especially chaps. 1, 3, 6-12, 17, 20-23. Her bibliography provides a good start toward an in-depth study of the early New Age thinkers. The work of those listed in the noted paragraph can be examined in the following: William James, *Varieties of Religious Experience* (1902; reprint New York: Mentor, 1958), lectures 16-17; C. G. Jung, *Modern Man in Search of a Soul* (New York: Harcourt Brace, 1933), esp. chap. 10; Abraham Maslow, *Religious Values and Peak Experiences* (Columbus: Ohio State University Press, 1962); Aldous Huxley, *The Doors of Perception and Heaven and Hell* (New York: Harper & Row, 1963); Stanislav Grof, "Beyond the Bounds of Psychoanalysis," *Intellectual Digest,* September 1972, pp. 86-88; for Andrew Weil see notes 17 and 19 above; John Lilly's most interesting book is *The Center of the Cyclone: An Autobiography of Inner Space* (New York: Julian, 1972).

[21]Groothuis, *Unmasking,* p. 80; see his chapter on New Age psychology, pp. 71-91.

[22]Theodore Roszak, *Where the Wasteland Ends: Politics and Transcendence in Postindustrial Society* (Garden City, N.Y.: Anchor, 1973), and *Unfinished Animal: An Adventure in the Evolution of Consciousness* (New York: Harper & Row, 1975); William Irwin Thompson, *At the Edge of History: Speculations on the Transformation of Culture* (New York: Harper & Row, 1971), and *Passages About Earth* (New York: Harper & Row, 1974); see also Thompson's *Darkness and Scattered Light* (Garden City, N.Y.: Anchor, 1978), and *The Time Falling Bodies Take to Light* (New York: St. Martin's, 1981).

In *anthropology* is Carlos Castaneda (1931-1998), whose books have been bestsellers both on university campuses and in general bookstores. *The Teachings of Don Juan* (1968) set the pace and was quickly followed by *A Separate Reality* (1971) and *Journey to Ixtlan* (1972). Other books came later but found a less interested public. Castaneda, who began by studying the effect of psychedelic drugs in Indian culture, apprenticed himself to Don Juan, a Yaqui Indian sorcerer. Having completed the initiation rites over several years, Castaneda became a sorcerer whose alleged experience with various kinds of new realities and separate universes makes fascinating, sometimes frightening, reading. In the 1970s and '80s Castaneda's works were one of the major doorways to the new consciousness.[23]

Even in *natural science* elements of New Age thinking are to be found. People involved professionally in physics often take the lead, perhaps be-

[23]Carlos Castaneda, *The Teachings of Don Juan: A Yaqui Way of Knowledge* (Berkeley: University of California Press, 1968); *A Separate Reality: Further Conversations with Don Juan* (New York: Simon & Schuster, 1971); *Journey to Ixtlan: The Lessons of Don Juan* (New York: Simon & Schuster, 1972); *Tales of Power* (New York: Simon & Schuster, 1974); *The Eagle's Gift* (New York: Pocket, 1982), *The Fire from Within* (New York: Simon & Schuster, 1984); *The Power of Silence* (New York: Simon & Schuster, 1987); *The Art of Dreaming* (New York: Harper Perennial, 1993); *Silent Knowledge* (Los Angeles: Cleargreen, 1996), *The Active Side of Infinity* (New York: HarperCollins, 1998); *Magical Passes: The Practical Wisdom of the Shamans of Ancient Mexico* (New York: HarperCollins, 1998); and *The Wheel of Time: The Shamans of Mexico: Their Thoughts About Life, Death and the Universe* (Los Angeles: LA Eidolona, 1998). The more recent of these books, while occasionally showing up on bestseller lists, did not have nearly the public impact of the first three.

Early on readers wondered if Castaneda had not created the Yaqui Indian sorcerer Don Juan out of his own fertile imagination; see the various viewpoints expressed by the critics such as Joyce Carol Oates anthologized in *Seeing Castaneda*, ed. Daniel C. Noel (New York: Putnam's Sons, 1976). Richard De Mille may be credited with convincingly unmasking the fictional character of Castaneda's books; see his *Castaneda's Journey: The Power and the Allegory* (Santa Barbara, Calif.: Capra, 1976). Nonetheless, in the foreword to *The Power of Silence* Castaneda maintains, "My books are a true account of a teaching method that Juan Matus, a Mexican Indian sorcerer, used in order to help me understand the sorcerers' world" (p. 8). Castaneda, always elusive, broke silence for an interview with Keith Thompson in *New Age Journal*, April 1994, pp. 66-71, 152-56. Here he again defends his work as an anthropologist-participant, but in the process he makes comments that raise more questions than are answered. Nonetheless, anthropologist Clifford Geertz probably speaks for many of his colleagues when he says, "Castaneda's books have no presence in anthropology" (quoted by Anupama Bhattacharya, "The Reluctant Sorcerer" <www.lifepositive.com/spirit/traditional-paths/sorcery/carlos-castaneda.asp>).

Confusion about Castaneda continued to characterize articles that appeared after news of his death. See, for example, Bhattacharya, "The Reluctant Sorcerer"; Keith Thompson, "To Carlos Castaneda, Wherever You Are" <www2.bcinternet.net/~newman/Castaneda.htm>; and Peter Applebome, "Carlos Castaneda, Mystical Writer, Dies 72," *New York Times*, June 19, 1998.

cause at its most theoretical it is the most speculative and least prone to falsification by fact. The case for a New Age interpretation of physics is most popularly put by physicist Fritjof Capra and popular science writer Gary Zukav.[24] More muted in their espousal of New Age ideas are Lewis Thomas and J. E. Lovelock. Thomas is a biologist and medical doctor whose *Lives of a Cell* has attained a solid status in the field of popular science writing.[25] And Lovelock is a specialist in gas chromatography whose *Gaia: A New Look at Life on Earth* is a seminal work on seeing Earth (Gaia is the ancient Greek earth goddess) as a single symbiotic system.[26]

In the *health* field the number of nonordinary therapies proposed in what has come to be called "holistic" or "alternative" medicine is legion. Acupuncture, Rolfing, psychic healing, kinesiology, therapeutic touch— these are just a few of the techniques used by New Age health practitioners.[27] Both doctors and nurses have been affected. Nursing education, in fact, may be the discipline most affected by New Age ideas and techniques. Under the guise of "spiritual care," a wide variety of New Age therapeutic techniques are now being taught to students of nursing.[28]

---

[24]Capra, *Tao of Physics*, and chap. 3 in *The Turning Point*; and Gary Zukav, *The Dancing Wu Li Masters* (New York: Bantam, 1980). See Stephen Weinberg, "Sokal's Hoax," *New York Review of Books*, August 8, 1996, pp. 11-15, and Victor J. Stenger, "New Age Physics: Has Science Found the Path to the Ultimate?" *Free Inquiry*, Summer 1996, pp. 7-11, for critiques of any attempt to draw metaphysical implications from physical theories such as quantum mechanics; see also Richard H. Bube, *Putting It All Together: Seven Patterns for Relating Science and the Christian Faith* (Lanham, Md.: University Press of America, 1995), pp. 150-62; and Nancy R. Pearcey and Charles B. Thaxton, *The Soul of Science: Christian Faith and Natural Philosophy* (Wheaton, Ill.: Crossway, 1994), pp. 189-219.

[25]See, for example, Thomas's speculation about what happens to human consciousness at death in Lewis Thomas, *The Lives of a Cell* (New York: Bantam, 1975), pp. 60-61. His frequent mention of the Gaia hypothesis—the idea that the earth is a single organism—is also common among New Age thinkers.

[26]J. E. Lovelock, *Gaia: A New Look at Life on Earth* (New York: Oxford University Press, 1979).

[27]An excellent discussion and critique of holistic medicine is found in Paul C. Reisser, Teri K. Reisser and John Weldon, *New Age Medicine* (Downers Grove, Ill.: InterVarsity Press, 1987). This book contains an extensive bibliography for those wishing to pursue the matter in depth.

[28]See, for example, Jean Watson, *Postmodern Nursing and Beyond* (New York: Churchill Livingstone, 1999); Vidette Todaro-Franceschi, *The Enigma of Energy: Where Science and Religion Converge* (New York: Crossroad, 1999); Barbara Blattner, *Holistic Nursing* (Englewood Cliffs, N.J.: Prentice-Hall, 1981); Margaret A. Newman, *Health as Expanded Consciousness* (St. Louis: C. V. Mosby, 1986); Lynn Keegan, *The Nurse as Healer* (Albany, N.Y.: Delmar, 1994); Dolores Krieger, *The Therapeutic Touch* (Englewood Cliffs, N.J.: Prentice-Hall, 1979); Kathleen Heinrich, "The Greek Goddesses Speak to Nurses," *Nurse Educator* 15, no. 5 (1990): 20-24. Two journals promote holistic nursing: *The Journal of Holistic Nursing* and *Nursing*

Weil, an advocate of "spontaneous healing," says that about 30 of 134 medical schools offer some instruction in alternative medicine; he now directs a program in integrative medicine linked to the University of Arizona Medical School.[29] Deepak Chopra, M.D., has also emerged as a popular teacher of New Age alternative healing.[30]

Science fiction as a genre has largely been dominated by naturalists whose hope for humanity's future lies in technology.[31] But a few of its writers have been prophetic. Arthur C. Clarke, for example, wrote two scenarios for a radical human transformation along New Age lines. *Childhood's End* (1953) is one of his most successful works of imagination. His script for *2001* (1968), which in its movie version is as much Stanley Kubrick's as his, ends with the dawning of the New Age in a new dimension with a new "man," the Star-Child.[32] And Robert A. Heinlein's *Stranger in a Strange Land* (1961), first an underground classic, became in the 1970s a tract for the New Age. Valentine Michael Smith, who *groks* reality in its fullness, is a prototype for the new humanity.[33] The final three novels of Philip K. Dick *(Valis, The Divine Invasion* and *The Transfiguration of Timothy Archer)* are fictional attempts to come to grips with

Science Quarterly. For a critique of New Age nursing therapies see Sharon Fish, "Therapeutic Touch: Healing Science of Metaphysical Fraud," and Sharon Fish, "A New Age for Nursing," *Journal of Christian Nursing,* Summer 1996, pp. 3-11; other critical articles appear in Winter 1998, Fall 2001 and Summer 2002 issues.

[29]Lemley, "My Dinner with Andy," p. 68; see as well the books written by Weil and listed in note 19.

[30]Though he has been involved for a number of years, Chopra is a recent newcomer to the New Age health limelight; the story of his leaving the Maharishi Mahesh's Transcendental Meditation movement and his rough reception by conventional medicine is told by Gregory Dennis, "What's Deepak's Secret?" *New Age Journal,* February 1994, pp. 50-54, 78-79, 128. Among his fifty books, see especially *Quantum Healing: Exploring the Frontiers of Mind and Body Medicine* (New York: Bantam, 1989) and *Ageless Body, Timeless Mind:The Quantum Alternative to Growing Old* (New York: Harmony Books, 1993) for introductions to his view of health. *How to Know God* (New York: Three Rivers Press, 2000) examines the religious dimension of life. For an analysis of Chopra's view of medicine, see "Deepak Chopra: The Think System and the Revival of Ayurveda" in Reisser, Mabe and Velarde, *Examining Alternative Medicine,* pp. 162-93; and Douglas Groothuis's review of Deepak Chopra's *The Seven Spiritual Laws of Success: A Practical Guide to the Fulfillment of Your Dreams* (San Rafael, Calif.: Amber-Allen/New World Library, 1995) in *Christian Research Journal,* Fall 1995, pp. 51, 41. The Library of Congress credits Chopra with over twenty titles since 2000.

[31]James A. Herrick's *Scientific Mythologies: How Science and Science Fiction Forge New Religious Beliefs* (Downers Grove, Ill.: InterVarsity Press, 2008) analyzes the symbiotic relationship between science fiction and the religious consciousness of the Western world.

[32]Shirley MacLaine calls Kubrick a "master metaphysician" in *Dancing in the Light* (New York: Bantam, 1985), p. 262.

[33]Robert A. Heinlein, *Stranger in a Strange Land* (1961; reprint, New York: Berkeley, 1968).

his own encounter with "a beam of pink light."[34]

In *movies,* one of the most effective communications media of the modern world, we should note the work of Steven Spielberg, especially *Close Encounters of the Third Kind,* and George Lucas, especially the Star Wars series. The Force, the divine power that pervades the world of these movies, is much like the Hindu Brahman, incorporating both good and evil, and Yoda, the lovable guru of *The Empire Strikes Back,* spouts pure New Age metaphysics. Not least among films encapsulating New Age thought is the brilliant, surprisingly interesting *My Dinner with André,* an autobiographical excursion into the mindset of André Gregory.[35] The movies of the 1990s and the early 2000s that venture into future scenarios have tended to be more postmodern than strictly New Age; witness the series of The Matrix movies.

It can be easily replied that those whose books and ideas I have just listed are on the fringe of Western society—the lunatic fringe. Their ideas do not represent the mainstream. Of course, that is to a large extent true. Some of the most popular New Age authors come from the Wow! school of journalism, and it is hard to take their ideas seriously. Moreover, establishment scholars, reviewers and critics—by which is largely meant naturalists whose naturalism is not yet pure nihilism—have been highly critical of New Age books of all kinds.[36] But that is actually a tribute to the power these ideas are beginning to have. The people whose work I have cited above have an enormous influence—by virtue of their position in key universities, hospitals and research centers, their personal charisma, or their celebrity status—sometimes by all three. In short, a worldview of immense cultural impact and penetration has been formulated and is be-

---

[34]Jay Kinney, "The Mysterious Revelations of Philip K. Dick," *Gnosis Magazine,* Fall/Winter 1985, pp. 6-11.

[35]The text of this latter movie reads well and has been published. See Wallace Shawn and André Gregory, *My Dinner with André* (New York: Grove, 1981).

[36]Critical reviews came early in the movement. See, for example, the review of Weil's *The Natural Mind* in *New York Times Book Review,* October 15, 1972, pp. 27-29. Critical reviews of Castaneda's work are legion. See *Time* magazine's cover story, March 5, 1973, pp. 36-45. Several more wide-ranging analyses of the whole movement toward a new consciousness deserve special mention for their penetrating insight: Os Guinness, *The Dust of Death* (Wheaton, Ill.: Crossway, 1994), chaps. 6-8; R. C. Zaehner, *Zen, Drugs and Mysticism* (New York: Vintage, 1974); Samuel McCracken, "The Drugs of Habit and the Drugs of Belief," *Commentary,* June 1971, pp. 43-52; Marcia Cavell, "Visions of a New Religion," *Saturday Review,* December 19, 1970; and Richard King, "The Eros Ethos: Cult in the Counterculture," *Psychology Today,* August 1972, pp. 35-37, 66-70.

ing promoted. In fact, perhaps the most influential promoter of New Age spirituality is Oprah Winfrey, not primarily through her own voice but through her television guests—Deepak Chopra, Marianne Williamson (A Course in Miracles), Gary Zukav and Iyanla Vanzant.[37] Her recent promotion of Eckhart Tolle's *A New Earth* has drawn millions of readers to his fairly standard New Age worldview.[38]

RELATIONSHIP TO OTHER WORLDVIEWS

The New Age worldview is highly syncretistic and eclectic. It borrows from every major worldview. Though its weirder ramifications and stranger dimensions come from Eastern pantheism and ancient animism, its connection with naturalism gives it a better chance to win converts than purer Eastern mysticism.

Like naturalism the new consciousness denies the existence of a transcendent God. There is no Lord of the universe unless it be each of us. There is only the closed universe. True, it is "peopled" by beings of incredible "personal" intelligence and power, and "human consciousness is not contained by the skull."[39] But these beings and even the consciousness of the cosmos are in no way transcendent in the sense required by theism. Moreover, some language about human beings retains the full force of naturalism.[40] Fritjof Capra, Gary Zukav and William Irwin Thompson point to the seeming corollaries between psychic phenomena and twentieth-century physics.[41]

Also borrowed from naturalism is the hope of evolutionary change for humanity. We are poised on the brink of a new being. Evolution will bring about the transformation.

Like both theism and naturalism, and unlike Eastern pantheistic monism, the New Age places great value on the individual person. Theism

---

[37]See Kate Maver, "Oprah Winfrey and Her Self-Help Saviors: Making the New Age Normal," *Christian Research Journal* 23, no. 4 (2001) <www.equip.org>; LaTonya Taylor, "The Church of O," *Christianity Today* (June 14, 2008) <www.christianitytoday.com/ct/2002/april1/1.38.html>; and Katelyn Beaty, "Another Brick in the Oprah Empire" <www.blog.christianityto day.com/ctliveblog/archives/2008/05/another_brick_i.html>.

[38]Eckhart Tolle, *A New Earth: Awakening to Your Life's Purpose* (New Yorik: Dutton/Penguin Group, 2005).

[39]Thompson, *Passages About Earth*, p. 124.

[40]John Lilly calls the brain a "biocomputer" and man a "beautiful mechanism," upsetting fellow new consciousness buff R. D. Laing (Lilly, *Center of the Cyclone*, pp. 4, 17, 29).

[41]Capra, *Tao of Physics*, and chap. 3 of *The Turning Point*; Zukav, *Dancing Wu Li Masters*; MacLaine, *Dancing in the Light*, pp. 323-24, 329, 351-53.

grounds this in each person's being made in the image of God. Naturalism, reflecting a memory of its theistic roots, continues to maintain the
value of individuals, grounding it in the notion that all human beings are
alike in their common humanity. If one is valuable, all are.

Like Eastern pantheistic monism, the new consciousness centers on a
mystical experience in which time, space and morality are transcended.
One could define new consciousness as a Western version of Eastern
mysticism in which the metaphysical emphasis of the East (its assertion
that Atman is Brahman) is replaced by an emphasis on epistemology
(seeing, experiencing or perceiving the unity of reality is what life is all
about). Moreover, like the East, the new consciousness rejects reason
(what Weil calls "straight thinking") as a guide to reality. The world is
really irrational or superrational and demands new modes of apprehension ("stoned thinking," for example).[42]

But the new consciousness is also related to animism, a worldview I
have not yet discussed in this book. Animism is the general outlook on
life that underlies primal or so-called pagan religions. To say the worldview is primal is not to say it is simple. Pagan religions are highly complex interplays of ideas, rituals, liturgies, symbol systems, cult objects
and so forth. But pagan religions tend to hold certain notions in common. Among them the following are reflected by the New Age: (1) the
natural universe is inhabited by countless spiritual beings, often conceived in a rough hierarchy, at the top of which is the Sky God (vaguely
like theism's God but without his interest in human beings); (2) thus
the universe has a personal dimension but not an infinite-personal
Creator-God; (3) these spiritual beings range in temperament from vi-
cious and nasty to comic and beneficent; (4) for people to get by in life
the evil spirits must be placated and the good ones wooed by gifts and
offerings, ceremonies and incantations; (5) witch doctors, sorcerers
and shamans, through long, arduous training, have learned to control
the spirit world to some extent, and ordinary people are much be-
holden to their power to cast out spirits of illness, drought and so forth;
(6) ultimately there is a unity to all of life—that is, the cosmos is a continuum of spirit and matter; "animals may be ancestors of men, people

---

[42]Weil, *Natural Mind*, chaps. 6-7, and *Spontaneous Healing*, pp. 113, 203-7. Many, if not most,
of New Age proponents recognize the close affinity of their notions to those of the East, and
some believe this to be a strong indication that they are on the right track, taking the best of
both worlds. The syncretist tendency of the East has already been noted in chapter seven.

may change into animals, trees and stones may possess souls."[43]

The new consciousness reflects every aspect of animism, though often giving it a naturalistic twist, or demythologizing it by psychology. That Roszak should call for a return to the "Old Gnosis" and the visions of William Blake and that Castaneda should take the long apprenticeship that ended in his becoming a sorcerer are indications that those in the New Age are well aware of its animistic roots.[44]

Can the New Age, with roots in three separate worldviews, be a unified system? Not really. Or not yet. In fact, not likely at all. Yet, though not all of the propositions I list below fit neatly together, there are many in virtually every area of culture who hold something like this way of looking at reality.

THE BASIC TENETS OF THE NEW CONSCIOUSNESS

Realizing the tenuousness of this set of propositions as an accurate description of the new consciousness worldview, we may yet begin, as with the other worldviews, with the notion of prime reality. Other worldview questions follow, but not in the stricter order found in previous chapters. Rather they are taken up as they naturally fall as one ponders this particular eclectic worldview, a mélange of elements derived from more orderly worldviews.

1. Worldview Questions 1, 2 and 3: *Whatever the nature of being (idea or matter, energy or particle), the self is the kingpin, the prime reality. As human beings grow in their awareness and grasp of this fact, the human race is on the verge of a radical change in human nature; even now we see harbingers of transformed humanity and prototypes of the New Age.*

If the transcendent God is the prime reality in theism and the physical universe the prime reality in naturalism, then in the New Age the self (the soul, the integrated, central essence of each person) is the prime reality.

A comparison (and contrast) with the central proposition of Eastern pantheistic monism is helpful. In essence the East says, "Atman is *Brah-*

---

[43]Eugene Nida and William A. Smalley, *Introducing Animism* (New York: Friendship, 1959), p. 50. This brief pamphlet is a remarkable repository of information on modern pagan animism.

[44]Roszak, *Where the Wasteland Ends*, p. xv.

man," putting the emphasis on Brahman. That is, in the East one loses one's self in the whole; the individuality of a drop of water (symbol of the soul) is lost as it falls into a pail of water (symbol of the whole of reality). In the New Age the same sentence reads in reverse: "*Atman* is Brahman." It is the single self that becomes important. Thus we see the influence of theism, in which the individual is important because made in the image of God, and naturalism, especially naturalistic existentialism, in which individuals are important because they are all that is left to be important.[45]

Just exactly what this self is is problematic. Is it idea, or spirit, or a "psychomagnetic field," or the unity that binds the diversity of cosmic energy? Proponents of the New Age do not agree, but they do insist that the self—the consciousness-center of the human being—is indeed the center of the universe. Whatever else exists besides the self, if in fact anything else does, exists for the self. The external universe exists not to be manipulated from the outside by a transcendent God but to be manipulated from the inside by the self.

John Lilly gives a long description of what it is like to realize that the self is in fact in control of all of reality. Here are his notes taken after experiencing what he believes to be the highest possible state of consciousness:

> We [he and other personal selves] are creating energy, matter and life at the interface between the void and all known creation. We are facing into the known universe, creating it, filling it. . . . I feel the power of the galaxy pouring through me. . . . I am the creation process itself, incredibly strong, incredibly powerful. . . . I am "one of the boys in the engine room pumping creation from the void into the known universe; from the unknown to the known I am pumping."[46]

When Lilly finally reaches the inner space he calls "+3"—the fullest, deepest penetration of reality—he becomes "God" himself. He becomes, so to speak, both the universe and the universe maker. So, he says, "why not enjoy bliss and ecstasy while still a passenger in the body, on this spacecraft? Dictate thine own terms as passenger. The transport com-

---

[45]Robert Bellah's study of individualism in America illuminates one major force behind the New Age emphasis on the self as the kingpin of reality. See Robert N. Bellah et al., *Habits of the Heart* (New York: Harper & Row, 1985).

[46]Lilly, *Center of the Cyclone*, p. 210.

pany has a few rules, but it may be that we dream up the company and its rules too. . . . There are no mountains, no molehills . . . just a central core of me and transcendent bliss."[47] For Lilly, imagination is the same as reality: *"All and every thing that one can imagine exists."*[48] For Lilly, therefore, the self is triumphantly in charge. Most people do not know that—it takes a technique of some sort to realize it—but the self is indeed king.

Shirley MacLaine speculates on whether in fact she has created her own reality (something she mentions many times in her books). She writes,

> If I created my own reality, then—on some level and dimension I didn't understand—I had created everything I saw, heard, touched, smelled, tasted; everything I loved, hated, revered, abhorred; everything I responded to or that responded to me. Then, I created everything I knew. I was therefore responsible for all there was in my reality. If that was true, than [sic] I *was* everything, as the ancient texts had taught. I was my own universe. Did that also mean I had created God and I had created life and death? Was that why I was all there was? . . .
>
> To take responsibility for one's power would be the ultimate expression of what we called the God-force.
>
> Was this what was meant by the statement I AM THAT I AM?[49]

She concludes that for all practical purposes that was the case. Most

---

[47]Ibid., p. 110.

[48]Ibid., p. 51, italics Lilly's. Laurence LeShan is more modest. He writes, concerning the way post-Einsteinian science views reality, that "within this view, man does not only discover reality; within limits he invents it" (*The Medium, the Mystic and the Physicist* [New York: Viking, 1974], p. 155).

[49]MacLaine, *It's All in the Playing*, p. 192. MacLaine continues to wonder at the vague boundaries between dream and reality throughout *Camino*, esp. p. 304. See also Houston, *Search for the Beloved*, pp. 25-26. The casual way MacLaine, Houston and others use the I AM language of God's self-revelation in Exodus 3:14 is deeply offensive to traditional Jews and Christians, for whom the term indicates a radical difference between the human and the divine, not the union of the human and the divine. David Spangler, spiritual leader at Findhorn, goes even further than MacLaine: "I AM now the Life of a new heaven and a new earth. Others must draw upon Me and unite with Me to build its forms. . . . There is always only what I AM, but I have revealed Myself in new Life and new Light and new Truth. . . . It is My function through this centre [Findhorn] to demonstrate what I AM through the medium of group evolution." See David Spangler, *Revelation: The Birth of a New Age* (Findhorn, 1971), pp. 110, 121, quoted in Thompson, *Passages About Earth*, p. 173. Such writing echoes the words of the god Krishna in the Bhagavad Gita (6.29-31). Thompson is hard put to know what to think of this strange elitist language, but he appears to see Spangler as one of the first of the transformed people of the New Age (Thompson, *Passages About Earth*, p. 174).

readers will, I presume, find all this to contain more than a touch of megalomania.

Deepak Chopra, who has become one of the more active and visible New Age promoters, in his recent book *The Third Jesus*, says that the essence of each of us is a "speck of God, the soul substance of everyone that never became separated from its source."[50] In the state of God-consciousness a person creates his or her own reality.[51]

We have already heard George Leonard, Jean Houston and Shirley MacLaine prophesy the coming of a New Age. And they are not alone. The hope—if not prophecy—is echoed by Marilyn Ferguson, Andrew Weil, Oscar Ichazo and William Irwin Thompson. Ferguson closes her book *The Brain Revolution* (1973) with a triumph of optimism: "We are just beginning to realize that we can truly open the doors of perception and creep out of the cavern."[52] Her later book *The Aquarian Conspiracy* (1980) charts the progress and contributes to it. What a glorious New Age is dawning: a new world peopled by healthy, well-adjusted, perfectly happy, absolutely blissed-out beings—no disease, no war, no famine, no pollution, just transcendent joy. What more could one want?

Critics of this utopian euphoria want one thing: some reasonable, objective assurance that such a vision is more than an opium pipe dream. But during the moments the self is immersed in subjective certainty, no reasons are necessary, no objectivity is required. Wilber describes the self-certitude of one's equality with all there is this way:

> When you step off the ladder altogether, you are in free fall in Emptiness. Inside and outside, subject and object, lose all ultimate meaning. You are

[50]Chopra, *Third Jesus*, p. 120; see also Chopra's *Jesus: A Story of Enlightenment* (New York: HarperOne, 2008).

[51]Ibid., p. 25.

[52]Marilyn Ferguson, *Brain Revolution*, p. 344; "Life at the Leading Edge: A *New Age* Interview with Marilyn Ferguson," *New Age*, August 1982; Weil, *Natural Mind*, pp. 204-5. Sam Keen ("A Conversation . . . ," *Psychology Today*, July 1973, p. 72) quotes Oscar Ichazo as saying, "Humanity is the Messiah." Weil, by the way, says, "I am almost tempted to call the psychotics the evolutionary vanguard of our species. They possess the secret of changing reality by changing the mind; if they can use that talent for positive ends, there are no limits to what they can accomplish" (*Natural Mind*, p. 182). LeShan would seem to agree (*The Medium, the Mystic and the Physicist*, pp. 211-12). Thompson in *Passages About Earth* is optimistic throughout, but see esp. p. 149; twelve years later in "A Gaian Politics," *Whole Earth Review*, Winter 1986, p. 4, he expressed some reservations, noting that the spirit of the age had replaced "'Star Trek' and 'Kung Fu' with 'Dynasty' and 'Dallas,' Joni Mitchell with Madonna, and 'Close Encounters' with 'Rambo.'"

no longer "in here" looking at the world "out there." You are not looking at the Kosmos, you are the Kosmos. The universe of One Taste announces itself, bright and obvious, radiant and clear, with nothing outside, nothing inside, an unending gesture of great perfection, spontaneously accomplished. The very Divine sparkles in every sight and sound, and you are simply that. The sun within your heart. Time and space dance as shimmering images on the face of radiant Emptiness, and the entire universe loses its weight. You can swallow the Milky Way in a single gulp, and put Gaia in the palm of your hand and bless it, and it is all the most ordinary thing in the world, and so you think nothing of it.[53]

Because of its absolute subjectivity, the I-am-God or I-am-the-Kosmos position remains beyond any criticism external to the subject.[54] It is easy enough for an outsider to be convinced—and on solid evidence—that MacLaine is not the infinite I AM THAT I AM and that Wilber has not swallowed the universe. But how does one break in on god-consciousness itself?

I could legitimately say that I created the Statue of Liberty, chocolate chip cookies, the Beatles, terrorism, and the Vietnam War. . . . And if people reacted to world events, then I was creating them to react so I would have someone to interact with, thereby enabling myself to know me better.

Shirley MacLaine, *It's All in the Playing*

Aldous Huxley suggests that such a breakthrough is possible. Not long before he died, he had second thoughts about the validity of the new consciousness. His wife, Laura, recorded on tape many of his final thoughts. Here is a transcript of his conversation two days before his death:

---

[53]Wilber, *Brief History of Everything*, p. 156. Parallel to this are Margaret Newman's remarks that "consciousness is coextensive with the universe and resides in all matter" and "the person does not *possess* consciousness—the person *is* consciousness" (*Health as Expanded Consciousness*, pp. 33, 36).

[54]According to Wilber (*Brief History of Everything*, pp. 217-19), only one trained in a discipline like Zen is capable of judging whether or not what one is experiencing is a transcendent reality. Knowledge is state-specific; in our ordinary waking consciousness we are unable to judge the reality of experiences of oneness with God, the One or the universe. Claims to the truth cannot be evaluated by ordinary reason; only the enlightened can know whether a claim is true.

It [an inner discovery he had just made] shows . . . the almost boundless nature of the ego ambition. I dreamed, it must have been two nights ago, . . . that in some way I was in a position to make an absolute . . . *cosmic* gift to the world. . . . Some *vast* act of benevolence was going to be done, in which I should have the sort of star role. . . . In a way it was absolutely terrifying, showing that when *one thinks one's got beyond one self one hasn't.*[55]

Still, Huxley did not abandon his quest. He died while on a "trip." For at his request his wife administered LSD to him and, after the manner of the *Tibetan Book of the Dead,* talked his spirit into rest on "the other side."

The danger of self-deception—theists and naturalists alike would add the *certainty* of self-deception—is the great weakness of the new consciousness at this point. No theist or naturalist, no one at all, can deny the "experience" of perceiving oneself to be a god, a spirit, a devil or a cockroach. Too many people give such reports. But so long as self alone is king, so long as imagination is presupposed to be reality, so long as seeing is being, the imagining, seeing self remains securely locked in its private universe—the only one there is. So long as the self likes what it imagines and is truly in control of what it imagines, others on the "outside" have nothing to offer.

The trouble is that sometimes the self is not king but prisoner. That's a problem we will take up under proposition 3 below.

2. Worldview Question 2: *The cosmos, while unified in the self, is manifested in two more dimensions: the visible universe, accessible through ordinary consciousness, and the invisible universe (or Mind at Large), accessible through altered states of consciousness.*

In the basic picture of the cosmos, then, the self (in the center) is surrounded first by the visible universe to which it has direct access through the five senses and which obeys the "laws of nature" discovered by natural science, and second by the invisible universe to which it has access through such "doors of perception" as drugs, meditation, trance, biofeedback, acupuncture, ritualized dance, certain kinds of music and so forth.

Such a metaphysical schema leads Huxley to describe every human group as "a society of island universes."[56] Each self is a universe floating in a sea of universes, but because each island universe is somewhat like

[55]Aldous Huxley, quoted in Laura Archera Huxley, *This Timeless Moment: A Personal View of Aldous Huxley* (1968; reprint, New York: Ballantine, 1971), pp. 249-51.
[56]Huxley, *Doors of Perception*, p. 13.

each other island universe, communication between them can take place. Moreover, because each universe is in its essence (that is, its self) the center of all universes, genuine comprehension is more than a mere possibility. Quoting C. D. Broad, who was himself relying on Henri Bergson, Huxley writes, "The function of the brain and nervous system and sense organs is in the main eliminative and not productive. Each person is at each moment capable of remembering all that has ever happened to him and of perceiving everything that is happening everywhere in the universe."[57] But because such perception would overwhelm us and appear chaotic, the brain acts as a "reducing valve" to filter out what at the moment is not useful. As Huxley says, "According to such a theory, each one of us is potentially Mind at Large."[58] In other words, each self is potentially the universe; each Atman is potentially Brahman. What comes through the reducing valve, says Huxley, is "a measly trickle of the kind of consciousness which will help us to stay alive on the surface of this particular planet."[59]

The New Age worldview is Western to a large degree and never more so than in its insistence that the visible universe, the ordinary external world, is really there. It is no illusion. Moreover, it is an orderly universe. It obeys the laws of reality, and these laws can be known, communicated and used. Most new consciousness proponents have a healthy respect for science. Ken Wilber, Aldous Huxley, Laurence LeShan and William Irwin Thompson are prime examples.[60] In short, the visible universe is subject to the uniformity of cause and effect. But the system is open to being reordered by the self (especially when it realizes its oneness with the One) that ultimately controls it and by beings from Mind at Large which the self may enlist as agents for change.

Mind at Large is a sort of universe next door, alternately called "ex-

---

[57]Ibid., p. 22.

[58]Ibid., p. 23.

[59]Ibid. Note the inner contradiction in what Huxley has said. On the one hand, without a new consciousness humanity will not be able to survive on this planet; on the other hand, the self, if it just realized it, is the center of the cosmos. Since the cosmos is eternal (a notion implicit in Huxley's system), the self is eternal. So why worry about life on earth? This why-worry attitude has been the position of the East for centuries; but it seems that when the West goes East for wisdom it cannot slough off all the Western baggage, one piece of which is firmly rooted in the Judeo-Christian notion that this present world (people on earth) counts for something.

[60]Ken Wilber insists that science is valid in its own domain of physical reality (*A Sociable God*, pp. 7-8).

panded consciousness" or "alternative consciousness" (MacLaine), "a
separate reality" (Castaneda), "clairvoyant reality" (LeShan), "other
spaces" (Lilly), "supermind" (Rosenfeld), "Emptiness/Original Face" (Wilber), "Universal Mind" (Klimo) or "God-consciousness" (Chopra).[61] This
Mind at Large does not obey the laws of the visible universe. The conscious self can travel hundreds of miles across the surface of the earth
and do so in the twinkling of an eye. Time and space are elastic; the universe can turn inside out, and time can flow backwards.[62] Extraordinary
power and energy can surge through a person and be transmitted to others. Physical healing can be effected, and if we are to include the black art
users of psychic abilities, enemies can be struck dead, sent mad or caused
physical, emotional or mental suffering.

MacLaine describes Mind at Large this way: "I was learning to recognize the invisible dimension where there are no measurements possible.
In fact, it is the dimension of no-height, no-width, no-breadth, and no-
mass, and as matter of further fact, no-time. It is the dimension of the
spirit."[63] Mind at Large, however, is not totally chaotic. It only appears so
to the self that operates as if the laws of the invisible universe were the
same as those of the visible universe. But Mind at Large has its own rules,
its own order, and it may take a person a long time to learn just what that
order is.[64]

To discover that the self itself, in Lilly's language, has made up the rules
that govern the game of reality may take time.[65] But when people discover
this, they can go on to generate whatever order of reality and whatever
universe they want. The sky is not the limit: "In the province of the mind,
what is believed to be true is true or becomes true, within limits to be
found experientially and experimentally. These limits are further beliefs to
be transcended. In the province of the mind, there are no limits."[66] Lilly's
Center of the Cyclone is his autobiography of inner space. To read it is to

[61]MacLaine, *Out on a Limb*, p. 74, and *It's All in the Playing*, p. 265; Castaneda, *A Separate Reality*; LeShan, *The Medium, the Mystic and the Physicist*, p. 34; Lilly, *Center of the Cyclone*, p. 25; Albert Rosenfeld, "Mind and Supermind," *Saturday Review*, February 22, 1975, p. 10; Wilber, *Brief History of Everything*, pp. 156, 240; Klimo, *Channeling*, pp. 174-76; Chopra, *Third Jesus*, p. 23.
[62]MacLaine, *It's All in the Playing*, p. 188.
[63]MacLaine, *Dancing in the Light*, p. 309.
[64]MacLaine, *It's All in the Playing*, p. 331.
[65]Lilly, *Center of the Cyclone*, p. 110.
[66]Ibid., p. 5.

journey through the geography of Lilly's mind as he opens various "doors of perception" and moves from space to space, from universe to universe.

Those who have never visited these spaces must rely on reports from those who have. Lilly records a number of them, and his book makes fascinating reading. Many others have visited such spaces as well, and their reports are similar in type though rarely in specific detail. I will take up the "feelings" associated with perceiving Mind at Large under proposition 3 below. Here the metaphysical aspect is the prime focus. What "things" appear in Mind at Large? And what characteristics do these "things" have? Huxley's report is a classic because his testimony has set the pattern for many others. The first characteristic of Mind at Large is its color and luminosity:

> Everything seen by those who visit the mind's antipodes is brilliantly illuminated and seems to shine from within. All colors are intensified to a pitch far beyond anything seen in the normal state, and at the same time the mind's capacity for recognizing fine distinctions of tone and hue is notably heightened.[67]

Whether the images in Mind at Large are otherwise ordinary objects such as chairs or desks or men and women or special beings such as ghosts or gods or spirits, luminosity is an almost universal characteristic. Lilly says, "I saw scintillating things in the air like champagne bubbles. The dirt on the floor looked like gold dust."[68] In eleven of sixteen separate accounts quoted by Ferguson, special mention is made of colors: "golden light," "sparkling lights," "intense white light," "ultra unearthly colors."[69] Castaneda sees a man whose head is pure light and in the climactic event in *Journey to Ixtlan* converses with a luminous coyote and sees the "lines of the world."[70]

These experiences of luminosity and color lend force to the feeling that what one is perceiving is more real than anything perceived in the visible universe. As Huxley puts it,

> I was seeing what Adam had seen on the morning of his creation—the miracle, moment by moment, of naked existence.... *Istigkeit*—wasn't that the word Meister Eckhart liked to use? "Is-ness" ... a transience that was

---

[67]Huxley, *Doors of Perception*, p. 89.
[68]Lilly, *Center of the Cyclone*, p. 180; also see pp. 10, 54.
[69]Ferguson, *Brain Revolution*, pp. 61-63.
[70]Castaneda, *Journey to Ixtlan*, pp. 297-98.

yet eternal life, a perpetual perishing that was at the same time pure Being, a bundle of minute particulars in which, by some unspeakable and yet self-evident paradox, was to be seen the divine source of all existence.[71]

For Huxley, Mind at Large was not so much a separate reality as the ordinary reality seen as it really is. But this new perception is so different that it appears as an entirely new thing; it appears as a thing apart.[72]

A second distinctive characteristic of Mind at Large is that special beings seem to populate this realm. In addition to seeing what she takes to be herself and others in her past lives, MacLaine sees her Higher Self: a person in "the form of a very tall, overpoweringly confident, almost androgynous human being."[73] He becomes her guide and interpreter of her experience. Castaneda encounters "allies," "helpers," "guardians" and "entities of the night."[74] Lilly frequently meets two "guardians," who instruct him on how to make the most of his life.[75] Similarly, in account after account, personal beings, or forces with a personal dimension, keep turning up—call them what you will: demons, devils, spirits or angels. Furthermore, some new consciousness aficionados recount experiences of being changed into a bird or an animal or of being made capable of flight or rapid travel, even interplanetary travel.

Indeed, Mind at Large is a very strange place. Do its inhabitants really exist? Are they figments of the self's imagination, projections of its unconscious fears and hopes? Does one really become a bird or fly? In the new consciousness worldview those questions are not important. Still, to theists and naturalists alike they are the obvious ones. I will, however, deal with them later under proposition 5.

3. Worldview Questions 5 and 6: *The core experience of the New Age is cosmic consciousness, in which ordinary categories of space, time and morality tend to disappear.*

---

[71]Huxley, *Doors of Perception*, pp. 17-18.

[72]Others do, however, emphasize the continuity, if not unity, of the self, the visible and the invisible universe. See Ferguson, *Brain Revolution*, p. 21; Thompson, *Passages About Earth*, pp. 97-103, 166; Lilly, *Center of the Cyclone*, p. 211; Wilber, *Brief History of Everything*, pp. 156, 240.

[73]Allusions to her past lives occur throughout MacLaine's writings, but a sort of litany of them appears in *Dancing in the Light*, pp. 366-84.

[74]Castaneda, *Teachings of Don Juan*, pp. 32, 136-38; *Separate Reality*, pp. 51, 140, 144, 158-59; *Journey to Ixtlan*, pp. 213-15; *Tales of Power*, pp. 46, 87-89, 239, 257.

[75]Lilly, *Center of the Cyclone*, pp. 27, 39, 55-57, 90-91, 199.

This proposition is the epistemological flip side of the metaphysical coin discussed under proposition 2. In a sense proposition 3 does not much advance our understanding of the New Age. But it does add a needed depth.

Underlying the unity that propositions 2 and 3 share is the presupposition discussed in proposition 1: that seeing (or perceiving) is being; anything the self sees, perceives, conceives, imagines or believes, exists. It exists because the self is in charge of everything that is: "I believe, therefore it is" or "I experience, therefore it is." Philosophically, the new consciousness offers a radical and simple answer to the problem of distinguishing between appearance and reality. It flatly claims there is no distinction. Appearance is reality. There is no illusion.[76]

Of course, perception takes two forms, one for the visible universe, another for the invisible universe. The first is called ordinary consciousness, waking consciousness or "straight thinking." It is the way ordinary people have ordinarily seen workaday reality. Space is seen in three dimensions. No two bodies can occupy the same space at the same time. Time is linear: yesterday is gone; here we are now; tomorrow is on the way. Two disparate events cannot happen to the same person at the same time; while I can sit and think at the same time, I cannot sit and stand at the same time. In ordinary consciousness some actions appear good, others less good, others bad, still others downright evil. And, of course, we assume they actually are as we perceive them. With all this we are all familiar.

The second state of consciousness is not so familiar. In fact, most of us in the West have hardly dreamed of it. To make it even more complicated, this second state of consciousness is really composed of many different states of consciousness; some say three, some six, some eight.[77] But before we consider any of its various subdivisions, we should grasp its general characteristics. Some of these characteristics are suggested by the various aliases for cosmic consciousness. They are legion: "timeless bliss" (R. C. Zaehner), "higher consciousness" (Weil), "peak experience" (Maslow), "nirvana" (Buddhists), "satori" (Japanese Zen), "Kosmic consciousness" (Wilber), "altered states of consciousness" or ASC (Masters

---

[76]MacLaine demonstrates this in *It's All in the Playing*, pp. 191-93.

[77]See Lilly's chart (*Center of the Cyclone*, pp. 148-49) detailing and describing his, George I. Gurdjieff's and I. K. Taimni's various levels of consciousness and their labels.

and Houston), "cosmic vision" (Keen).

Two of these labels seem more apt than the others, one for theoretical, the other for historical reasons. Theoretically, *altered states of consciousness* carries the most universally accepted understanding of the phenomenon. The states of consciousness involved are, indeed, not ordinary. The other apt label, *cosmic consciousness,* is often used because it is one of the oldest in modern writing on the subject. It was introduced in 1901 by Canadian psychiatrist R. M. Bucke and was given popularity by its inclusion in William James's classic study of mysticism:

> The prime characteristic of cosmic consciousness is a consciousness of the cosmos, that is, of the life and order of the universe. Along with the consciousness of the cosmos there occurs an intellectual enlightenment which alone would place the individual on a new plane of existence— would make him a member of a new species. . . . With these come what may be called a sense of immortality, a consciousness of eternal life, not a conviction that he shall have this but the consciousness that he has it already.[78]

The label *cosmic consciousness* comes bearing a metaphysical explanation of the experience, one widely accepted among proponents of the new consciousness worldview. The point is this: when the self perceives itself to be at one with the cosmos, it is at one with it. Self-realization, then, is the realization that the self and the cosmos not only are of a piece but are the same piece. In other words, cosmic consciousness is experiencing Atman as Brahman.

Central to cosmic consciousness is the unitary experience: first, the experience of perceiving the wholeness of the cosmos; second, the experience of becoming one with the whole cosmos; and finally, the experience of going beyond even that oneness with the cosmos to recognize that the self is the generator of all reality and in that sense is both the cosmos and the cosmos-maker.[79] *"Know that you are God; know that you are the universe,"* says MacLaine.[80]

---

[78]Richard Maurice Bucke, *Cosmic Consciousness: A Study in the Evolution of the Human Mind* (1901; reprint, New York: Penguin, 1991), p. 3, as quoted in James, *Varieties of Religious Experience,* p. 306. Bucke also mentions "a quickening of the moral sense," but this is unusual, as we shall see below.

[79]Again, see Lilly's various levels (*Center of the Cyclone,* pp. 148-49).

[80]MacLaine, *Dancing in the Light,* p. 350, italics hers. Houston had such an experience at age six: "It seemed to me as if I knew everything, as if I *was* everything" (*Godseed,* p. xvii).

Still, other "things" appear under the states of cosmic consciousness. Even after reading countless records of these experiences, I can do no better than to quote Ferguson's exhaustive list of characteristics:

> Loss of ego boundaries and the sudden identification with all of life (a melting into the universe); lights; altered color perception; thrills; electrical sensations; sense of expanding like a bubble or bounding upward; banishment of fear, particularly fear of death; roaring sound; wind; feeling of being separated from physical self; bliss; sharp awareness of patterns; a sense of liberation; a blending of the senses (synesthesia), as when colors are heard and sights produce auditory sensations; an oceanic feeling; a belief that one has awakened; that the experience is the only reality and that ordinary consciousness is but its poor shadow; and a sense of transcending time and space.[81]

Ferguson goes on to quote a number of interesting accounts of cosmic consciousness, each one illustrating many, if not all, of these characteristics.

On one aspect of proposition 3, however, there is disagreement. Not all proponents of the new consciousness will agree that the category of morality disappears. Theoretically, it must, for cosmic consciousness implies the unity of all reality and that must be a unity beyond moral as well as metaphysical distinctions, as shown in the analysis of Eastern pantheistic monism in the preceding chapter.[82] MacLaine, for example, argues vigorously for the disappearance of the distinction between good and evil as she finds herself in heated arguments with Vassy, one of her lovers, who retains an emotional attachment to Russian Orthodoxy.[83] Bucke, Thompson and Wilber would take exception to this, but MacLaine, Lilly and Huxley agree.[84] Chopra adds: "When God-consciousness dawns, . . . there

---

[81]Ferguson, *Brain Revolution*, p. 60. See also the descriptions in Lilly, *Center of the Cyclone*, chaps. 11-18; James, *Varieties of Religious Experience*, pp. 292-328; LeShan, *The Medium, the Mystic and the Physicist*, pp. 86-87, 250; Zaehner, *Zen, Drugs and Mysticism*, pp. 89-94; Wilber, *Brief History of Everything*, pp. 156, 240; virtually every discussion of altered states of consciousness will mention many, if not all, of those characteristics. For a more scientific approach to the characteristics of altered states of consciousness, see Arnold M. Ludwig, "Altered States of Consciousness," in *Altered States of Consciousness: A Book of Readings*, ed. Charles Tart (New York: John Wiley & Sons, 1969), pp. 9-22.

[82]See pp. 144-65.

[83]MacLaine, *Dancing in the Light*, pp. 202-3, 242-43, 248-49, 269, 341-42, 345, 351, 363-64, 383; and *It's All in the Playing*, pp. 173-75.

[84]James, *Varieties of Religious Experience*, p. 306; Thompson, *Passages About Earth*, pp. 29, 82; Wilber, *Brief History of Everything*, pp. 189, 233, 235; Lilly, *Center of the Cyclone*, pp. 20,

is no longer a battle between good and evil."[85] Still, like Hesse's Siddhartha and all people who remain perceivably people, MacLaine, Huxley, Chopra and Lilly speak as if it were better to be enlightened—that is, cosmically conscious or God-conscious—than unenlightened, better to love than to hate and better to help usher in the New Age than merely to watch the old one collapse.

Finally, we must note that not every altered state of consciousness is euphoric. Naive proponents of the new consciousness worldview often lose sight of this grim fact, but accounts of bad trips are readily available. Huxley himself knew the terrors of a "bummer":

> Confronted by a chair which looked like the Last Judgment—or, to be more accurate, like a Last Judgment which, after a long time and with considerable difficulty, I recognized as a chair—I found myself all at once on the brink of panic. This, I suddenly felt, was going too far. Too far, even though the going was into more intense beauty, deeper significance. The fear, as I analyze it in retrospect, was of being overwhelmed, of disintegrating under a pressure of reality greater than a mind, accustomed to living most of the time in a cosy world of symbols, could possibly bear.[86]

Huxley, though, was convinced that only those who have had "a recent case of jaundice, or who suffer from periodical depressions or a chronic anxiety" need fear the mescaline experience.[87] Few today would agree.

Lilly's various bouts with the "demonic" along with Castaneda's experiences document the lows of "hell."[88] Even the ever-optimistic MacLaine wrestled with visions she did not like, at least at first.[89] To avoid the regions of inner hell, Huxley, Lilly and Castaneda (as well as many others) strongly urge the presence of a guide during early attempts to experience cosmic consciousness.[90] This is the New Age counterpart to one of the

---

171, 180; Huxley, *Doors of Perception*, p. 39. Wilber, for example, says the more evolved is the better: "The Base Moral Intuition is protect and promote the greatest depth for the greatest span" (*Brief History of Everything*, p. 335). Evil is possible inasmuch as "we want to be *whole* [have rights] without being a *part* of anything [have responsibility]" (ibid., p. 333).

[85]Chopra, *Third Jesus*, p. 209.

[86]Huxley, *Doors of Perception*, p. 55; see also pp. 51, 54-58, 133-40.

[87]Ibid., p. 54.

[88]Lilly, *Center of the Cyclone*, pp. 24-25, 33, 88-90, 169; and Castaneda, throughout his first four books.

[89]MacLaine, *It's All in the Playing*, pp. 162-71.

[90]Lilly, *Center of the Cyclone*, p. 35; L. Huxley, *This Timeless Moment*, pp. 275-88; Weil, *Natural Mind*, pp. 83, 95.

major functions performed by a guru or a Perfect Master in more fully Eastern forms of mysticism.

There is, of course, a blatant contradiction here. If seeing is being and imagination is reality, then an experienced hell is simply reality. Or to put it another way, if the self is king, it is in control of creation and can create as it wishes. If one experiences hell, one can destroy it and create heaven. God should need a guide?

But like devotees of the East, New Age proponents may respond that while it is true that the self is "god," the self does not always realize it. It is a sleeping god and needs to awaken, or it is a "fallen" god and needs to arise.[91] Our task, then, as human beings is to reverse this "fall." Such a view fits well with the evolutionary motif of the New Age, but it does not resolve the basic contradiction. If the self is really god, how could it not be manifest as god? Still, there is no more contradiction here than in the Eastern version of pantheistic monism, and that has multitudes of adherents.

4. Worldview Question 4: *Physical death is not the end of the self; under the experience of cosmic consciousness, the fear of death is removed.*

Again, I mention this characteristic separately because the notion of death is so central a concern to all of us. We are not just our physical body, says the New Age. Human beings are a unity beyond the body. States of cosmic consciousness confirm this over and over, so much so that Stanislav Grof has experimented with LSD, giving it to patients before they die so that they can experience cosmic unity as they breathe their last breath.[92]

Perhaps the most well-known student of death, however, is psychiatrist Elisabeth Kübler-Ross, whose *On Death and Dying* (1969) has attained a deserved acclaim. In the 1970s Kübler-Ross studied near-death out-of-body experiences and acquired her own spirit guides, who have assured her that death is just a transition to another stage of life.[93] Inter-

---

[91]Keen recounts Ichazo's notion of the "fall" of man in "Conversation," p. 67.

[92]Grof, "Beyond the Bounds of Psychoanalysis," pp. 86-88; Lilly, *Center of the Cyclone*, pp. 17, 35; LeShan, *The Medium, the Mystic and the Physicist*, pp. 232-64; James, *Varieties of Religious Experience*, p. 306; Zaehner, *Zen, Drugs and Mysticism*, p. 44.

[93]Elisabeth Kübler-Ross, *On Death and Dying* (New York: Macmillan, 1969). For an explanation of her views and a critique from a Christian perspective see Phillip J. Swihart, *The Edge of Death* (Downers Grove, Ill.: InterVarsity Press, 1987), pp. 25-31; this book contains a useful

est in near-death experiences was fueled by the very popular *Life After Life*, written by medical doctor Raymond J. Moody Jr.[94]

Another witness to death as transition to another state is provided by past-life recall, such as that MacLaine recounts at considerable length in her books, especially *Dancing in the Light.* Through acupuncture that triggers past-life recall and by consulting channelers such as Kevin Ryerson—through whom speak the voices of Tom McPherson (who says he was once a pickpocket in the Elizabethan age) and John of Zebedee (who identifies himself as the author of Revelation and the Gospel of John)—MacLaine says she has either learned about or "seen" herself in former incarnations. She claims, for example, to have lived thousands of lives before, having been a harem dancer, "a Spanish infant wearing diamond earrings, and in a church, . . . a monk meditating in a cave, . . . a ballet dancer in Russia . . . an Inca youth in Peru." She was also "involved with voodoo" and, as "princess of the elephants" in India, once saved a village from destruction and taught her people a higher level of morality.[95] In *It's All in the Playing* she has a vision of cremation vases which her Higher Self tells her contain "both child and grandfather." She had been both.[96]

The ultimate basis for the belief that death is just a transition to another form of life is, however, the notion that "consciousness" is more than one's physical manifestation. If one is the all or the maker of the all, and if this is "known" intuitively, then a person surely has no need to fear death. Past-life recall and most near-death accounts, so the New Age holds, justify this lack of fear. There is, however, negative evidence from out-of-body experiences that is not considered by New Age proponents, and the idea of reincarnation has been weighed and found wanting as well.[97]

---

bibliography of books on near-death and other out-of-body experiences.

[94]Raymond J. Moody Jr., *Life After Life* (New York: Bantam, 1976). Some New Age bookstores have a special section dealing solely with out-of-body experiences.

[95]MacLaine, *Dancing in the Light*, pp. 353-59, 366.

[96]MacLaine, *It's All in the Playing*, p. 166.

[97]See Christian critics Swihart, *Edge of Death*, pp. 41-82, esp. 67-69; and Mark Albrecht, *Reincarnation* (Downers Grove, Ill.: InterVarsity Press, 1982); for a secular humanist perspective see Melvin Harris, "Are 'Past-Life' Regressions Evidence of Reincarnation?" *Free Inquiry*, Fall 1986, pp. 18-23; and Paul Edwards's three-part article "The Case Against Reincarnation," *Free Inquiry*, Fall 1986, pp. 24-34; Winter 1986-1987, pp. 38-43, 46-48; Spring 1987, pp. 38-43, 46-49.

5. Worldview Questions 1 and 2: *Three distinct attitudes are taken to the metaphysical question of the nature of reality under the general framework of the New Age: (1) the occult version, in which the beings and things perceived in states of altered consciousness exist apart from the self that is conscious, (2) the psychedelic version, in which these things and beings are projections of the conscious self, and (3) the conceptual relativist version, in which the cosmic consciousness is the conscious activity of a mind using one of many nonordinary models for reality, none of which is any "truer" than any other.*

This proposition of the new consciousness worldview takes up the question that has been screaming to be answered from the very beginning: What do all these strange experiences mean? Are they real? I've never had one, some say. So am I missing something?

One thing must be clear: there is no use denying that people have the experiences reported. Experience is private. None of us has each other's experience. If a person reports a strange experience, he or she may be lying, misremembering, embellishing, but we will never be able to critique the account. Even if it appears to us to be intrinsically self-contradictory, we can deny its existence only on an a priori basis—that such and such a state of affairs is inherently impossible. If a person holds to his or her report, say, under cross-examination, then at least for that person the experience remains what it was or is remembered to have been. Monitoring a person's brain with an electrical recording device is of no help whatsoever. It can tell us that electrical activity is or is not going on; it cannot tell us anything about the nature of the existence of the things the self is conscious of.

We can also agree, I believe, that states of altered consciousness have many general details in common—light, timelessness, "magic" beings and so forth. So while each self has a private universe or a set of them when her consciousness is altered, each private universe is at least analogous to others. Huxley's description—"every human group is a society of island universes"—is apt.[98]

The upshot is that we have a host of witnesses to what appears to be a universe next door, a separate reality. The maps of this reality are not well drawn, but if we were to enter it ourselves, I think we would know where

---

[98]Huxley, *Doors of Perception*, p. 13.

we had been—at least when we returned, and assuming we remembered. So the question: where is this separate reality?

Three answers are given. The first is the oldest, but ultimately not acceptable to many modern New Agers. Ultimately deriving from animism, this view is that cosmic consciousness lets you see, react to, receive power from and perhaps begin to control spiritual beings that reside in a sort of fifth dimension parallel to our normal four (three of space and one of time). This dimension exists as truly and as "really" as the other four. Altered states of consciousness allow us to perceive that dimension.

This first answer I call the occult version because it is the intellectual framework for most, if not all, mediums, witches, warlocks, sorcerers, shamans, witch doctors and so forth. The assumption of the ever present and increasingly popular occultists is that by certain means—trances, crystal balls, tarot cards, Ouija boards and other objects with occult powers—a person can consult "the other side" and enlist its aid. But let the beginner beware, say the occultists. Without initiation into the rites and system of the occult, those who toy with incantation and even Ouija boards may bring down on themselves the wrath of the spirit world. When that happens, all hell may break loose.

This occult version has modern-minded adherents. Huxley's understanding is clearly occult. He talks about doors of perception opening on Mind at Large and describes how he saw this Mind at Large in its multi-colored, multidimensional nature. Moreover, he closes *Heaven and Hell* with these words:

> My own guess is that modern spiritualism and ancient tradition are both correct. There *is* a posthumous state of the kind described in Sir Oliver Lodge's book *Raymond* but there is also a heaven of blissful visionary experience; there is also a hell of the same kind of appalling visionary experience suffered here by schizophrenics and some who take mescaline; and there is also an experience, beyond time, of union with the divine Ground.[99]

As noted earlier, Huxley and his wife Laura applied their knowledge of the *Tibetan Book of the Dead* at his death, as she "talked" him into peace on the other side. MacLaine also seems to accept this occult dimension in her theories of new consciousness.

---

[99]Ibid., p. 140. See also Huxley's novel *Island*, where he gives many of these new consciousness notions a fuller, imaginative treatment.

Lilly is more attracted to the alternate explanations discussed below, but he considers the occult version a serious option:

> In my own far-out experiences in the isolation tank with LSD and in my close brushes with death I have come upon the two guides. . . . They may be entities in other spaces, other universes than our consensus reality. . . . They may be representatives of an esoteric hidden school. . . . They may be members of a civilization a hundred thousand years or so ahead of ours. They may be a tuning in on two networks of communication of a civilization way beyond ours, which is radiating information through-out the galaxy.[100]

So the occult version of the new consciousness is an important alternative. If it is correct, however, it stands in contradiction to the notion that the self is both universe and universe maker. It means that there are beings other than the self; there are other centers of consciousness that make claim on one's own self. Viewed as less of a challenge, however, the occult version may yet hold that the self is king to the extent that it can—by whatever means—wrest control from the powerful beings that inhabit the separate universe. Occult bondage is nonetheless a frequent problem. Those who would control may themselves become controlled, locked in the jaws of a demonic trap whose strength is as the strength of ten be-cause its heart is evil.

The second answer I call the *psychedelic* version because it is relatively recent and points to the origin of reality in the psyche of the person who experiences it. The psychedelic version is much more consistent with proposition 1 than is the occult version, for the psychedelic version merely says that the reality perceived under altered states of consciousness is spun out by the self. This reality, in other words, is self-generated. One does not so much open doors of perception as create a new reality to perceive.

We have seen this view described in various ways above, but Lilly's description of his own bad trip is instructive. Early in his work with drugs, Lilly became so confident that he could handle his inner experience that he took LSD without the careful controls of an external and trustworthy guide. As a result, he had a delayed reaction, collapsed in an elevator and almost died. He attributes this collapse to a failure to control his aggres-

---

[100]Lilly, *Center of the Cyclone*, p. 39. The omitted sentences suggest several nonoccult alternatives, including conceptual relativism.

sive instincts. On LSD, he turned against himself and, after the manner
of Freud's death wish, almost wished himself out of existence. Lilly's
death would never have been ruled a suicide by doctors, but as far as Lilly
is concerned it was indeed his own internal programming that put him in
this fix. For Lilly both heaven and hell are inner constructs. Whether one
sees himself as the freaked-out edges of the universe (hell) or as "one of
the boys in the engine room pumping creation from the void" (heaven), it
is one's self that is the creator of the vision.

The third answer to the question of the nature of reality involves *conceptual relativism*. Essentially this is the view that there is a radical disjunction between objective reality (reality as it really is) and perceived
reality (the way we understand that reality by virtue of our symbol system). That is, reality is what it is; the symbols we use to describe it are
arbitrary. In the following chapter we will see this as a major part of the
postmodern perspective. But it must be treated here too.

An example of conceptual relativism is in order. In our Western society we generally conceive of time as "a smooth flowing continuum in
which everything in the universe proceeds at an equal rate, out of a future, through a present, into a past."[101] Hopi Indians have no such general
notion, for their language has "no reference to 'time,' either explicit or
implicit."[102] It is not that reality is really different but that our Western
language system with its overlay of cultural conceptions does not allow
us to see otherwise. This has led Benjamin Whorf to the hypothesis that
in linguistics is now associated with his name: "The structure of the language one habitually uses influences the manner in which one understands his environment. The picture of the universe shifts from tongue
to tongue."[103]

How does conceptual relativism work out in a practical situation? Robert Masters gives an illustration: "There are peoples who live in close
surroundings, like a dense forest, and who therefore believe it's impossible to see beyond a few thousand yards. And if you take them out into the
open, they still can only see that far. But if you persuade them that there's
more to see, why then the scales fall away and great vistas are opened." So
Masters concludes, "All perception is a kind of symbolic system. . . . There

[101]Benjamin Whorf, *Language, Thought and Reality*, ed. John B. Carroll (Cambridge, Mass.:
MIT Press, 1951), p. 57.
[102]Ibid., p. 58.
[103]Stuart Chase, foreword to ibid., p. vi.

is no direct awareness of reality at all."[104]

In modern philosophy Ernst Cassirer describes this skeptical view of language and its implication as "the complete dissolution of any alleged truth content of language, and the realization that this content is nothing but a sort of phantasmagoria of the spirit."[105] In such a system concepts are creations of thought and "instead of giving us the true forms of objects, show us rather the forms of thought itself." As a result "knowledge, as well as myth, language, and art, has been reduced to a kind of fiction— to a fiction that recommends itself by its usefulness, but must not be measured by any strict standard of truth, if it is not to melt away into nothingness."[106] On the other hand, while objective truth may be unattainable, this idea has a more positive counterpart: each symbol system "produces and posits a world of its own."[107] To have a new world, one need have only a new symbol system.

At this point the relevance of our excursion into philosophy and language analysis should be obvious. The conceptual relativist version of the new consciousness worldview simply claims that altered states of consciousness allow people to substitute one symbol system for another symbol system, that is, one vision of reality for another.

The Western world's symbol system has dominated our vision for centuries. It has claimed to be not only *a* symbol system but *the* symbol system—the one leading to objective truth, the truth of correspondence. What a proposition asserts is or is not true, does or does not correspond to reality. Theism and naturalism have insisted that there is no other way to think. So cosmic consciousness—the seeing of the world in a different symbol system—has had a hard time coming. But with theism and naturalism losing their grip, other conceptual orders are now possible.

Many of the proponents of the conceptual relativist version of the new consciousness are well aware of its philosophic roots and its counterpart in modern theories of physics. Laurence LeShan's "general theory of the paranormal" is a specific version of conceptual relativism. When mediums perform the mediumistic task, says LeShan, they assume the follow-

---

[104]Robert Masters, *Intellectual Digest,* March 1973, p. 18. That his conclusion does not follow from his illustration is beside the point here.

[105]Ernst Cassirer, *Language and Myth,* trans. Susanne K. Langer (New York: Dover, 1946), p. 7.

[106]Ibid., pp. 7-8.

[107]Ibid., p. 8.

ing basic mystical worldview: "1. That there is a better way of gaining
information than through the senses. 2. That there is a fundamental
unity to all things. 3. That time is an illusion. 4. That all evil is mere
appearance."[108] At other times when they are ordinary inhabitants of the
visible universe, they accept more commonsense notions of reality. Le-
Shan quotes liberally from modern scientists, especially physicists who
call on the notion of complementarity to explain why an electron appears
to behave sometimes like a particle and at other times like a wave, depending on the instrument they are using to "observe" it.[109] All the time,
the assumption is, it remains the same as it was. But what that is, no one
knows. We know only that it appears in some of our equations as one
thing and in other formulations as another. Wilber's elaborate schemata
picturing the whole of reality in four quadrants, each with its own type of
language, is a recent variant.[110]

But Erwin Schrödinger raises an important consequence of assuming
that symbol systems can be so easily put on and cast off. He points out
that that means no true model of reality exists: "We can think it, but
however we think it, it is wrong."[111] The only category left to help us distinguish between the value of two symbol systems is the purely practical
issue: does it get you what you want?

As there are no true models of reality in science, according to some
versions of the notion of complementarity, so there are no true models of
reality for humanity in general.[112] And just as the value of a scientific

---

[108]LeShan, *The Medium, the Mystic and the Physicist*, p. 43. He is relying on Bertrand Russell for the list, but he documents from his own experience and that of clairvoyants he has
interviewed.

[109]I strongly suspect that there is nothing but a metaphoric relationship between the concept
of complementarity used by scientists and the version of conceptual relativism advocated by
LeShan and other new consciousness theorizers. See Weinberg, "Sokal's Hoax," and Stenger,
"New Age Physics," cited in note 24 above, for confirmation. But it is always a good rhe-
torical ploy to appeal to the prestige of science—even while advocating a worldview that, if
practiced, would destroy scientific initiative.

[110]The whole of Wilber's *Brief History of Everything* is devoted to an elaboration of this schemata.

[111]Erwin Schrödinger, quoted in Ferguson, *Brain Revolution*, p. 19. Of course, if there is no
way of measuring the truth of a model of reality, there is no way of measuring its falsity. So
the idea that all of our models of reality are wrong is a denial of all meaning and a case of
ciphered nihilism (see Thielicke, *Nihilism*, pp. 63-65). To say there are no "true models" of
reality in science is not a devastating criticism for those who understand scientific description as providing valid insights into what reality *is like* but not what reality *is* (see Bube,
Putting It All Together, pp. 15-20).

[112]For a different view of the notion of complementarity, see Donald MacKay, *The Clockwork*

model is measured by its practicality, so pragmatic value is the measure of the worth of a particular altered state of consciousness or a particular theory about it. On this there is a chorus of agreement among new consciousness theorists and practitioners alike.[113] LeShan states the view succinctly: "If the application of a theory produces results in the predicted direction, its fruitfulness has been demonstrated."[114] So much for the theories of cosmic consciousness. Weil applies the pragmatic test to the experience itself: "It would seem obvious that the only meaningful criterion for the genuineness of any spiritual experience . . . is the effect it has on a person's life."[115] Readers who detect in this elements of postmodernism, especially of the sort represented by Richard Rorty, are not far off the target, as we will see in the following chapter.

The practical consequence of the conceptual relativist view of the new consciousness is that it frees a person to believe anything that will bring the desired results. So where do you want to go? What do you want to do? When Lilly accepted the naturalist's notion of the universe, he took a journey to hell. When he accepted the notion that there were civilizations beyond ours, he was "precipitated into such spaces."[116] Believing was being. No vision of reality is more real than another. Schizophrenia is one way of seeing things; normality is another, says R. D. Laing. "But who is to say which is the madness, especially considering the results of normality have been so disastrous in the West."[117]

Moreover, it may be that some of our *normal* distinctions and ways of perceiving bring us personal as well as social and environmental problems: "Suppose someone gets a feeling, and then he makes some distinction about that feeling. Say he calls it anxiety to distinguish it from other feelings. Then that first feeling is followed by a second which he distinguishes as shame."[118] In a spiraling cycle he feels both more anxious and

---

Image (Downers Grove, Ill.: InterVarsity Press, 1974), pp. 91-92; and Bube, *Putting It All Together*, pp. 167-87.

[113]See Ferguson, *Brain Revolution*, p. 83; Weil, *Natural Mind*, p. 67; LeShan, *The Medium, the Mystic and the Physicist*, pp. 99, 124, 139, 150; James, *Varieties of Religious Experience*, 308; Ichazo quoted by Keen, "Conversation . . . ," p. 70; Lilly, *Center of the Cyclone*, throughout.

[114]LeShan, *Center of the Cyclone*, p. 125.

[115]Weil, *Natural Mind*, p. 67. This pragmatic criterion also governs the judgment of Charles Tart and Jon Klimo (Klimo, *Channeling*, pp. xiv, 23).

[116]Ibid., pp. 48, 87.

[117]R. D. Laing, quoted by Peter Mezan, "After Freud and Jung, Now Comes R. D. Laing: Popshrink, Rebel, Yogi, Philosopher-King?" *Esquire*, January 1972, p. 171.

[118]Ibid.

more depressed. Laing concludes, "Now, in a sense it's his distinctions that are making him unhappy. Sometimes I think a great deal of people's suffering wouldn't exist if they didn't have names for it."[119] The solution is obvious: Get rid of distinctions or symbol systems which have them. Imagine a worldview in which you could not tell the difference between pain and pleasure, for example. The consequences of doing this might be severe, but why not figure out a way of adopting such a worldview when one is ill in one's ordinary state of consciousness? Different worldviews have different values at different times. Why not employ them as needed? Play the sexton—different chimes for different times.

6. Worldview Question 5: *Human beings can understand reality because in a state of God-consciousness they directly perceive it. Nonetheless, when New Age teachers present this view to others, they often cite the authority of ancient Scriptures and other religious teachers.*

As we have seen above, a person in the state of God-consciousness knows reality directly. That knowledge is not mediated by rational argument or any external authority: "I experience (whatever), therefore it is." No such conscious argument lies behind the experience itself; rather, the conscious present experience is the source and authority for the knowledge. This authority is like that for recognizing your best friend when he or she appears in your field of vision.

Most people, however, do not have a direct knowledge of their own

---

The teachings of the Bible, the Mahabharata, the Koran and all the other spiritual books that I had tried to understand flooded back to me. The Kingdom of heaven is within you. Know thyself and that will set you free; to thine own self be true; to know self is to know all; know that you are God; know that you are the universe.

SHIRLEY MACLAINE, *Dancing in the Light*

---

divinity; they have to be convinced. As we have seen, New Age proponents suggest various methods of meditation to achieve this direct knowledge. But many of them also cite the external authority of other New Age

---

[119]Ibid.

proponents and especially texts that Christians or other religious believers call scripture. Among the most cited religious authorities are the Buddha and Jesus. Credence for New Age teachings is thereby enhanced. For Christians especially, if Jesus said it or if it's in the Bible, then it must be true. Virtue by association, one might say.

Deepak Chopra provides a clear example. In a recent book, *The Third Jesus,* Chopra turns from promoting alternative medicine to teaching his religious views directly.[120] There are three Jesuses, he says. The first Jesus is the man who lived in Palestine centuries ago. About him we today know almost nothing. He was "swept away by history."[121] The second Jesus is the Jesus largely invented by the church to "fulfill their agenda"; this is the theological Jesus, the Jesus of the creeds, the Jesus preached in sermons.[122] He is so far from the historical Jesus that he can be dismissed as mostly fabrication. The third Jesus is the "one who taught his followers to reach God-consciousness."[123] He had reached this state and spent his life teaching others how to do so. He "asked his followers to see themselves as souls rather than as fallible individuals whose desires conflicted with one another."[124]

How does Chopra know his Jesus is the real Jesus? Nowhere is it more apparent that Chopra's knowledge is based on the authority of his own God-consciousness. How does he know that the historical Jesus is not a well-attested figure? How does he know which Scripture texts accurately portray Jesus and which don't? Not only does he cite no biblical scholarship, he seems not to know that it exists.[125] The historical Jesus is dismissed with a wave of the hand. The Jesus of the church is rejected as a

---

[120]Carl Olson's "Chopra's Christ: The Mythical Creation of a New Age Panthevangelist" is a long, detailed, critical, and logically and theologically astute review of *The Third Jesus* <www.ignatiusinsight.com/features2008/colson_chopra_may08.asp>.

[121]Chopra, *Third Jesus*, p. 8.

[122]Ibid.

[123]Ibid., p. 9.

[124]Chopra, *Third Jesus*, p. 10.

[125]As Carl E. Olson puts it, "no arguments are given, no scholars are quoted, no effort is made to show how and why Chopra accepts one verse [of the Bible] as authentic while dismissing others as somehow distorted or corrupted for ideological ends" (Olson, "Chopra's Christ"). There are no end of creditable books on the Jesus of history. Chopra might have consulted the work of N. T. Wright, some of whose massive scholarship is found in Christian Origins and the Question of God, 3 vols., *The New Testament and the People of God* (1992), *Jesus and the Victory of God* (1996) and *The Resurrection of the Son of God* (2003); all are published by Minneapolis: Fortress Press. Paul Barnett, *Is the New Testament Reliable?* (Downers Grove, Ill.: InterVarsity Press, 1985) is a more popular but still scholarly book.

fabrication. But who today is more likely to know about Jesus: those who pay attention to the data of history—texts written a few years after his death—or those who, with no other authority than their own intuition or imagination, reduce a profoundly detailed figure to a mere ghostly absence? Only if Chopra really is the God of his own God-consciousness can he have the authority to proclaim a Third Jesus.

When Chopra does turn to ancient sources, he quotes Gnostic texts as if they were more authoritative than biblical texts, claiming, for example, that the *Gospel of Thomas* comes from the same period of time. It doesn't. The latest New Testament book is probably the Gospel of John (c. A.D. 90); the *Gospel of Thomas* and other Gnostic texts date from the middle of the second century.

The biblical texts Chopra quotes are lifted from their original theistic context and dropped into the context of an ancient Gnostic or modern New Age worldview. When Jesus says that "the kingdom of God is within you" (Luke 17:21 KJV), Chopra says this means that the kingdom of God is solely individual and immaterial, which he finds conflicts with the book of Revelation.[126] Later he cites John 5:39-40 (NRSV): "You search the Scriptures because you think that in them you have eternal life; and it is they that testify on my behalf. Yet you refuse to come to me to have life." Here, Chopra says, "Jesus is reinforcing his message that the Kingdom of God is within."[127] Not so. Jesus is telling his critics that because they use the Scripture as their authority, they should recognize him as one who has come from the Father.

Even John 3:16-17 (NRSV) gets twisted beyond recognition: "For God so loved the world that he gave his only Son, so that everyone who believes in him may not perish but may have eternal life. Indeed, God did not send the Son into the world to condemn the world, but in order that the world might be saved through him." Chopra comments: "Jesus bolsters his divine identity in the strongest, most eloquent terms. Higher consciousness saves a person from the illusion of death, and this gift comes from a loving God."[128] No, higher consciousness does not save us; Jesus himself does that.

Or again, take John 14:6-7: "Jesus answered, 'I am the way and the truth

[126]Chopra, *Third Jesus*, p. 39.
[127]Ibid., p. 73.
[128]Ibid., p. 125.

and the life. No one comes to the Father except through me. If you really knew me, you would know my Father as well. From now on, you do know him and have seen him.'" This declaration of the exclusivity of the Christian faith stands in direct contradiction to Chopra's main teaching that each of us is capable of God-consciousness and of creating our own reality. Still, he says, "If we sift out the element of Church doctrine, Jesus is saying, 'If you have been seeking, seek no further. This is how the spirit looks when it has been realized.' In other words, he brings God-consciousness down-to-earth by being its living exemplar."[129] No, in the context of the Gospel of John, Jesus is not an exemplar of God-consciousness. He is the one and only eternal Son of God. We ourselves are not God. To think we are God or that we can become God or a god is the primal sin of pride.

7. Worldview Question 7: *History as a record of events that actually occurred in the past is of little interest, but cosmic history which ends with the deification of humanity, especially the individual human self, is seen as a great vision and a great hope.*

New Age proponents do not hesitate to consider accounts of experience from throughout human history. But they are more interested in the "experience" induced by these events than with the significance of these events themselves. How were these events perceived? That is the important matter. Experience is all.

The overall pattern of human history—the impact of events on human experience—is, however, of considerable interest.[130] There is, first of all, the general evolutionary history of cosmic formation—big bang, galactic and planetary formation, the formation of the earth. Then comes the emergence of organic life, its evolution into humanity's present state, its teetering on the edge of a transition to cosmic consciousness. Cosmic history's future is finally foreseen as the arrival of the New Man, the New Woman and the universal New idyllic Age.

8. Worldview Question 8: *New Agers are committed to realizing their own individual unity with the cosmos, creating and recreating it in their own image.*

---

[129]Ibid., pp. 125-26.
[130]See pp. 169-73 above.

As is the case with other worldviews, not all who name themselves New Agers (or allow themselves to be named that by others) would claim to have realized that their self is the kingpin of the cosmos. By no means would all of them imitate Shirley MacLaine as she runs up a California beach shouting, "I am God. I am God." But behind the specific beliefs and practices of fully New Age practitioners is the hope that they—each one of them—are in the center of reality even though they have not yet achieved a fully cosmic consciousness. Their implicit, if not explicit, commitment is to realize this goal.

This is a very tall order and there are many reasons why New Age optimism may overstep whatever cosmic and human reality is now or comes to be.

CRACKS IN THE NEW CONSCIOUSNESS

Is the New Age worldview a step beyond nihilism? Does it deliver what it promises—a new life, a new person, a new age? One thing is clear: it hasn't yet, and the mañana argument is not reassuring. We have had visionaries before, and they and their followers have not done much to save either the world or themselves. Tomorrow is always on the way. As Alexander Pope said, "Hope springs eternal in the human breast."[131]

We have little assurance now that with cosmic consciousness will come the new society. Far greater is the case for pessimism, for the new consciousness worldview is shot through with inner inconsistencies, and it does not even begin to solve the dilemmas posed by naturalistic nihilism or Eastern mysticism. It simply ignores them.

The first major difficulty with the New Age worldview is shared with naturalism and pantheistic monism. The notion of a closed universe—the absence of a transcendent God—poses the problem. William Irwin Thompson says, "God is to the universe what grammar is to language."[132] God is just the structure of the universe. We have already seen how such a situation makes ethics impossible, for either there is no value at all in the external universe (pure naturalism), or God is inseparable from all its activities, and at the level of the cosmos distinctions between good and evil disappear.

New Age proponents have not solved this problem at all. To be sure,

---

[131]Pope, *Essay on Man* 1.95.
[132]Thompson, *Passages About Earth*, p. 99.

many assume that the survival of the human race is a prime value, and they insist that unless humanity evolves, unless people become radically transformed, humanity will disappear. But few discuss ethical issues, and some admit that in the New Age categories of good and evil disappear, just as do categories of time and space, illusion and reality. Even those who opt for moral distinctions are careful not to be fastidious. If human survival means submission to the new elite, then the finer ethical distinctions may be too costly. To survive people may have to abandon traditional notions of freedom and dignity.[133]

The reason ethical questions receive little attention is clear from proposition 1. If the self is king, why worry about ethics? The king can do no wrong. If the self is satisfied, that is sufficient. Such a conception allows for the grossest cruelty. The New Age worldview falls prey to all the pitfalls of solipsism and egoism. Yet virtually no proponent of the system pays any attention to that problem. Why? Because, I presume, they buy the consequences and are unconcerned. Let go and let be. Be here now. There is simply no place for ethical distinctions.

Wilber, however, does argue for an ethical intuition—that is, those who are more evolved toward higher consciousness are better. He makes ethical judgments that find some human beings of less value than some animals. It would be better to kill Al Capone, Wilber says, than a dozen apes: "Nothing is sacrosanct about a human holon [unit]."[134]

A second major difficulty in the new consciousness worldview comes with what it borrows from animism: a host of demigods, demons and guardians who inhabit the separate reality or the inner spaces of the mind. Call them projections of the psyche or spirits of another order of reality: either way, they haunt the New Age and must be placated with rituals or controlled by incantation. The New Age has reopened a door closed since Christianity drove out the demons from the woods, desacralized the natural world and generally took a dim view of excessive interest in the affairs of Satan's kingdom of fallen angels. Now they are back, knocking on university dorm-room doors, sneaking around psychology laboratories and chilling the spines of Ouija players. Modern folk have fled from Grandfather's clockwork universe to Great-great-

---

[133]At this point there is little difference between B. F. Skinner and William Irwin Thompson; see *Beyond Freedom and Dignity*, pp. 180-82, and *Passages About Earth*, pp. 117-18.

[134]Wilber, *Brief History of Everything*, p. 336. By "human holon" Wilber means the whole/part complex that constitutes a human being.

grandfather's chamber of gothic horrors.

Theism, like animism, affirms the existence of spirits, for the Old and New Testaments alike attest to the reality of the spirit world. There are both angels under the command of God and demons (or fallen angels) under their own command or at the beck and call of the master fallen angel, Satan. But biblical teaching about this spirit world is sketchy, and what there is is often cast in the form of sidelong allusions to pagan religious practices and of warnings not to toy with the realm of spirits.

It may seem strange that Christian theism does not have a well-developed angelology. If there exist dynamic powerful beings whose nature is beneficent, why should we not contact them, employ them as guides and harness their power for our human ends? The major reason is simple: God alone is to be our source of power, wisdom and knowledge. How easy it would be for us to worship the angels and forget God!

This is precisely what happened in the early years of the Christian church. The Gnostics, borrowing perhaps from Chaldean astrological lore, taught that God is too exalted, too far away to be personally interested in mere human beings. But other beings exist—"principalities" and "powers"—who are higher than humans but lower than God. We must, so the argument goes, learn to placate the more unfriendly of these beings and to call on the more friendly for help. Vestiges of this idea remain in the Roman Catholic Church's notion of saints. Beseech Mary, for she is human and knows our need; she will in turn ask God to help us: *Sancta Maria, ora pro nobis.* The challenge to this has been that it tends both to overexalt the departed saints and to denigrate God.

Saints and angels play quite a different role in the Bible. The word *saint* simply means church member or Christian, and angels are solely at the command of God. They are not given to human beings for their own manipulation. God's infinite love is manifest in many finite ways, but he alone is our helper. Though he sometimes employs angels to do his bidding, he needs no intermediaries. He himself became human, and he knows us inside out.

So the Bible contains no model—no counterpart to the Lord's Prayer—for enlisting angels in our plans. But it does contain warnings against enlisting the aid of spirits or "other gods." One of the earliest and clearest is in Deuteronomy:

When you enter the land the LORD your God is giving you, do not learn to imitate the detestable ways of the nations there. Let no one be found among you who sacrifices his son or daughter in the fire, who practices divination or sorcery, interprets omens, engages in witchcraft, or casts spells, or who is a medium or spiritist or who consults the dead. Anyone who does these things is detestable to the LORD, and because of these detestable practices the LORD your God will drive out those nations before you. You must be blameless before the LORD your God.

The nations you will dispossess listen to those who practice sorcery or divination. But as for you, the LORD your God has not permitted you to do so. (Deut 18:9-14)

This instruction was given just before Israel entered the Promised Land. Canaan is full of false religion, full of occult practices. So watch out. Have nothing to do with this. Yahweh is God—the one God. Israel needs no other. There is no other. To think so—or to cover all bets by seeking the services of diviners, soothsayers, sorcerers, wizards, charmers, mediums or whatever—is blasphemy. God is God, and Israel is his people.

The New Testament likewise forbids divination and recounts many instances of demon possession.[135] One of the most instructive is the account of Jesus' casting the demons from the Gerasene demoniac (Mk 5:1-20). From this account it is clear that many demons had possessed the man; they were not a projection of his psychosis, since when they left him they entered a herd of swine; demons are personal beings who can use language and communicate with people; and they have the very worst in mind for humanity. It is also clear—and this is most important—that Jesus had complete control over them. It is in this that Christians have hope.

Many modern men and women who have become involved in the occult have found freedom in Christ. The apostle Paul himself assures us:

If God is for us, who can be against us? . . . Who shall separate us from the love of Christ? . . . I am convinced that neither death nor life, neither angels nor demons, neither the present nor the future, nor any powers, neither height nor depth, nor anything else in all creation, will be able to separate us from the love of God that is in Christ Jesus our Lord. (Rom 8:31, 35, 38-39; see also Col 2:15)

---

[135]See, for example, Mt 7:21-23; Lk 10:20; Acts 8:9-24; 13:8-11; 19:11-20; Gal 5:19-21; Jas 3:13-18; Rev 21:8. See also J. S. Wright and K. A. Kitchen, "Magic and Sorcery," in *New Bible Dictionary*, ed. I. Howard Marshall et al., 3rd ed. (Downers Grove, Ill.: InterVarsity Press, 1961), pp. 713-17.

No natural force, no spiritual being, absolutely nothing can overcome God. God is our refuge, not because we, like some superstar magician, can command him to help us, but because he wants to. "God is love," says the apostle John. "In him there is no darkness at all" (1 Jn 4:8; 1:5). So the demonic can be overcome and will be overcome.

While spirit activity has been constant in areas where Christianity has barely penetrated, it has been little reported in the West from the time of Jesus. Christ is said to have driven the spirits from field and stream, and when Christianity permeates a society the spirit world seems to disappear or go into hiding. It is only in the last few decades that the spirits of the woods and rivers, the air and the darkness have been invited back by those who have rejected the claims of Christianity and the God of Abraham, Isaac and Jacob. Perhaps it will be a case of sowing to the wind and reaping the whirlwind.

A third major difficulty with the new consciousness is its understanding of the nature of reality and the nature of truth. Some of the most sophisticated new consciousness proponents, like Ken Wilber, are not occultists in the usual sense. They do not cast I Ching or consult tarot cards. Rather they accept the languages of all systems of reality—the languages of sorcery and science, of witchcraft and philosophy, of drug experience and waking reality, of psychosis and normality—and they understand them all to be equally valid descriptions of reality.[136] In this version of New Age thought there is no truth of correspondence in the Mind at Large or higher levels of consciousness, only a pattern of inner coherence. So there is no critique of anyone's ideas or of anyone's experience. Each system is equally valid; it must only pass the test of experience, and experience is private.

Taken to its logical conclusion, this notion is a form of epistemological nihilism.[137] For we can never know what really is. We can know only what we experience. The flip side is that the self is kingpin—god, if you will—and reality is what any god takes it to be or makes it to be.

We are caught in an impasse. The issue is primary: either the self is god and the New Age is a readout of the implications of that, or the self is not god and thus is subject to the existence of things other than itself.

---

[136]The word *valid* goes through some interesting permutations in LeShan, *The Medium, the Mystic and the Physicist*, pp. 99, 108, 150, 154, 210.

[137]Perhaps Thielicke would call it ciphered nihilism; see Thielicke, *Nihilism*, pp. 36, 63-65.

To the self that opts for its own godhead, there is no argument. The naturalist's charge that this is megalomania or the theist's accusation that it is blasphemy is beside the point. Theoretically such a self accepts as real only what it decides to accept. It would be theoretically futile (but perhaps not practically so) to try to shock out of their delusion those who suppose themselves to be a god. Pouring a pot of hot tea on their head should produce no particular response. Still, it might be worth a try!

Perhaps (but how can we know?) this is the situation of psychotics who have totally withdrawn from conversation with others. Are they making their own universe? What is their subjective state? Only if they waken may we find out, and then memory is often dim if present at all. Their reports may be quite useless. If they waken, they waken into our universe of discourse. But perhaps this universe is our made-up universe, and we ourselves are alone in a corner of a hospital ward unwittingly dreaming we are reading this book, which actually we have made up by our unconscious reality-projecting machinery.

Most people do not go that route. To do so is to recede down corridors of infinite regress. Nausea lies that way, and most of us prefer a less queasy stomach. So we opt for the existence of not only our own self but the selves of others, and thus we require a system that will bring not only unity to our world but knowledge as well. We want to know who and what else inhabits our world.

But if we are not the unity-giver (god), who or what is? If we answer that the cosmos is the unity-giver, we end in naturalistic nihilism. If we say it is God who is the one and all, we end in pantheistic nihilism. So we need, says Samuel McCracken in his brilliant essay on the mindset of the drug world, "a certain simpleminded set of working assumptions: that there is a reality out there, that we can perceive it, that no matter how difficult the perception, the reality is finally an external fact."[138] We also need a basis for thinking that these needs can be met. Where do we go for that? Not postmodernism, as we will see next.

---

[138]Samuel McCracken, "The Drugs of Habit," *Commentary*, June 1971, p .49.

Chapter 9

THE VANISHED HORIZON

"Whither is God," he [the madman] cried.
"I shall tell you. We have killed him—you and I.
All of us are his murderers. But how have we done this?
How were we able to drink up the sea?
Who gave us the sponge to wipe away the entire horizon? . . .
Are we not straying as through an infinite nothing?
Do we not feel the breath of empty space? . . .
Do we not smell anything yet of God's decomposition?
Gods too decompose. God is dead. God remains dead.
And we have killed him. How shall we, the murderers
of all murderers, comfort ourselves? . . .
I come too early," he said then; "my time has not come yet.
This tremendous event is still on its way,
still wandering—it has not yet reached the ears of man."

FRIEDRICH NIETZSCHE, "THE MADMAN"

In a brilliant parable written over a hundred years ago, Friedrich Nietzsche saw it all.[1] A culture cannot lose its philosophic center without the most serious of consequences, not just to the philosophy on which it was based but to the whole superstructure of culture and even each person's notion of who he or she is. Everything changes. When God dies, both the substance and the value of everything else die too.

---

[1]Friedrich Nietzsche, "The Madman," *Gay Science* 125, in *The Portable Nietzsche*, trans. Walter Kaufmann (New York: Viking, 1954), pp. 95-96.

The acknowledgment of the death of God is the beginning of postmodern wisdom. It is also the end of postmodern wisdom. For, in the final analysis, postmodernism is not "post" anything; it is the last move of the modern, the result of the modern taking its own commitments seriously and seeing that they fail to stand the test of analysis.[2]

As I commented earlier, Socrates said that the unexamined life is not worth living, but for a naturalist he is wrong.[3] For a naturalist it is the examined life that is not worth living. Now, over a hundred years after Nietzsche, the news of God's death has finally reached "the ears of man." The horizon defining the limits of our world has been wiped away. The center holding us in place has vanished. Our age, which more and more is coming to be called postmodern, finds itself afloat in a pluralism of perspectives, a plethora of philosophical possibilities, but with no dominant notion of where to go or how to get there. A near future of cultural anarchy seems inevitable.

Enough gloomy talk. This book is supposed to be a catalog of worldviews. Catalogs should be dispassionate. Get a grip!

THE PROBLEM OF DEFINITION

Getting a grip is hard. How does one define the indefinite? Certainly the term that now fits is *postmodernism*.[4] But what does it mean? It is used by so many people to focus on so many different facets of cultural and intellectual life that its meaning is often fuzzy, not just around the edges but at the center as well (as if a term defining a worldview without a center could have a center).

Though literature professor Ihab Hassan was one of the first scholars to write about postmodernism, he confesses, "I know less about postmodernity today than I did thirty years ago [1971], when I began to write about it. . . . [Still today] no consensus obtains on what postmodernism

---

[2]Anthony Giddens calls postmodernity the "radicalising of modernity" (*The Consequences of Modernity* [Stanford, Calif.: Stanford University Press, 1990], p. 52).

[3]See chapter five, p. 113.

[4]In the writing of this chapter I have found the following presentations and critiques helpful; the list should be considered to extend to all the other sources cited in the footnotes to this chapter: Steven Best and Douglas Kellner, *Postmodern Theory* (New York: Guilford, 1991); Steven Connor, *Postmodernist Culture* (Oxford: Blackwell, 1989); Fredric B. Burnham, *Postmodern Theology: Christian Faith in a Pluralist World* (San Francisco: HarperSanFrancisco, 1989); Albert Borgmann, *Crossing the Postmodern Divide* (Chicago: University of Chicago Press, 1992); and Stephen Toulmin, *Cosmopolis: The Hidden Agenda of Modernity* (New York: Free Press, 1990).

really means." After being locked in a room for a week of discussion, he says, the major scholars writing about it would reach no agreement, "but a trickle of blood might appear beneath the sill." Still he notes some common elements: "fragments, hybridity, relativism, play, parody, pastiche, an ironic anti-ideological stance, an ethos bordering on kitsch and camp."[5] Mark Lilla makes a similar claim about "academic postmodernism," describing it as "a loosely structured constellation of ephemeral disciplines like cultural studies, gay and lesbian studies, science studies and postcolonial theory." It "borrows freely," he says, "from a host of works (in translation) by such scholars as Jacques Derrida, Michel Foucault and Jean-François Lyotard." Then he adds, "Given the impossibility of imposing logical order on ideas as dissimilar as these, postmodernism is long on attitude and short on argument."[6]

The term *postmodernism* is usually thought to have arisen first in reference to architecture, as architects moved away from unadorned, impersonal boxes of concrete, glass and steel to complex shapes and forms, drawing motifs from the past without regard to their original purpose or function.[7] But when French sociologist Jean-François Lyotard used the term *postmodern* to signal a shift in cultural legitimation, the term became a key word in cultural analysis.

In short, Lyotard defined *postmodern* as "incredulity toward metanarratives."[8] No longer is there a single story, a metanarrative (in our terms a worldview), that holds Western culture together. It is not just that there have long been many stories, each of which gives its binding power to the social group that takes it as its own. The naturalists have their story, the pantheists theirs, the Christians theirs, ad infinitum. With

---

[5]Ihab Hassan, "Postmodernism to Postmodernity" <www.ihabhassan.com/postmodernism_to_postmodernity.htm>. His first major work on postmodernism was *The Dismemberment of Orpheus: Toward a Postmodern Literature* (New York: Oxford University Press, 1971).

[6]Mark Lilla, "The Politics of Jacques Derrida," *New York Review of Books*, June 25, 1998, p. 36. Lilla is professor of social thought at the University of Chicago.

[7]Modern architecture is the application of mechanical reason to the shaping of space. This results in form following function—giant boxes of concrete, glass and steel with ninety-degree corners and not a curve in sight. The centers of many American cities—Atlanta, Dallas, Minneapolis—major in these highly formal and impersonal stacks of blocks. Postmodern architects rebelled against the impersonal, bringing back motifs from every earlier era of architecture from every culture—rose windows, classical columns, modernized gargoyles—tacking them on to structural forms that have no obvious organizing principle.

[8]Jean-François Lyotard, *The Postmodern Condition: A Report on Knowledge*, trans. Geoff Bennington and Brian Massumi (Minneapolis: University of Minnesota Press, 1984), p. 24.

postmodernism no story can have any more credibility than any other. All stories are equally valid, being so validated by the community that lives by them.

I cannot catalog postmodernism as I have earlier worldviews. Even more than existentialism, postmodernism is both more than and less than a worldview. In major part this is due to the origin of the term within the discipline of sociology rather than philosophy. Sociologists are concerned with how people behave as part of society. They do not use categories of being (metaphysics) or knowing (epistemology) or ethics; that is, they do not ask what is true about reality, but how notions of being and knowing and ethics arise and function in society. To understand postmodernism, therefore, we will have to ask and answer not simply the seven worldview questions posed in chapter one but a question about the questions themselves.

But first let us get one thing clear. Postmodernism has influenced religious understanding, including that characteristic of Christian theism, but it accepts the foundation at the heart of naturalism: *Matter exists eternally; God does not exist.*

THE FIRST THING: BEING TO KNOWING

I have apologized before for approaching an explanation by first making a summary statement that seems opaque. I will do so again in hope that the ensuing explanation will clarify the vision.

1. A Worldview Question About Worldview Questions: *The first question postmodernism addresses is not what is there or how we know what is there but how language functions to construct meaning. In other words, there has been a shift in "first things" from being to knowing to constructing meaning.*

Two major shifts in perspective have occurred over the past centuries: one is the move from the "premodern" (characteristic of the Western world prior to the seventeenth century) to the "modern" (beginning with Descartes); the second is the move from the "modern" to the "postmodern" (whose first major exponent was Friedrich Nietzsche in the last quarter of the nineteenth century). Take the following as an example of these shifts, others of which we will see below. There has been a movement from (1) a "premodern" concern for a just society based on revelation from a just God to (2) a "modern" attempt to use universal reason as the guide to justice to (3) a "postmodern" despair of any universal standard for justice. Society then moves from medieval hierarchy to Enlightenment, universal democracy to postmodern privileging of the self-defining values of individuals and communities. This is a formula for anarchy. It is hard to think of this as progress, but then progress is a "modern" notion. The "premodern" Christian had too clear a view of human depravity, and the "postmodern" mind has too dim a view of any universal truth.

One of the ways to understand these shifts is to reflect on our reflecting.[9] For us that means to identify the preconceptions on which this book's analysis so far has been based.

Some readers of earlier editions of this book have challenged the way I posed the worldview questions of chapter one. Their concern is whether a set of seven questions (now eight) commits this particular worldview analysis to the confines of one worldview.[10] This is an astute observation.

The heart of the issue is the order of the questions. I placed question 1 (*What is prime reality—the really real?*) first for a good reason. I take metaphysics (or ontology) to be the foundation of all worldviews. Being is prior to knowing. If nothing is there, then nothing can be known. So, in defining theism, I began with God, defined as infinite and personal (triune), transcendent and immanent, omniscient, sovereign and good.[11] All else in theism stems from this commitment to a specific notion of what is fundamentally there. Question 2 asked about the nature of the external universe, and questions 3 and 4 about the nature of human beings and their destiny. It was not till question 5 that "how we know" was dealt with. Then came ethics—how we should behave—in question 6, and finally an overall question about our human historical significance in question 7. Now question 8 focuses on the end toward which we live our lives.

---

[9]Giddens writes, "What is characteristic of modernity is not an embracing of the new for its own sake, but the presumption of wholesale reflexivity—which of course includes reflection upon the nature of reflection itself" (*Consequences of Modernity*, p. 39). I have, for example, been reflecting throughout this book on the worldviews that shape our understanding; now I am looking at my looking, reflecting on my reflecting. Another way to put this is to say I will step back from my analysis to make a meta-analysis.

[10]I have dealt with this issue in *Naming the Elephant: Worldview as a Concept* (Downers Grove, Ill.: InterVarsity Press, 2004).

[11]Above, chapter two, pp. 28-31.

The fact is that this order of questions is *premodern* in general and *theistic* in particular. Theism puts being before knowing. Enlightenment naturalism puts knowing before being.[12] The shift came early in the seventeenth century with Descartes. Descartes is seen as the first modern philosopher, not the least because he was more interested in *how* one knows than in *what* one knows. For his philosophic approach—and the approach of almost every major philosopher from his time on—knowing is prior to being.[13] Descartes was not rejecting the theistic notion of God. Quite the contrary, he held a notion of God essentially the same as that of Thomas Aquinas.[14] But his interest in being certain about this notion had major consequences.

Descartes's approach to knowing is legendary. He wanted to be completely certain that what he thought he knew was actually true. So he took the method of doubt almost (but not quite) to the limit. What can I doubt? he asked himself in the quietness of his study. He concluded that he could doubt everything except that he was doubting (doubting is thinking). So he concluded, "I think, therefore I am." He then further considered whether there was anything other than his own existence that he could be sure of. After a series of arguments he eventually wrote,

> I do not now admit anything which is not necessarily true: to speak accurately, I am not more than a thing which thinks, that is to say a mind or a soul, or an understanding, or a reason, which are terms whose significance was formerly unknown to me. I am, however, a real thing and really exist; what thing? I have answered: a thing which thinks.[15]

Here is the essence of the modern: the autonomy of human reason. One individual, Descartes, declares on the foundation of his own judgment that he knows with philosophic certainty that he is a thinking thing. From this foundation Descartes goes on to argue that God necessarily

---

[12]Recently some naturalist philosophers (such as Paul M. Churchland and Patricia Smith Churchland) have, however, moved back toward a new emphasis on the mechanisms inherent in the material order. See "Naturalistic Epistemology," in *The Cambridge Dictionary of Philosophy*, ed. Robert Audi (Cambridge: Cambridge University Press, 1995), pp. 518-19.

[13]I devote chap. 3 of *Naming the Elephant*, pp. 51-73 , to this issue.

[14]Over thirty years ago I wrote a paper for a graduate course in seventeenth-century philosophy in which I demonstrated to my own and my professor's satisfaction that Descartes and Aquinas held identical views of God. What I didn't see then is that Descartes's interest in how he knew such a God existed had had such consequences.

[15]René Descartes, "Meditation II," in *Philosophical Works*, trans. Elizabeth S. Haldane and G. R. T. Ross, 2 vols. (New York: Dover, 1955), 1:152.

exists and that reality is dual—matter and mind.

The notion of the autonomy of human reason liberated the human mind from the authority of the ancients. Scientific and technical progress came not from notions revealed in Scripture but from the assumption that human reason could indeed find its way toward the truth. Such knowledge was power, instrumental power, power over nature, power to get us what we want. In science, the results were stellar. In philosophy, however, the move from being to knowing, from the primacy of God who creates and reveals to the primacy of the self that knows on its own, was fatal. It both set the agenda for modern philosophy from Locke to Kant and sparked as well the recoil of postmodern philosophy from Nietzsche to Derrida as humanistic optimism flirted with despair.

THE FIRST THING: KNOWING TO MEANING

As knowing became the focus, knowing how one knew became a major issue. David Hume (1711-1776) cast into doubt the existence of cause and effect as objective reality. Immanuel Kant (1724-1804) tried to answer Hume but ended by both exalting the knowing self to the position of "creating" reality and removing from it the ability to know things in themselves.[16] Georg W. F. Hegel (1770-1831) and, for a brief period of optimism, the German Idealists exalted the human self to almost divine dimensions. Finally Friedrich Nietzsche (1844-1900) delivered the coup de grâce to the modern self-confidence that what we think we know we really do know. Apart from New Age enthusiasts, today there is little hope that any optimism about the human condition can be sustained.

The larger story of modern philosophy can be read in many places.[17] We are concerned with a single but central theme: the shift from *knowing* to *meaning*. It is in Nietzsche that this is first most evident. Nietzsche completed what Descartes started; he took doubt beyond Descartes, re-

---

[16]For Kant, of course, "creating reality" must not be understood in the manner of New Age thought; the categories by which we understand reality—space, time, etc.—are part of our endowment as human beings; they form the structure of our knowledge.

[17]I am painfully aware that my comments about Descartes, Hume and Kant are superficial perhaps beyond forgiveness. But though the strokes are broad, I think they take the right shape. For the story of modern philosophy I have found Copleston's *History of Philosophy* of special value (Frederick Copleston, *A History of Philosophy*, vols. 4-9 [London: Burns and Oates, 1958-1974]). In particular for the issues dealt with here, however, see Robert C. Solomon, *Continental Philosophy Since 1750: The Rise and Fall of the Self* (New York: Oxford University Press, 1988).

jecting his argument for certitude about the existence of the self.

Look again at Descartes's "I think, therefore I am." What if it is the thinking that creates or causes the *I* rather than the *I* that creates or causes the thinking? What if the activity of thinking does not require an agent but produces only the illusion of an agent?[18] What if there is only thinking—a fluid flow of language without discernible origin, determinate meaning or direction?

Regardless of whether Nietzsche's specific critique is a fair analysis of Descartes's search for certitude, Nietzsche's more radical doubt does radical damage to human certitude. After Nietzsche, no thoughtful person should have been able to secure easy confidence in the objectivity of human reason. But as Nietzsche pointed out in the parable of the madman, it takes a long time for ideas to sink in to culture. The madman says he came too soon. The deed had been done, but in the 1880s the news was still on the way. By the 1950s and 1960s it was beginning to be heard in the voices of Jean-Paul Sartre and Albert Camus. By the 1990s everyone in the Western world and much of the East came to see that confidence in human reason is almost dead. True, most philosophers have not capitulated, not perhaps because they have the most to lose but because they have everything to lose.[19] Many scientists and technologists continue in their confidence that science gives sure knowledge, but they seem to be the last part of the intellectual world to do so.

THE DEATH OF TRUTH

Knowing itself comes under fire, especially the notion that there are any truths of correspondence. Conceptual relativism, discussed in the previous chapter, now serves not just religious experience but all aspects of reality.[20]

---

[18]"For, formerly, one believed in 'the soul' as one believed in grammar, and the grammatical subject: one said, 'I' is the condition, 'think' is the predicate and conditioned—thinking is an activity to which thought *must* supply a subject as cause. Then one tried with admirable perseverance and cunning to get out of this net—and asked whether the opposite might not be the case: 'think' the condition, 'I' the conditioned; 'I' in that case [am] only a synthesis which is *made* by thinking" (Friedrich Nietzsche, *Beyond Good and Evil*, sec. 54, in *The Basic Writings of Nietzsche*, ed. Walter Kaufmann [New York: Modern Library, 1969], p. 257); see also a much longer critique in secs. 16-17, pp. 213-14.

[19]Richard Rorty, for example, moved from a philosophy post at Princeton University to become professor of humanities at the University of Virginia.

[20]See chapter eight, pp. 200-204.

2. Worldview Question 5: *The truth about the reality itself is forever hidden from us. All we can do is tell stories.*

If we begin with the seemingly knowing self and follow the implications, we are left first with a solitary self (solipsism) and then not even that. Literary theorist Edward Said put it this way:

> No longer a coherent *cogito* [thinking thing], man now inhabits the interstices, "the vacant interstellar spaces," not as an object, still less as a subject; rather man is the *structure*, the generality of relationships among those words and ideas that we call the humanistic, as opposed to the pure, or natural sciences.[21]

Of course, we still tell personal stories about our lives, where we have been and where we intend to go. And we tell larger stories too. Some of us—say, Christians, optimistic naturalists, secular humanists, chemists, for example—may cling to our metanarratives, but they are just wishful

---

What, then, is truth? A mobile army of metaphors, metonyms, and anthropomorphisms—in short, a sum of human relations, which have been enhanced, transposed, and embellished poetically and rhetorically, and which after long use seem firm, canonical, and obligatory to a people: truths are illusions about which one has forgotten that this is what they are; metaphors which are worn out and without sensuous power; coins which have lost their pictures and now matter only as metal, no longer as coins.

NIETZSCHE, "On Truth and Lie in an Extra-Moral Sense"

---

thinking. The language we use to tell our stories is, as Nietzsche put it, "a mobile army of metaphors."

We have a continued "urge for truth," but now "to be truthful means using the customary metaphors—in moral terms: the obligation to lie according to fixed convention, to lie herd-like in a style obligatory for all."[22]

---

[21]Edward Said, *Beginnings: Intention and Method* (New York: Basic Books, 1975), p. 286, quoted by Stanley Grenz, *A Primer on Postmodernism* (Grand Rapids: Eerdmans, 1996), p. 120.
[22]Nietzsche, "On Truth and Lie in an Extra-Moral Sense," in *The Portable Nietzsche*, p. 47.

Those who hang on to their metanarrative as if it really were the master story, encompassing or explaining all other stories, are under an illusion. We can have meaning, for all these stories are more or less meaningful, but we cannot have truth.

According to postmodernism, nothing we think we know can be checked against reality as such. Now we must not think that postmodernists believe that there is no reality outside our language. We are not to abandon our ordinary perception that a bus is coming down the street and we'd better get out of the way. Our language about there being a "bus" that is "coming down" a "street" is useful. It has survival value! But apart from our linguistic systems we can know nothing. All language is a human construct. We can't determine the "truthfulness" of the language, only the usefulness.

This basic notion has many varied expressions, depending on the postmodern theorist. Richard Rorty will serve as an illustration.

> The world does not speak. Only we do. The world can, once we have programmed ourselves with a language, cause us to hold beliefs. But it cannot propose a language for us to speak. Only other human beings can do that. . . . *Languages* are made rather than found, and . . . truth is a property of linguistic entities, of sentences.[23]

Truth is whatever we can get our colleagues (our community) to agree to. If we can get them to use our language, then—like the "strong poets" Moses, Jesus, Plato, Freud—our story is as true as any story will ever get.

Of course if our story doesn't "work," if we fail to have a language that allows us safely to "cross a street when a bus is coming," few of us will be around long in a modern city. Some languages will pass out of existence because the language framers did not survive long enough to have children to whom they taught it. But since many languages—from Hindi to Mandarin to Swahili—keep us alive in the cities, they have all the truth value needed to keep us from being hit by a bus.

Philosopher Willard Quine compares the language of modern science to Homer's stories of the gods:

---

[23]Richard Rorty, *Contingency, Irony and Solidarity* (Cambridge: Cambridge University Press, 1989), pp. 6-7. Compare Rorty's statement with this one by Michel Foucault: "'Truth' is to be understood as a system of ordered procedures for the production, regulation, distribution, circulation, and operations of statements" ("Truth and Power" [from *Power/Knowledge*], in *The Foucault Reader*, ed. Paul Rabinow [New York: Pantheon, 1984], p. 74).

For the most part I do, qua lay physicist, believe in physical objects and not in Homer's gods; and I consider it a scientific error to believe otherwise. But in point of epistemological footing the physical objects and the gods differ only in degree and not in kind. Both sorts of entities enter our conception only as cultural deposits. The myth of physical objects is epistemologically superior to most in that it has proved more efficacious than other myths as a device for working a manageable structure into the flux of experience.[24]

In short, the only kind of truth there is is pragmatic truth. There is no truth of correspondence.

It is easy to see how this notion, when applied to religious claims, triggers a radical relativism.[25] No one's story is truer than anyone else's story. Does the story work? That is, does it satisfy the teller? Does it get you what you want—say, a sense of belonging, a peace with yourself, a hope for the future, a way to order your life? It's all one can ask.

There is as well a problem with the stories themselves. How is the language in which they are expressed to be interpreted? Within the deconstructionist segment of postmodernism, the stories we tell ourselves and others do not have a determinate meaning. They are not only subject to normal misreading through lack of intelligence or basic background, or difference between the writer's or speaker's background or context and that of the reader or listener. There is an inherent indeterminacy to language itself. Stories all contain the seeds of self-contradiction.[26] Texts and statements mean only what readers take them to mean.[27]

So in postmodernism there is a movement from (1) the Christian "premodern" notion of a revealed determinate metanarrative to (2) the "modern" notion of the autonomy of human reason with access to truth of correspondence to (3) the "postmodern" notion that we create truth as we construct languages that serve our purposes, though these very languages deconstruct upon analysis.

---

[24]Willard Van Orman Quine, "Two Dogmas of Empiricism," in *From a Logical Point of View*, 2nd ed. (Cambridge, Mass.: Harvard University Press, 1980), p. 44. Quine adds, "Epistemologically these are myths on the same footing with physical objects and gods, neither better nor worse except for differences in the degree to which they expedite our dealings with sense experience" (ibid., p. 45). I am indebted to C. Stephen Evans for this observation.

[25]I have discussed religious relativism in more detail in chaps. 5-6 of *Chris Chrisman Goes to College* (Downers Grove, Ill.: InterVarsity Press, 1993), pp. 45-68.

[26]Lilla, "Politics of Jacques Derrida," p. 38.

[27]A brief, helpful introduction to this notion is found in Harold K. Bush Jr., "Poststructuralism as Theory and Practice in the English Class Room," *ERIC Digest* (1995), available at <www.indiana.edu/~ericrec/ieo/digests/d104.html>.

3. Worldview Question 3: *Stories give communities their cohesive character.*

If, then, claims to truth are not seen as the way things really are, if all we have are humanly constructed stories that we believe and tell, total anarchy is not necessarily the result. This is true for two reasons. First, people believe these stories to be true, so they function in society as if they were true. Second, groups of people believe the same basic story, and the result is more or less stable communities. Communities begin to fall apart when different people within them believe substantially different stories.

Christians, for example, believe that God is triune. The postmodernist may say that this story cannot be known to accord with reality, but a Christian thinks it does anyway. A naturalist really believes that "the cosmos is all there is," regardless of how the postmodernist may explain that this belief cannot in principle or practice be substantiated. One might say, too, that a postmodernist really believes that this explanation is true, though if it is, then it can't be (but this anticipates the critique of postmodernism that follows below). In any case, stories have great social binding power; they make communities out of otherwise disparate bunches of people.[28] The result is that though in postmodernism there is an "incredulity toward metanarratives" (Lyotard), in every culture there is a sufficiently agreed upon story that acts as a metanarrative. So much is this so that these stories, acting as metanarratives, mask a play for power by those in any society who control the details and the propagation of the story.

LANGUAGE AS POWER

The shift is now complete: from being to knowing to meaning. But the implications keep piling up.

4. Worldview Questions 5 and 6: *All narratives mask a play for power. Any one narrative used as a metanarrative is oppressive.*

---

[28]In a self-reflective postmodern society, Lyotard points out, "most people have lost the nostalgia for the lost narrative. It in no way follows that they are reduced to barbarity. What saves them is their knowledge that legitimation can only spring from their own linguistic practice and communicated interaction" (*Postmodern Condition*, p. 41). Lyotard seems not to be aware that his "postmodern" story is itself a story acting as a metanarrative (something that has lost credibility in a postmodern society, according to him) and therefore no more credible than any other story, any other explanation.

"Knowledge is power," Francis Bacon said in a peculiarly prophetic moment. He was right; "modern" scientific knowledge has demonstrated its power for three centuries. With postmodernism, however, the situation is reversed. There is no purely objective knowledge, no truth of correspondence. Instead there are only stories, stories that, when they are believed, give the storyteller power over others.

Several major postmodern theorists, notably Michel Foucault, emphasize this relationship. Any story but one's own is oppressive. Every modern society, for example, defines "madness" such that those who fall into that category are put out of the way of the rest of society. Since there is no way to know what madness as such really is, all we have are our definitions.[29] To reject oppression is to reject all the stories society tells us. This is, of course, anarchy, and this, as we will see, Foucault accepts.

Here then we can trace a movement from (1) a "premodern" acceptance of a metanarrative written by God and revealed in Scripture to (2) a "modern" metanarrative of universal reason yielding truth about reality to (3) a "postmodern" reduction of all metanarratives to power plays.

THE DEATH OF THE SUBSTANTIAL SELF

The question of human identity is thousands of years old. "What is man?" the psalmist asked. Created "a little lower than the heavenly beings and crowned . . . with glory and honor," came the answer.[30] But not in postmodernism.

5. Worldview Question 3: *There is no substantial self. Human beings make themselves who they are by the languages they construct about themselves.*

If this sounds like existentialism, that's because existentialism is a step in the postmodern direction. Sartre said, "Existence precedes essence."[31] We make ourselves by what we choose to do. The *I* is an activity. The postmodern pundit says, "We are only what we describe ourselves to be." The *I* is not a substance, not even an activity, but a floating construct

[29]"Knowledge is violence. The act of knowing, says Foucault, is an act of violence" (Grenz, *Primer on Postmodernism*, p. 133).
[30]Psalm 8:4-5; some translations say, "a little lower than God."
[31]Jean-Paul Sartre, "Existentialism," in *A Casebook on Existentialism*, ed. William V. Spanos (New York: Thomas Y. Crowell, 1966), p. 289. For Sartre, however, the authentic self is never encompassed by its cultural context or any metanarrative; it is rather radically free.

dependent on the language it uses. If we are "strong poets," we create new ways of speaking or modify the language of our society. Freud, for example, was a strong poet. He got a whole society to talk about human reality in terms like "the Oedipus complex" or the "id, the ego and the superego."[32] Jung created the "collective unconscious." There is no way to know whether any of these "things" exist. But we use the language to describe ourselves, and that becomes the truth.

> Foucault claims that we are now realizing that "humanity" is nothing more than a fiction composed by the modern human sciences.... The self is no longer viewed as the ultimate source and ground for language; to the contrary, we are now coming to see that the self is constituted in and through language.[33]

In postmodernism the self is indeed a slippery concept. For Nietzsche the only self worth living was the self of the *Übermensch,* the Overman (sometimes misleadingly translated Superman), the one who has risen above the conventional herd and has fashioned himself. *Thus Spake Zarathustra* is the voice of such a "man beyond man." But few can do this. Most of us have our selves constructed by the conventional language of our age and society.

So again there is a shift from (1) the "premodern" theistic notion that human beings are dignified by being created in the image of God to (2) the "modern" notion that human beings are the product of their DNA template, which itself is the result of unplanned evolution based on chance mutations and the survival of the fittest, to (3) the "postmodern" notion of an insubstantial self constructed by the language it uses to describe itself.

BEING GOOD WITHOUT GOD

Postmodernism follows the route taken by naturalism and existentialism, but with a linguistic twist.

---

[32]See Rorty's discussion of Freud as a "strong poet" in *Contingency,* pp. 20, 28, 30-34, and his comments on the power of poetry (pp. 151-52) and on truth as "whatever the outcome of undistorted communication happens to be" (p. 67; also pp. 52, 68).

[33]Grenz, *Primer on Postmodernism,* p. 130. Grenz also quotes Foucault as follows: "To all those who still wish to think about man, about his reign, or his liberation, to all those who still ask themselves questions about what man is in his essence, to all those who wish to take him as their starting-point in their attempts to reach the truth . . . to all these warped and twisted forms of reflection we can answer only with a philosophical laugh—which means, to a certain extent, a silent one" (from *The Order of Things* [New York: Random House-Pantheon, 1971], pp. 342-43, quoted by Grenz, *Primer on Postmodernism,* p. 131).

6. Worldview Question 6: *Ethics, like knowledge, is a linguistic construct. Social good is whatever society takes it to be.*

There is little reason to elaborate on this notion. On the one hand, it is a postmodern version of a much older cultural relativism.[34] On the other hand, it is the ethical extension of the notion that truth is what we decide it is. Rorty's comment will serve to show that this position is not necessarily a happy one for people of what we normally call goodwill:

> There is nothing deep down inside us except what we have put there ourselves, no criterion that we have not created in the course of creating a practice, no standard of rationality that is not an appeal to such a criterion, no rigorous argumentation that is not obedience to our own conventions.[35]

This means, he admits, that if some future society decides that fascism is what it wants, a liberal democrat or anyone else is without appeal. So there is no appeal to a higher good outside the human family. One is left with a radical ethical relativism. The good is whatever those who wield the power in society choose to make it. If a person is happy with how society draws its ethical lines, then individual freedom remains. But what if an individual refuses to speak the ethical language of his or her community?

Take Foucault, in many ways the most radical anarchist of all the major postmodern theorists. For him the greatest good is an individual's freedom to maximize pleasure.[36] Foucault is so fearful that "society constitutes a conspiracy to stifle one's own longings for self-expression" that "he agonizes profoundly over the question of whether rape should be regulated by penal justice." For him, writes Ronald Beiner, "law = repression; decriminalization = freedom."[37] Postmodernism can make no normative judgment about such a view. It can only observe and comment: so much the worse for those who find themselves oppressed by the majority.

---

[34]See the brief discussion in chapter five, pp. 108-9.

[35]Richard Rorty, *The Consequences of Pragmatism* (Minneapolis: University of Minnesota Press, 1982), p. xlii. Derrida runs into the same problem. Mark Lilla writes, "Derrida places enormous trust in the ideological goodwill or prejudices of his readers, for he cannot tell them why he chooses justice over injustice or democracy over tyranny, only that he does" (Lilla, "Politics of Jacques Derrida," p. 40).

[36]Ronald Beiner, "Foucault's Hyper-liberalism," *Critical Review*, Summer 1995, pp. 349-70.

[37]Ibid., pp. 353-54.

Even value in literature is seen as the creation of the reader. It is now a common belief, writes Kevin J. H. Dettmar, "that artistic value is not transcendent but contingent: that value resides not strictly within a text, but in a complex interaction between what a text says and does, and what the reader wants and needs."[38]

Again we see the shift from (1) the "premodern" theistic ethics based on the character of a transcendent God who is good and has revealed that goodness to us to (2) the "modern" ethics based on a notion of universal human reason and experience and the human ability to discern objective right from wrong to (3) the "postmodern" notion that morality is the multiplicity of languages used to distinguish right from wrong.

POSTMODERNISM'S CUTTING EDGE

7. Worldview Questions 7 and 8: *Postmodernism is in flux, as is postmodernism's take on the significance of human history, including its own history. This means that the core committments of many postmodernists are in flux as well. Postmodernists, in short are committed to an endless stream of shifting "whatevers."*

Given the six previous characteristics of postmodernism, it is easy to see why it is always in flux. As Lyotard says, "All that has been received, if only yesterday . . . must be suspected. . . . A work can become modern only if it is first postmodern. Postmodernism thus understood is not modernism at its end but in the nascent state, and this state is constant."[39] The story of postmodernism's development is too long to be told here. I can only offer a few short episodes, told, as any postmodern would point out, from one perspective—my own.

In the Middle Ages, theology was the queen of the sciences. In the Enlightenment, philosophy, and especially science, became the leading edge of intellectual cultural change. In the postmodern age, literary theory once led the way.

To anyone who did graduate work in English in the early 1960s this move seems both sudden and surprising. But in the 1960s literary theory

---

[38]Dettmar notes that this view "has been articulated most influentially" by Barbara Herrnstein Smith in *Contingencies of Value* (Cambridge, Mass.: Harvard University Press, 1988). See Kevin J. H. Dettmar, "What's So Great About Great Books," *Chronicle of Higher Education*, September 11, 1998, p. B6.

[39]Lyotard, *Postmodern Condition*, p. 79.

began to become both sophisticated and culturally relevant.[40] While scientists continued to do what they had done for over a hundred years, and philosophers trained their focus on smaller and smaller matters of analytic philosophy, a new mode of thinking about thinking emerged and quickly evolved. A kind of Precambrian burst of new ideas fired the imagination of backwater English departments, whose younger scholars did not just move into the mainstream but became the mainstream.

The babbling brooks of Marx and Freud fed into the sedate pools of Southern gentlemanly New Criticism and historical criticism, stirring the waters. Then fresh springs from anthropology (Claude Lévi-Strauss), sociology (Foucault, Lyotard), feminism (Kate Millet, Elaine Showalter) and linguistics (Ferdinand de Saussure) came with such force that the eddies of literary study became the mainstream of intellectual life. Scholars like Jacques Derrida (deconstruction) and Stanley Fish (reader response) became hot on campus. Literary critics became intellectual celebrities. "The hunger for social status has always seemed to me more pronounced in English professors than in other academics," charges literature professor Mark Krupnick. The postmodernist baby boomers have won, he says. "Now there are fewer clashes in the English departments because nearly everyone is a theorist or cultural-studies specialist."[41]

Nonetheless, some backlash has ensued. The Association of Literary Scholars (ALSC), what some would call a retrograde movement founded and dominated by older scholars, began forming in 1991, led by John M. Ellis, whose own *Against Deconstruction* is a sharp critique of Derrida's work, among others.[42] This organization is still active in its emphasis on

---

[40]What follows is a broad-stroke picture of recent literary theory. Details can be found in Roger Lundin, *The Culture of Interpretation* (Grand Rapids: Eerdmans, 1993). Bonny Klomp Stevens and Larry L. Stewart's survey designed to introduce graduate students to literary study is also helpful; see their *A Guide to Literary Criticism and Research*, 3rd ed. (New York: Harcourt Brace College, 1996). I have also found helpful critiques and countercritiques of postmodern literary theory in numerous articles in recent volumes of *The Christian Scholar's Review* and *Christianity and Literature*. See especially the survey of recent Christian approaches to literature and theory in Harold K. Bush Jr., "The Outrageous Idea of Christian Literary Study: Prospects for the Future and a Meditation on Hope," *Christianity and Literature*, Autumn 2001, pp. 79-103. The following books are especially helpful: Clarence Walhout and Leland Ryken, *Contemporary Literary Theory: A Christian Appraisal* (Grand Rapids: Eerdmans, 1991); and W. J. T. Mitchell, *Against Theory* (Chicago: University of Chicago Press, 1985).

[41]Mark Krupnick, "Why Are English Departments Still Fighting the Culture Wars?" *Chronicle of Higher Education*, September 20, 2002, p. B16.

[42]John M. Ellis, *Against Deconstruction* (Princeton, N.J.: Princeton University Press, 1989); Caleb Crain, "Inside the MLA: or, Is Literature Enough?" *Lingua Franca*, March 1999, pp.

the traditional study of literature as "literature," not as linguistics, politics or an instrument of social change. Ilan Stavans even harks back to Matthew Arnold, who defined literary criticism as "a disinterested endeavor to learn and propagate the best that is known and thought in the world."[43] Perhaps of even more interest is the automatic backlash that comes when postmodern scholars themselves are subjected to postmodern critique. Gender, political and psychological causes are now being found or speculated to account for their theories. The snake appears to be swallowing its own tail.[44]

Finally I note one rather bizarre twist. Daniel Barash and Nanelle Barash suggest a literary approach that is at once postmodern in that it is new (as far as I know) and retrograde—a return to scientific modernity. They suggest that the theory of biological evolution be the "organizing principle" of literary criticism. "Literature does not so much construct an arbitrary array of disconnected imaginings as it reflects the interaction (whether actual or imagined) of living organisms with the world in which they evolved and to which they are adapted."[45] Four years later, D. T. Max outlines the work of a small cadre of scholars devoted to literary Darwinism. Heartedly promoted by sociobiologist E. O. Wilson, they are developing a variety of mostly speculative hypotheses they hope may be confirmed by what they describe as a scientifically conducted analysis of literary texts.[46] Both traditional and postmodern scholars are highly dubious. But proponents such as Jonathan Gottschall are euphoric with expectation:

> If we literary scholars can summon the courage and humility to do so, the potential benefits will reverberate far beyond our field. We can generate more reliable and durable knowledge about art and culture. We can reawaken a long-dormant spirit of intellectual adventure. We can help spur a process whereby not just literature, but the larger field of the humanities

35-43.

[43]Ilan Stavans, "A Literary Critic's Journey to the Culture at Large," *Chronicle of Higher Education,* August 9, 2003, p. B7.

[44]Morris Dickstein, "Literary Theory and Historical Understanding," *Chronicle of Higher Education,* May 23, 2003, pp. B7-10.

[45]David P. Barash and Nanelle Barash, "Biology as a Lens: Evolution and Literary Criticism," *Chronicle of Higher Education,* October 2002, pp. B7-9.

[46]D. T. Max, "The Literary Darwinists," *The New York Times Magazine,* November 6, 2006 <www.nytimes.com/2005/11/06/magazine>; Britt Peterson, in "Darwin to the Rescue," *The Chronicle Review,* August 1, 2008, p. B 7-9, surveys further work of literary Darwinists.

recover some of the intellectual momentum and "market share" they have lost to the sciences. And we can rejoin the oldest, and still the premier, quest of all the disciplines: to better understand human nature.[47]

In any case, as literary study has in general backed off from some of its wilder irrational theorizing, there are hundreds of graduate students of English literature who have been schooled in these once cutting-edge theories and have brought them into the undergraduate classroom. Even if fifteen years ago there was a discernible backlash, these approaches will have a long-term effect.[48] Moreover, Jeffrey J. Williams has recently detected a return to interest in postmodern literary theory of thirty years ago. Today's literary theory, he says, is in a "holding pattern"; it is an "eclectic mix" that is "memorializing the past."[49]

The cutting edge is of course always moving. Postmodern core commitments are ephemeral. Today's hot intellectual ploy is tomorrow's forgotten foolishness. And what's next is up for grabs. For one thing the whole postmodern movement may be in trouble. As we shall see, its internal contradictions are almost as rife as those in New Age thought. But then, if history proceeded from one good reason to the next better reason, the story told in this book, let alone this chapter, would be different. We can, however, see why much of postmodernism may not be with us for the long haul.

THE PANORAMIC SWEEP OF POSTMODERNISM

The effects of postmodern perspectives can be seen almost everywhere in Western culture. I have already mentioned literary study. We will look briefly now at history, science and theology.[50]

In the discipline of history, for example, the pastness of the past disappears in the mists of the present moment. Historians are moving from a

---

[47]Jonathan Gottschall, "Measure for Measure," *The Boston Globe*, May 11, 2008.

[48]Karen J. Winkler surveys the lash and backlash of postmodern literary theory in "Scholars
Mark the Beginning of the Age of 'Post-theory,'" *Chronicle of Higher Education*, October 13,
1993, p. A9. See also Frank Lentricchia, "Last Will and Testament of an Ex-Literary Critic,"
Lingua Franca, September/October 1996, pp. 59-67.

[49]Jeffrey J. Williams, "Why Today's Publishing World Is Reprising the Past," *The Chronicle
Review* in *The Chronicle of Higher Education*, June 13, 2008, pp. B8-10.

[50]In *The Death of Truth* (Minneapolis: Bethany House, 1996), Dennis McCallum has collected
a series of critical essays on postmodernism in healthcare, literature, education, history, psychotherapy, law, science and religion, each written by an expert in the field.

modern historicism (the notion that the meaning of events is to be found in their historical context) to a postmodern "denial of the fixity of the past, of the reality of the past apart from what the historian chooses to make of it, and thus any objective truth about the past."[51] The postmodern historian does not use imagination to re-create for readers a sense of the past itself but creates "a past in the image of the present and in accord with the judgment of the historian."[52] The move away from using footnotes in scholarly writing only exacerbates the situation.[53] Who can check the historian's judgment?

With postmodern historian Keith Jenkins, history becomes a hall of mirrors: "In the post-modern world, then, arguably the content and context of history should be a generous series of methodologically reflexive

---

History is a shifting problematic discourse, ostensibly about an aspect of the world, the past, that is produced by a group of present-minded workers (overwhelmingly in our culture salaried historians) who go about their work in mutually recognizable ways that are epistemologically, methodologically, ideologically and practically positioned and whose products once in circulation, are subject to a series of uses and abuses that are logically infinite but which in actuality generally correspond to a range of power bases that exist at any given moment and which structure and distribute the meanings of histories along a dominant-marginal spectrum.

KEITH JENKINS, *Re-thinking History*

---

studies of the makings of the histories of post-modernity itself."[54] History becomes reflection on histories of reflection.

---

[51]Gertrude Himmelfarb, "Tradition and Creativity in the Writing of History," *First Things*, November 1992, p. 28. Himmelfarb's essay, which ranges over history, law, philosophy and culture in general, deserves reading in its entirety (pp. 28-36).

[52]Ibid., p. 30.

[53]Gertrude Himmelfarb, "Where Have All the Footnotes Gone?" in *On Looking into the Abyss* (New York: Alfred A. Knopf, 1994).

[54]Keith Jenkins, *Re-thinking History* (London: Routledge, 1991), p. 70 (the last sentence in the book). For a plea for pulling back from postmodern historiography, see Jeffrey N. Westerstrom, "Are You Now or Have You Ever Been . . . Postmodern?" *Chronicle of Higher Education*, September 11, 1998, p. B4.

Postmodernism has made little impact on science itself—either on how it is conducted or on how it is understood by most scientists. Nonetheless, postmodernism has begun to rewrite our understanding of what science is despite what scientists do or say. Most scientists, whether naturalists or Christian theists, are critical realists. They believe that there is a world external to themselves and that the findings of science describe what the world is like more or less accurately. Accuracy increases as scientific study progresses or it discovers a better paradigm to organize and interpret the data. Postmodernists are antirealists; they deny that there is any known or knowable connection between what we think and say with what is actually there.[55]

Scientific truth is the language we use to get us what we want. "There is no other proof that the rules [of scientific practice] are good than the consensus extended to them by the experts," wrote Lyotard.[56] Science is what the scientists say it is.[57] To which one scientist wag has replied, "Just step outside that ten-story window and say that again." But this is to misunderstand the postmodern theorists. They are not saying that no physical world exists; they are rather giving a "report" on the status and nature of scientific claims to knowledge in light of the impossibility of directly accessing reality with our epistemic equipment. The world does not speak to us. Our minds do not access the essences that make reality determinate, the essences that make wood wood and metal metal. We speak to the world. We say "wood" or "metal" and put these words in sentences that often get us what we want. When they don't, we say that these sentences are false. We should rather say that they don't work.

Much postmodern writing about science has been couched in highly obscure language. This has both frustrated practicing scientists and bamboozled the editors of at least one postmodern journal. Alan Sokal, a physicist at New York University, submitted an article titled "Transgressing the Boundaries: Toward a Transformative Hermeneutics of Quantum

---

[55]For a survey of these issues in the philosophy of science, see Del Ratzsch, *Philosophy of Science* (Downers Grove, Ill.: InterVarsity Press, 1986).

[56]Lyotard, *Postmodern Condition*, p. 29.

[57]In a statement guaranteed to enrage traditional scientists and philosophers, literary critic Terry Eagleton wrote, "Science and philosophy must jettison their grandiose metaphysical claims and view themselves more modestly as just another set of narratives" (quoted from "Awakening Modernity," *Times Literary Supplement*, February 20, 1987, by Alister McGrath, *A Passion for Truth* [Downers Grove, Ill.: InterVarsity Press, 1996], p. 187).

Gravity" to the journal *Social Text.*[58] The editors, not noticing that the article was riddled with inanities from the standpoints of both physics and sociology, accepted it for publication. Sokal then announced in *Lingua Franca* that the article was a hoax, written to expose the absurdity of much postmodern cultural analysis in general and science in particular. Claiming himself to be on the "left" socially, he said that he was only trying to keep cultural studies from obscurantism and overweening ambition. The joy the hoax incited among modern-minded scientists and the furor it caused among the editors and their intellectual friends points up the personal stake today's social critics and their subjects have in postmodern approaches to science. The whole affair merited a further comment in Sokal and Bricmont's *Fashionable Nonsense: Postmodern Intellectual's Abuse of Science* and *The Sokal Hoax,* a collection of comments by both American and foreign scholars and pundits, edited by the editors of *Lingua Franca.*

The postmodern sociologists might, however, get at least an echoing giggle. Two French scientists without Ph.D. credentials slipped a pseudo-scientific, jargon-laden paper past the professional referees of a scientific journal. Whether their discussion of the singularity at the heart of the big bang was intended as a hoax or just bad, presumptuous science is not clear. But it did show that nonsense can get past the intellectual guards posted at the gates of journals of both the natural and the human sciences.[59]

The reactions of theologians to postmodernism have run the gamut. Some accept its central claims and write not theologies but a/theologies

---

[58]The original article appeared in *Social Text,* Spring/Summer 1996, pp. 217-52; Sokal's revelation of the hoax was "A Physicist Experiments with Cultural Studies," *Lingua Franca,* May/June 1996, pp. 62-64; Sokal's "afterword" giving "his own account of the political significance of the debate," which was sent to *Social Text* at the same time as his article in *Lingua Franca* but rejected by the editors, was published as "Transgressing the Boundaries: An Afterword," *Dissent,* Fall 1996, pp. 93-97. The story of this hoax was widely broadcast in journals in the summer of 1996. See, for example, "Mystery Science Theater," *Lingua Franca,* July/August 1996, pp. 54-64; Bruce V. Lewenstein, "Science and Society: The Continuing Value of Reasoned Debate," *Chronicle of Higher Education,* June 21, 1996, pp. B1-2; Liz McMillan, "The Science Wars," *Chronicle of Higher Education,* June 28, 1996, pp. A8-9, 13; Steven Weinberg, "Sokal's Hoax," *New York Review of Books,* August 8, 1996, pp. 11-15; "Sokal's Hoax: An Exchange," *New York Review of Books,* October 3, 1996, pp. 54-56; "Footnotes," *Chronicle of Higher Education,* November 22, 1996, p. A8. See as well Alan Sokal and Jean Bricmont, *Fashionable Nonsense: Postmodern Intellectuals' Abuse of Science* (New York: Picador, 1998), and *The Sokal Hoax: The Sham That Shocked the Academy,* ed. the editors of *Lingua Franca* (Lincoln: University of Nebraska Press, 2000).

[59]Richard Monastersky, "The Emperor's New Science: French TV Stars Rock the World of Theoretical Physics," *Chronicle of Higher Education,* November 15, 2002, pp. A16-18.

(neither theologies nor nontheologies but theologies that stem from the interstice between the two). Don't try to understand that without reading Mark C. Taylor.[60] Other theologians accept the postmodern critique of modernism, see much contemporary Christian theology as being too "modern" and attempt to recast theology. Among these are postliberals who revise the notion of what theology is and can do (George Lindbeck), those who see in the postmodern emphasis on story a chance for the Christian story to get a hearing (Diogenes Allen), and evangelicals who revision evangelical theology (Stanley Grenz, John Franke, Merold Westphal and James K. A. Smith) or who emphasize the narrative nature of theology (Richard Middleton and Brian Walsh).[61] Still others reject the entire postmodern program and call for a return to Scripture and the early church (Thomas Oden) or to a Reformation program that continues to value human reason (Carl F. H. Henry, David F. Wells and Gene Edward Veith Jr.).[62]

In evangelical circles postmodernism continues to prove controver-

---

[60]Mark C. Taylor, *Erring: A Postmodern A/theology* (Chicago: University of Chicago Press, 1984). Here's a taste of Taylor: "Ideas are never fixed but are always in transition; thus they are irrepressibly transitory. . . . The words of a/theology fall in between; they are *always* in the middle [between the beginning and the end]. The a/theological text is a tissue woven of threads that are produced by endless spinning" (p. 13). Taylor has since branched out from theology to cybernetics; see his profile in "From Kant to Las Vegas to Cyberspace: A Philosopher on the Edge of Postmodernism," *Chronicle of Higher Education*, May 29, 1998, pp. A16-17.

[61]A collection of essays on this topic by some of the theologians mentioned here plus others is Timothy R. Phillips and Dennis L. Okholm, eds., *The Nature of Confession* (Downers Grove, Ill.: InterVarsity Press, 1996). See also George A. Lindbeck, *The Nature of Doctrine* (Philadelphia: Westminster Press, 1984); Diogenes Allen, *Christian Belief in a Postmodern World* (Louisville, Ky.: Westminster John Knox, 1989); Stanley Grenz, *Revisioning Evangelical Theology* (Downers Grove, Ill.: InterVarsity Press, 1993), and *Renewing the Center*, 2nd ed. (Grand Rapids: Baker, 2006); Stanley Grenz and John Franke, *Beyond Foundationalism: Shaping Theology in a Postmodern Context* (Louisville, Ky.: Westminster John Knox Press, 2001); Merold Westphal, *Overcoming Onto-theology: Toward a Postmodern Christian Faith* (New York: Fordam University Press, 2001); James K. A. Smith: *Who's Afraid of Postmodernism? Taking Derrida, Lyotard, and Foucault to Church* (Grand Rapids: Baker, 2006); and J. Richard Middleton and Brian J. Walsh, *Truth Is Stranger Than It Used to Be* (Downers Grove, Ill.: InterVarsity Press, 1995).

[62]Thomas C. Oden, *After Modernity . . . What?* (Grand Rapids: Zondervan, 1990); Carl F. H. Henry, "Truth: Dead on Arrival," *World*, May 20-27, 1995, p. 25; David F. Wells, *God in the Wasteland* (Grand Rapids: Eerdmans, 1994); and Gene Edward Veith Jr., *Postmodern Times* (Wheaton, Ill.: Crossway, 1994). Oden uses the term *postmodern* to describe his own approach, but he does so because he takes what I have been calling *postmodern* not to be "post" modern but ultramodern. What he recommends for the church today actually does, he believes, go beyond the modern and so can legitimately be called *postmodern*.

sial.[63] Some younger scholars such as Robert Greer have surveyed the Christian options and call for a recognition of the true insights of post-modernism and a fresh approach he calls "post-postmodernism."[64] Older scholars such as Merold Westphal and Douglas Groothuis disagree over what postmoderns like Lyotard are saying, sometimes, so it seems, talking past one another in their dialogue. While both affirm the central teachings of the Christian faith, they take remarkably different views on how much the mind is able to accurately know what is true about God, humans and the universe.[65] It is clear that the last word on postmodernism and theology has yet to be written.

POSTMODERNISM: A CRITIQUE

I will start my critique by pointing out some aspects of the postmodern perspective that seem true, not just useful, and continue with more critical remarks.

First, postmodernism's critique of optimistic naturalism is often on target. Too much confidence has been placed in human reason and the scientific method. Descartes's attempt to find complete intellectual certitude was fatal. As a Christian he might well have been satisfied with a confidence based on the existence of a good God who made us in his image and wants us to know. He should not have expected to be certain apart from the givenness of God. Subsequent intellectual history should be a lesson to all who wish to replace the God who declares "I AM THAT I AM" with individual self-certitude. There is a mystery to both being and knowing that the human mind cannot penetrate.

Second, the postmodern recognition that language is closely associated with power is also apt. We do tell "stories," believe "doctrines," hold "philosophies" because they give us or our community power over others. The public application of our definitions of madness does put people in mental health wards. Indeed, we should suspect our own motives for be-

---

[63]See Charlotte Allen's somewhat sensational "Is Deconstruction the Last Best Hope of Evangelical Christians?" *Lingua Franca*, January 2000, pp. 47-59.

[64]Robert Greer, *Mapping Postmodernism: A Survey of Christian Options* (Downers Grove, Ill.: InterVarsity Press, 2003).

[65]See Merold Westphal, "Blind Spots: Christianity and Postmodern Philosophy," *Christian Century*, June 14, 2003, pp. 32-35; Douglas Groothuis, "Modern Fallacies: Response to Merold Westphal," and Merold Westphal, "Merold Westphal Replies," *Christian Century*, July 26, 2003, pp. 41-42. See also Douglas Groothuis, *Truth Decay: Defending Christianity Against the Challenges of Postmodernity* (Downers Grove, Ill.: InterVarsity Press, 2000).

lieving what we do, using the language that we do, telling the stories that inform our lives. We may just as well suspect the motives of others.

If, however, we adopt the radical form this suspicion takes in Foucault, we will end up in a contradiction or, at least, an anomaly. If we hold that all linguistic utterances are power plays, then that utterance itself is a power play and no more likely to be proper than any other. It prejudices all discourse. If all discourse is equally prejudiced, there is no reason to use one rather than another. This makes for moral and intellectual anarchy. Moreover, Foucault's prime value—personal freedom to intensify pleasure—is belied by his reduction of all values to power itself. The truth

---

Truth isn't outside power . . . it's produced by virtue of multiple forms of constraint. . . . Each society has . . . its "general politics" of truth: that is, the types of discourse which it accepts and makes function as true; the mechanisms and instances which enable one to distinguish true and false statements, the means by which it is sanctioned; the techniques and procedures accorded value in the acquisition of truth; the status of those who are charged with saying what counts as true.

. . . By truth I do not mean "the ensemble of truths which are to be discovered and accepted" but rather "the ensemble of rules according to which the true and the false are separated and specific effects of power attached to the true," it being understood also that it is not a matter . . . "on behalf" of the truth, but of a battle about the status of truth and the economic and political role it plays.

"Truth" is to be understood as a system of ordered procedures for the production, regulation, distribution, circulation and operations of statements. "Truth" is indeed linked . . . with systems of power which produce and sustain it. . . . A "regime" of truth.

MICHEL FOUCAULT, *Power/Knowledge**

*The passage is abridged and quoted in Keith Jenkins, *Re-thinking History* (London: Routledge, 1991), pp. 31-32.

---

question cannot be avoided. Is it true, for example, that *all* discourse is a masked power play? If we say no, then we can examine with care where power is an undue factor. If we say yes, then there is one sentence that makes sense only if it is seen not as a power play. A radical postmodernism that says yes is self-refuting.[66]

Third, attention to the social conditions under which we understand the world can alert us to our limited perspective as finite human beings. Society does mold us in many ways. But if we are only the product of the blind forces of nature and society, then so is our view that we are only the product of the blind forces of nature and society. A radical sociology of knowledge is also self-refuting.

Nonetheless, though often flawed in its approach, postmodernism does make several positive contributions to our understanding of reality. I turn now to more critical comments.

First, the rejection of all metanarratives is itself a metanarrative. The idea that there are no metanarratives is taken as a first principle, and there is no way to get around this except to ignore the self-contradiction and get on with the show, which is what postmodernism does.

Second, the idea that we have no access to reality (that there are no facts, no truths-of-the-matter) and that we can only tell stories about it is self-referentially incoherent. Put crudely, this idea cannot account for itself, for it tells us something that, on its own account, we can't know. Charles Taylor puts the matter more carefully in his analysis of Richard Rorty:

> Rorty offers a great leap into non-realism: where there have hitherto been thought to be facts or truths-of-the-matter, there turn out to be only rival languages between which we end up plumping, if we do, because in some way one works better for us than the others. . . .
>
> But to believe something is to hold it true; and, indeed, one cannot consciously manipulate one's beliefs for motives other than their seeming to be true to us.[67]

Likewise, when Nietzsche says "truth is a mobile army of metaphors" or conventional "lies," he is making a charge that implicitly claims to be true but on its own account cannot be.[68]

---

[66]McGrath comments, "Postmodernism thus denies in fact what it affirms in theory. Even the casual question 'Is postmodernism true?' innocently raises fundamental criteriological questions which postmodernism finds embarrassingly difficult to handle" (*Passion for Truth*, p. 195).

[67]Charles Taylor, "Rorty in the Epistemological Tradition," in *Reading Rorty*, ed. Alan R. Malachowski (Oxford: Blackwell, 1990), p. 258.

[68]Nietzsche, "On Truth and Lie," pp. 46-47. Bernard Williams's comment about Rorty could

Third, as Lilla points out, deconstructive postmodernism's view of the indeterminacy of language (a text can be read in a variety of ways, some contradictory) raises a question: "How then are we to understand the deconstructionist's own propositions? As more than one critic has pointed out, there is an unresolvable paradox in using language to claim that language cannot make unambiguous claims."[69]

Fourth, postmodernism's critique of the autonomy and sufficiency of human reason rests on the autonomy and sufficiency of human reason. What is it that leads Nietzsche to doubt the validity of Descartes's "I think, therefore I am"? That is, what leads him to doubt that the *I* is an agent that causes thought? Answer: Nietzsche's thought. What if Nietzsche's thinking is not produced by Nietzsche, if it is merely the activity of thought? Then Nietzsche's *I* is being constructed by language. There isn't any Nietzsche accessible to Nietzsche or us. In fact, there is no substantial us. There is only the flow of linguistic constructs that construct us. But if there are only linguistic constructs, then there is no reason we should be constructed one way rather than another and no reason to think that the current flow of language that constructs us has any relationship to what is so. The upshot is that we are boxed into subjective awareness consisting of an ongoing set of language games.

SPIRITUALITY IN A POSTMODERN WORLD

It is true, as we have seen, that some people seem to get along well with the notion that there is no God. Bertrand Russell, Carl Sagan and Kai Nielsen are cases in point.[70] Others have more difficulty. Nietzsche replaces God with himself. Václav Havel attributes to Being a character

---

serve as well for Nietzsche: "Sometimes he [Rorty and, I would add, Nietzsche] seems quite knowing about the status of his own thoughts. . . . At other times, he seems to forget altogether about one requirement of self-consciousness, and like the old philosophies he is attempting to escape, naively treats his own discourse as standing quite outside the general philosophical situation he is describing. He thus neglects the question whether one could accept his account of various intellectual activities, and still continue to practice them" ("Auto-da-Fé: Consequences of Pragmatism," in *Reading Rorty*, ed. Alan R. Malachowski [Oxford: Blackwell, 1990], p. 29). For an extensive, sophisticated critique of postmodern epistemology, see Alvin I. Goldman, *Knowledge in a Social World* (Oxford: Oxford University Press, 1999), pp. 3-100.

[69]Lilla, "Politics of Jacques Derrida," p. 38.

[70]See Bertrand Russell, "A Free Man's Worship" <www.philosophicalsociety.com/Archives/A Free Man's worship.htm>; Carl Sagan, *Cosmos* (New York: Random House, 1980), p. 8, n. 9; Kai Nielsen, *Ethics Without God*, rev. ed. (Buffalo, N.Y.: Prometheus, 1900).

that presents itself in theistic terms but is not really a personal God.[71] Postmodern scholar Ihab Hassan briefly encourages a vague spirituality. "This I know," he pleads, "without spirit the sense of cosmic wonder, of being and morality at the widest edge, which we all share, existence quickly reduces to mere survival."[72] Science writer John Horgan surveys the possible connection between science and spirituality, concluding rather vaguely that mystical experience bestows on us a great gift:

> To see—really see—all that is right with the world. Just as believers in a beneficent deity should be haunted by the problem of natural evil, so Gnostics, atheists, pessimists, and nihilists should be haunted by the problem of friendship, love, beauty, truth, humor, compassion, fun.[73]

How atheists and nihilists are to be so haunted, he does not say.

Still, the predominant stance of recent naturalists is humanistic to the core. Somehow after the death of God we will muddle through. At the end of his massive book *The Modern Mind,* Peter Watson looks to a chastened postmodernism, a chastened science and a chastened Western humanism to provide a way from cultural anarchy to societies in which all can find meaning and significance.[74] He cites both philosopher Bryan Magee and sociobiologist E. O. Wilson. For Magee no justification by God or reason is required for a moral stance or belief in human decency. We can just act as we intuitively know we should.[75] For Wilson, future science pursuing its current course will blend with humanistic studies and the arts in a "consilience" that will support human values and aspirations. Wilson believes that discovering the material causes for our sense of morality will provide a sufficient justification for acting as we should. Actually, despite his disclaimer, he has committed the naturalistic fallacy of deriving *ought* from *is.* Few have found his materialistic reductionism convincing.[76]

[71]Václav Havel, *Letters to Olga: June 1979-September 1982,* trans. Paul Wilson (New York: Henry Holt, 1989), pp. 331, 346, 358-59; see also James W. Sire, *Václav Havel: Intellectual Conscience of International Politics* (Downers Grove, Ill.: InterVarsity Press, 2001), pp. 55-59.
[72]Hassan, "Postmodernism to Postmodernity," final paragraph.
[73]John Horgan, "Between Science and Spirituality," *Chronicle of Higher Education,* November 29, 2002, p. B9.
[74]Peter Watson, *The Modern Mind: An Intellectual History of the Twentieth Century* (New York: Perennial, 2001), pp. 767-72.
[75]Bryan Magee, *Confessions of a Philosopher* (London: Phoenix, 1977), pp. 590-92.
[76]E. O. Wilson, *Consilience: The Unity of Knowledge* (New York: Alfred A. Knopf, 1998), esp.

Finally, Alan Sokal and Jean Bricmont consider three possible out-
comes to the challenge to postmodernism. First is "a backlash leading to
some form of dogmatism, mysticism (e.g. New Age), or religious fundamentalism." Second is "that intellectuals will become reluctant (at least
for a decade or two) to attempt any thoroughgoing critique of the existing
societal order." Third is "the emergence of a culture that would be rationalistic but not dogmatic, open-minded but not frivolous, and politically
progressive but not sectarian." But Sokal and Bricmont are realistic. They
add that "this is only a hope, and perhaps only a dream."[77] And a dream it
most probably is. Where in scientific rationalism is there a foundation for
such hope?

In any case, the challenge of the death of God, the death of reason, the
death of truth and the death of the self—all dominant in current postmodernism—is likely to be with us for a very long time. Thinking people
of every age refuse to stop wondering about what is really real and how
we can know. If we are only material beings, a product of unintentional,
uncaring sources, why do we think we can know anything at all? And
why do we think we should be good?

If postmodernism has not taken us beyond naturalism but rather has
enmeshed us in a web of utter uncertainty, why should we think it describes us as we really are? Is there a way beyond postmodernism?

BEYOND POSTMODERNISM

Postmodernism is, of course, not a full-blown worldview. But it is such a
pervasive perspective that it has modified several worldviews, most notably naturalism. In fact, the best way to think about most of postmodernism is to see it as the most recent phase of the "modern," the most recent
form of naturalism. In postmodernism the essence of modernism has not
been left behind. Both rest on two key notions: (1) that the cosmos is all
there is—no God of any kind exists—and (2) the autonomy of human
reason. Of course 2 follows from 1. If there is no God, then human beings, whatever else they are, are the only "persons" in the cosmos; they
have the only rational minds for which there is any evidence. We are
therefore on our own. The first moderns were optimistic; the most recent

pp. 238-65. See, for example, the responses of postmodernist Richard Rorty and biologist
Paul R. Gross in "Is Everything Relative?" *Wilson Quarterly*, Winter 1998, pp. 14-49.
[77]Sokal and Bricmont, *Fashionable Nonsense*, p. 211.

ones are not. The distinctions between the early and late moderns are certainly important enough not just to note but to signal the latter with a term like *postmodern*.

Postmodernism pulls the smiling mask of arrogance from the face of naturalism. The face behind the mask displays an ever-shifting countenance: there is the anguish of Nietzsche railing against the herd mentality of the mass of humanity, the ecstatic joy of Nietzsche willing into being the Overman, the leering visage of Foucault seeking the intensification of sexual experience, the comic grin of Derrida as he deconstructs all discourse including his own, and the play of irony around the lips of Rorty as he plumps for a foundationless solidarity. But no face displays a confidence in truth, a trust in reality or a credible hope for the future.

If our culture is to move toward a hopeful future, it will first have to move back to a more realistic past, pick up from where we began to go wrong, take into account the valuable insights derived from what has happened since and forge a more adequate worldview.[78]

One worldview has been on center stage in the Middle East, North Africa and Southeast Asia for centuries. But its presence as an intellectual and social challenge to the modern Western world has been minimal—until recently. But the event called 9/11, the date in 2001 when terrorists flew commercial airline planes into the World Trade Center in New York, has changed all that. Islam has now come to front and center stage in the West as well. Its worldview can no longer be ignored.

---

[78] I end this chapter on a cryptic note. It is not my intention now or later to contribute much to what I have briefly envisioned. Others (see those mentioned in footnotes 61-62 above) are working on this, and I will leave the task to them and their colleagues.

Chapter 10

A VIEW FROM THE MIDDLE EAST
by Winfried Corduan, Ph.D.

ISLAMIC THEISM

*There is no God but Allah
and Muhammad is the Prophet of God.*

MUSLIM DECLARATION OF FAITH

Events of the past thirty years have brought on stage in North America and Europe a worldview that to that point had been very much alive and well from North Africa across the globe east to Indonesia, but had been treated as only a quaint aberration in contrast to the "real" struggle between Communism and capitalism. Though the Western world had never been able to ignore it in foreign policy, the general populace even in Europe could largely discount its contribution to modern thought. In the Middle Ages, of course, its scholars had contributed to Western thought by preserving, commenting on and advancing the philosophical thought of the ancient Greeks. But this intellectual influence on Europe and subsequently on the New World largely disappeared by the seventeenth century. Politically, of course, the Middle East posed a continued challenge to the West, but it did not seriously threaten the Western worldviews of Christianity, deism, naturalism and existentialism. However, in 1979 radical Muslims in Iran took over the American embassy, followed shortly by skirmishes with other Muslims in Lebanon and Libya. Then as the twenty-first century was just dawning, two commercial planes flown by Middle-Eastern terrorists crashed into the World Trade Center in New York. The worldview of Islam could no longer be ignored.

There has indeed been renewed interest in Islam, both in general and in particular with regard to specific groups, such as the Taliban and Al-Qaeda. Unfortunately, popular descriptions of Islam are frequently driven by polemics, and one may find many conflicting descriptions of the religion and the worldview it entails. Thus, it is important to provide a careful discussion of Islamic theism.

To do so, however, brings up an obvious question: Since theism has already been treated in this book, does it really make sense to retread the same material again? The answer to that question would be a clear "no" if all forms of theism were alike and if we would simply be repeating the identical information. But there are no *generic* worldviews, and there is no such thing as *generic* theism in real life. Nobody holds to "just theism," or, for that matter, to any other worldview without bringing in matters of heritage and environment. Worldviews always occur in a specific context and are susceptible to various forms of expression depending on the culture of origin and the culture in which they are practiced. Consequently, it should be no surprise that there are important differences between Christian theism and Islamic theism.

A Christian writer undertaking this description can easily err by going in one of two directions. One is to point to the differences between Christian theism and Islamic theism with the implicit agenda of demonstrating that in all such cases simply being different from Christianity is a flaw in Islam. Such an inference is unwarranted, even for a committed Christian, since not all points of difference are issues of truth and falsehood. The other direction into which one can stray is to make Islam look more like Christianity than it actually is, maybe by overemphasizing superficial commonalities or perhaps by letting a minority group stand for the broader consensus. Ultimately, that attitude reveals the same prejudice, namely that the worth of Islam as a religion is dependent on its similarity to Christianity. On the other hand, if Islamic theism turns out to entail a difficulty that would be resolved by Christian theism, it appears to me to be legitimate to point out the Christian version as a potential resolution.

I will attempt to let Islam speak for itself as much as possible by holding myself to the teachings of the Qur'an and Hadith. Where there are differences among various Islamic groups, I will make my best attempt to represent what I take to be the more widely held interpretation and, if that's not realistic, give some priority to the more literal reading of the Qur'an. If doing so seems to be a limitation, let me point out why it is actually an asset. Since the Islamic groups that have dominated the news, and about whom we are curious, are also among the more conservative ones, by using this approach we may actually receive a clearer picture of their worldview than if we gave all factions equal coverage.[1]

BASIC ISLAMIC THEISM

1. Worldview Question 1: *The fundamental reality of Islam is God (Allah), described as monotheistic, infinite, personal, transcendent, immanent, omniscient, sovereign and good. Of these attributes Islam emphasizes his oneness, transcendence and sovereignty. There has been debate as to what extent the Qur'an should be included in the category of fundamental reality.*

The word *Allah* is simply the Arabic word for "God" or, to be completely literal, a contraction of *al-ilāh, the* God.[2] It is technically not a proper name, but it is used generically, just as "God" is in English. Normally, when Christians or others refer to the God of the Bible in Arabic, the best option is to use the word *Allah*. Consequently, by itself, to say that the fundamental reality in the Islamic version of theism is Allah is not to say anything distinctive about its theism. We need to look closer at the descriptions of Allah to see if there is any difference between

---

[1]More technically, there are four schools of Islamic law *(shari'a)*, of which the most conservative is the Hanbalite school, named after its founder Ibn-Hanbal, who lived around A.D.800. About a hundred years after his death, his approach was pushed to the forefront by Abu al-Hasan al-Ash'ari, whose followers are known as Ash'arites. This conservative strain was revived in Saudi Arabia in the eighteenth century by the very strict reformer Muhammad Ibn Abd al-Wahhab. Wahhabite Islam became the only acceptable school of Islam in Saudi Arabia and eventually gave birth to the Taliban in Afghanistan. To some extent, it also stands in the background of Al-Qaeda because its leader, Osama bin Laden has personal roots in Wahhabism. Since I am taking an intentionally conservative approach in my account, it will mirror the Hanbalite and Ash'arite beliefs most closely. But it is precisely this conservative form of Islam that has been held by the groups creating the most interest of late, so we can hardly go wrong if our description of the teachings of the Qur'an sheds light on their understanding of the religion.
[2]Frederick Mathewson Denny, *An Introduction to Islam*, 2nd ed. (New York: Macmillan, 1994), p. 387.

Christian theism and Islamic theism in this regard.[3]

Now, to approach the study of Allah and Islam on a comparative basis is not to do it an injustice. A great amount of the content of the Qur'an consists of demonstrating that Islam is better than any other religion, and that God, as portrayed in Islam, is greater than any other deity that human beings may have imagined. Islam arose in the context of rivalry. Muhammad was proclaiming monotheism as he understood it against the polytheism that dominated Mecca in his day, the monotheism of Judaism, which he considered to be hypocritical, and the trinitarian monotheism of Christianity, which he censured as both idolatrous and absurd. Islam did not so much define itself internally as externally against the other existing options.

> O People of the Book! Commit no excesses in your religion: Nor say of God aught but the truth. Christ Jesus the son of Mary was (no more than) an apostle of God, and His Word, which He bestowed on Mary, and a spirit proceeding from Him: so believe in God and His apostles. Say not "Trinity": desist: it will be better for you: for God is one God: Glory be to Him: (far exalted is He) above having a son. To Him belong all things in the heavens and on earth. And enough is God as a Disposer of affairs. (4:171)[4]

The comparative impulse in Islam comes out in one of the most well-known phrases associated with Islam: *Allahu akbar.* It is a part of the call to prayer repeated five times a day, and faithful believers may use it as an

---

[3]I shall use *God* and *Allah* interchangeably, partly for the sake of variety in style (if I were to write extensively on the biblical God I would use such synonyms as *the Lord* or *Yahweh*) and partly to keep us alert to the fact that there are both similarities and differences between Christian theism and Islamic theism.

[4]All quotations from the Qur'an come from the translation by Yusuf Ali, which is now available in many editions as well as in multiple locations on the Internet. Islam holds that the Qur'an is only the Qur'an in its original Arabic form because any translation must interpret, and to interpret is potentially to distort. There is much debate as to which translation/interpretation is more accurate than others. Yusuf Ali's version has come in for some criticism, but it continues to be the one that is handed out by mosques and Islamic centers to visitors, and thus it is a fair inference that it must be accurate enough to represent their faith. Furthermore, Yusuf Ali was a devout Muslim, whose study notes reflect a commonly accepted conservative approach, and it can thus be trusted to represent a sound Islamic view in its phrasing and teachings.

However, one must be aware of Yusuf Ali's manner of translation. When moving from one language to another, sometimes a single word needs to be translated by several words, or a short phrase by a longer one. Usually translators just make these adjustments automatically and expect readers to be aware of such things. Yusuf Ali puts such words or phrases in parentheses, even though they are clearly an integral part of the meaning conveyed. Furthermore, his use of capitalization is somewhat unusual.

exclamation in response to anything out of the ordinary, whether good or
ill. It is usually translated simply as "God is great." What is notable about
this expression is that *akbar* does not actually mean "great" in the
straightforward sense. "Great" by itself would simply be *kabir*. In order to
get closer to its meaning, one has to translate it as either "greater" (the
comparative degree) or "the greatest" (the superlative degree).

But even those two options do not do complete justice to the way that
akbar is used in this context. After all, something can be greater without
being greatest, and language allows that there could be two or more beings that share a superlative, such as two greatest beings. To use a simple
English illustration, George may run faster than Fred (comparative), but
that doesn't mean that he is the fastest runner (superlative), and if both
Michael and Stephen share the record, they are both the fastest runners,
and therefore they both partake of the superlative. In Arabic there is another grammatical form, called the *elative*, which, as used in this context[5], that is, as applied to Allah, raises the degree of an adjective above
all other applications. Thus, *Allahu akbar* actually implies "God is greater
than all others," or "God is the one and only supreme being." We see,
then, that at the very foundation of Islam is the conviction that Allah's
greatness is understood by way of contrast to all other inferior beings.

This mindset makes itself felt wherever Islam presents itself. In the
Qur'an there are very few places where the praise of Allah is not immediately connected to statements simultaneously condemning either false
views of God or the people who hold them. Certainly insofar as the scriptures of other religions show awareness of other faiths, they, too, are likely
to make contrasts, but they do not do so as constantly as the Qur'an does.

The unequaled greatness of Allah becomes the linchpin of all further
considerations of his nature. Anything that could conceivably be con-
strued as detracting from his greatness must be considered to be false, or
even offensive. The worst sin in Islam is *shirk*, which is commonly translated as "idolatry," but literally means "association" and thus implies far
more than the common understanding of idolatry, such as worshiping
statues of deities. *Shirk* means to conjoin Allah with any of his creatures,
to ascribe a partner to him, or to understand him to possess limitations

---

[5]Please note that, strictly grammatically, in other settings the elative may carry no more force
than the comparative or superlative degrees, but that, on this point at least, it includes the
exclusivist meaning.

that are characteristic of his creatures but not of him.

Not only does this prohibition rule out notions such as an incarnation or any direct revelation of God himself in any humanly apprehensible form, but it also means that whatever attributes God has revealed about himself cannot be measured by human standards. For example, Allah is just, but if we come up with a definition of justice and then think that, therefore, we can understand what it means for Allah to be just, we are overstepping the bounds of what is allowable. Similarly, Allah is merciful, gracious and forgiving, but knowing these truths about Allah does not give us any warrant for drawing implications concerning how he should be expected to act toward any specific person. Allah is not unknowable, but it would be presumptuous for us to infer from his attributes specifically how he would manifest them in any particular cases.

An integral part of any theism is that God is both transcendent (beyond the world) and immanent (present and active within the world). In the case of Islamic theism, God's transcendence far outweighs his immanence. Any notion of a possible relationship with Allah must respect this boundary. God and a human person can never meet on the same plane. In the (perhaps slightly overstated) words of Isam'il Ragi al Faruqi,

> Islam is transcendentalist. It repudiates all forms of immanentism. It holds that reality is of two generic kinds—transcendent and spatiotemporal, creator and creature, value and fact—which are metaphysically, ontologically unlike as different from each other. These two realms of being constitute different objects of two modes of human knowledge, namely, the a priori and the empirical. Consciousness of this duality of being is as old as man; but it has never been absolutely free of confusion, absolutely clear of itself, as in Islam. . . . Islam takes its distinguishing mark among the world religions precisely by insisting on an absolute metaphysical separation of transcendent from the spatiotemporal.[6]

We saw earlier in this book that in Christian theism there is no direct contradiction between God's transcendence and our finitude. In fact, Christians maintain that an important aspect of what it means to be human is to have the capacity for an intimate relationship with God, namely to know him as we would know our brother or father. Even though the Qur'an allows us to know of Allah's presence and to recognize his guid-

[6]Isam'il Ragi al Faruqi, "Islam," in *The Great Asian Religions*, ed. by Wing-tsit Chan, Isam'il Ragi al Faruqi, Joseph M. Kitagawa and P. T. Raju (Indianapolis: Macmillan, 1969), p. 309.

ance, his availability and his kindness, it keeps a much wider gap between a person's relationship with Allah compared to Christian theism. In Christian theism one could say that, because of God's indwelling of us through his Spirit (Jn 14:17, 19; Rom 8:9; 1 Cor 6:16), we have an even more intimate relationship with God than with other people; such a statement would be impossible in the Qur'an. Even though Allah is immanent insofar as he acts in the world, the Christian notions of God's incarnation in a human being (Christ) or his direct indwelling of all who believe in him would bring him too far down to the level of creatures for Islamic theism.

Of course, we need to be clear on the fact that the Qur'an does state that God is close to us, but we also need to recognize what this means.

> When My servants ask thee concerning Me, I am indeed close (to them): I listen to the prayer of every suppliant when he calleth on Me: Let them also, with a will, Listen to My call, and believe in Me: That they may walk in the right way. (2:186)

Hammudah Abdalati asserts on the basis of this verse.

> God is High and Supreme, but He is very near to the pious thoughtful people; He answers their prayers and helps them. He loves the people who love Him and forgives their sins. . . . Because He is so Good and Loving, He recommends and accepts only the good and right things. The door of His mercy is always open to any who sincerely seek His support and protection.[7]

This verse is considered to be of great comfort to Muslims in the struggles of everyday life, and, thus, must be considered to contribute to the total Islamic worldview. Nevertheless, we may also take cognizance of its context and its overall intent. The verse occurs in the midst of various rules concerning the observance of Ramadan. Its immediate predecessor enjoins fasting during Ramadan and allows for those who are sick or on a journey to make up their obligation later. It is followed by the instructions not to have sexual relations during fasting hours and not to overindulge oneself during the times when eating is permitted. In short, even though the verse carries reassurance of God's presence, in its setting its primary purpose seems to be to provide conditions under which believers' prayers will be heard during Ramadan. Thus, it is a word of com-

---

[7]Hammudah Abdalati, *Islam in Focus* (Indianapolis: American Trust Publications, 1975), p. 5.

fort, but it is also bound up with an exhortation to obedience.

To provide an even more drastic example, Muslim apologists to Western Christians sometimes attempt to counter the perception of distance between God and people by quoting a part of a verse from the Qur'an (50: 16): "We are nearer to him than (his) jugular vein," where "We" is Allah speaking using the "royal we." This statement certainly seems to imply an intimate personal relationship. However, a look at the immediate context shows that what might by itself look like an assurance of God's comforting presence is actually a threat. Let us quote the entire verse and the two that follow it,

> It was We Who created man, and We know what dark suggestions his soul makes to him: for We are nearer to him than (his) jugular vein. Behold, two (guardian angels) appointed to learn (his doings) learn (and noted them), one sitting on the right and one on the left. Not a word does he utter but there is a sentinel by him, ready (to note it). (50:16-18)

Not only does this verse not teach anything like an intimate personal relationship, God's presence as depicted in this passage is also not immediate, but mediated by two angels.

A possible exception to this apparent lack of an intimate relationship with Allah is provided by Sufism, the mystical side of Islam. Sufi teachings have had a profound influence on Islam as a whole by going far beyond the Qur'an in emphasizing a loving relationship between God and his believers. It even teaches that a person can attain a direct vision of Allah. But this is not something that is simply given to every Muslim. It is an outcome that requires a lot of labor and is not an experience that one can attain simply by deciding to do so. It takes many years of following the strict Sufi rule to get to this point.[8] One must not only follow all of the normal rules for Islam, but one must also reach and maintain a state of absolute purity. Then it may be possible to attain a moment of being directly in the presence of God. But even so, Sufism does not supply an exception to the emphasis on God's transcendence because its goal is not for God to move downward in order to be closer to the human being, but for the Sufi monk to rise up in his spiritual state until he finally attains the height sufficient to experience God.

---

[8]Menahem Milson, trans. and ed., *A Sufi Rule for Novices* (Cambridge, Mass.: Harvard University Press, 1975).

But of course despite al-Faruqi's statement above, Islam does not do away completely with the immanence of God. As we shall see below, even from afar he regulates the events of the universe, and he has consistently revealed himself throughout human history. The most important revelation from Allah is the Qur'an, but Islam even allows for a certain amount of general revelation.

> Behold! in the creation of the heavens and the earth; in the alternation of the night and the day; in the sailing of the ships through the ocean for the profit of mankind; in the rain which God Sends down from the skies, and the life which He gives therewith to an earth that is dead; in the beasts of all kinds that He scatters through the earth; in the change of the winds, and the clouds which they Trail like their slaves between the sky and the earth;—(Here) indeed are Signs for a people that are wise. (2:164)

Note that the perception of these divine clues is already limited to those "people that are wise," which is just another way of saying "people who believe in Allah already." In fact, what follows this verse immediately is a condemnation of anyone else who may see the signs, but winds up worshiping them rather than Allah.

Still, the fact of revelation shuts the door on the idea that because of God's transcendence we must be agnostic concerning God's attributes. We can know some things about Allah. However, at all times we must acknowledge that this knowledge is only general. We can know *that* God is merciful, but we should in no way pretend that we comprehend what this means sufficiently to draw implications from it.

Having seen all of the above concerning the exclusive nature of Allah, you may be surprised to learn that we need to add one other item to our exploration of what constitutes fundamental reality in Islam, at least as an issue that is debated among Muslims. Our answer so far consists of the fact that God is the ultimate reality, that God in himself is quite remote from us, and that God has revealed himself to us through the Qur'an. It is the nature of the Qur'an that has raised another puzzle. It is generally accepted that the Qur'an is eternal. In its true form it exists in heaven as the *Mother of the Book* (*Umm-al-kitab*). When Gabriel first commissioned Muhammad, the angel presented him with excerpts out of the *Umm-al-kitab* and commanded him to read and subsequently recite these portions (sura 96). This order seriously perplexed Muhammad at first because he was illiterate. The angel reassured him that the same

God who creates people out of a mere clot of blood (i.e., the fertilized ovum), would also give him the ability to read the book and to repeat its content with complete precision. This is one of the reasons why Muslims refer to the Qur'an as a miracle (the other one being its perceived perfection in form and content). At the same time, the nature of the book-behind-the-book, the true Qur'an in heaven, has caused a lot of discussion among Muslims.

The major contenders in this debate historically were known as the Mu'tazilites and the Ash'arites.[9] We cannot possibly do justice to the entire debate in this chapter and must content ourselves with assessment by John L. Esposito that "in time the [the Ash'arites] came to be regarded as the dominant school of Sunni theology,"[10] and thus focus on their point of view. The conundrum of the *Umm-al-Kitab*, as already alluded to, concerns its eternality. If it really is an eternal book, then we could actually have two foundational realities, namely both Allah and the Qur'an, and the latter would then detract from Allah's greatness. The easiest way of dealing with this unwanted outcome would be to say that the Qur'an is created and, therefore, temporal, which was the position of the Mu'tazilites. But the notion of the *Umm-al-Kitab* as eternal had become so engrained in Islamic thought that to deny it reduced the authority of the book in Muslim eyes. The most commonly accepted solution, which is the Ash'arite position, is to say that the Qur'an is indeed eternal, though not as an independent reality. Rather, the words of the Qur'an are the thoughts of Allah himself, and so it has existed as long as there has been God, which makes the Qur'an eternal, but does not stipulate the book as a second reality.

---

[9]The Mu'tazilites arose in the early eighth century A.D. among philosophically literate converts to Islam, who attempted to make a rational case *(kalām)* for Islam. They took uncommon stances on two issues: the eternity of the Qur'an and the freedom of individual persons (to which we will come later in this chapter). Concerning the Qur'an, the Mu'tazilites asserted that the Qur'an was created. They were opposed by the Ash'arites (see note 1 above), who advocated the understanding that the Qur'an was eternal, but only as the thoughts of God, not as a separately existing reality. Although the Ash'arites managed to have the Mu'tazilites eventually declared to be heretics, Mu'tazilite ideas have been revived to a certain extent by contemporary Muslims. Nevertheless, it does not make much sense to consider either the Mu'tazilites or Ash'arites to have "solved" the problem for Islam, though the Ash'arite view has been the more enduring one. The debate is still ongoing. David S. Noss, *A History of the World's Religions* (Upper Saddle River, N.J.: Prentice Hall, 2008), pp. 569-72.

[10]John L. Esposito, *Islam: The Straight Path*, 3rd ed. (New York: Oxford University Press, 1998), p. 73.

Given this point of view, the Qur'an not only contains God's thoughts, but it also mediates God's thoughts to us. Consequently, one has to think of the Qur'an on two levels, distinguishing between it as the content of

---

The place of the Qur'an in the life of the Muslims is only in limited ways like that of the Bible in the lives of Jews and Christians. Scholars have observed that in relation to Christianity, the Qur'an may be usefully compared with Christ, in that it is believed to be God's Word that has miraculously come down into the world in history and humankind. If in Christianity the "Word became flesh," in Islam it became a book. And the book is properly appropriated and applied only where it is recited live in a context of belief and obedience.

FREDERICK MATHEWSON DENNY, *An Introduction to Islam*

---

the mind of God (which is never accessible to us) and as divine revelation (which is the only way to have accurate knowledge about God).

It is not necessary for us to take sides in this debate among Muslim scholars, but it is important for us, when we try to identify what constitutes fundamental reality in Islam, that we may need to include the Qur'an as expressive of the mind of God for some schools of Islam.

2. Worldview Question 2: *God (Allah) created the universe ex nihilo, and all creatures are responsible to him. However, the world is a closed system insofar as nothing happens in the world outside of his divine decrees.*

The magnificence of Allah's greatness is brought out clearly in the miracle of his creation of the universe.

> Men who celebrate the praises of Allah, standing, sitting, and lying down on their sides, and contemplate the (wonders of) creation in the heavens and the earth, (With the thought): "Our Lord! not for naught Hast Thou created (all) this! Glory to Thee! Give us salvation from the penalty of the Fire." (3:191)

His creation is not just limited to material things. In the very first sura,

God is praised as "the Cherisher and Sustainer of the worlds" (1:2), and Richard C. Martin points out that "the plural, worlds, does not refer to other planets and stars as we think of them, but rather to other sacred realms of angels and unseen spiritual beings." [11] Prior to the creation of humans, God already had brought angels and *jinn* into existence. The latter are malicious spirits of relatively limited power, but sufficiently strong to ruin someone's life if left unchecked.

Allah's method of creation is simply to speak a thing into existence. This understanding is illustrated in two verses in the Qur'an. Thus, we read concerning the creation of Adam,

> He created him from dust, then said to him: 'Be.' And he was. (3:59)[12]

Similarly, when the angel announced to Mary that she would bear Jesus even though she was a virgin, Mary was understandably puzzled. The angel reproved her skepticism by saying,

> Even so: Allah createth what He willeth: When He hath decreed a plan, He but saith to it, 'Be,' and it is! (3:47)

Since Allah has created the universe, he has absolute discretion over it. Think of a child who has built a sandcastle at the beach. She may decorate it with sea shells, protect it from the water, add to it, or she may trample it, let the water wash it away or preserve half of it but let the other half stand. The decision is entirely hers, and she owes nothing to the sandcastle, but the structure owes everything to her. Insofar as she does take care of it, it is purely a matter of her good nature, which she is not obligated to maintain. Such is the relationship between God and his creation.

God is the creator and owner of the universe, and nothing happens within it that would be outside of his plan. This doctrine is called *Qadr*, which literally means "power." In this case it refers to God's power to know and govern the universe. There are no surprises for Allah. This much is given, but there are multiple ways of understanding this concept,

---

[11]Richard C. Martin, *Islam: A Cultural Perspective* (Englewood Cliffs, N.J.: Prentice-Hall, 1982), p. 92.

[12]Please note that here and in several other places, the Qur'an goes along with the biblical notion that Adam was created from dust or clay. The statement in sura 96 that God created man from a clot of blood does not refer to the creation of Adam, but to the miracle of each human being from the fertilized ovum, which initially appears to be nothing more than a clot of blood.

and Muslim scholars have debated its implications right from its first
century of existence up to the present moment. Again, historically, the
two main contenders were the Mu'tazilites and Ash'arites, and again,
without wanting to minimize the significance of the Mu'tazilite position,
we need to note that the Ash'arite view became dominant and is, therefore, more representative of the whole. And, once again, for our purposes,
we need not take sides in this discussion about who is right. Furthermore,
it would take an entire book just to describe all of the variations in its
interpretation.

Allah's providence begins with his exhaustive knowledge of every last
detail about the universe. All of this knowledge is maintained in a permanent data bank.

> Not a leaf doth fall but with His knowledge: there is not a grain in the
> darkness (or depths) of the earth, nor anything fresh or dry (green or with-
> ered), but is (inscribed) in a record clear (to those who can read). (6:59b)

But knowledge for God is never just his taking cognizance of certain
states of affairs or holding all correct propositions to be true. With him,
to know a thing or an event is to control it.

> No misfortune can happen on earth or in your souls but is recorded in a
> decree before We bring it into existence: That is truly easy for Allah. In
> order that ye may not despair over matters that pass you by, nor exult over
> favours bestowed upon you. For Allah loveth not any vainglorious boast-
> ers. (57:22-23)

Mahmoud Murad defends a fairly strict interpretation of *Qadr* and
insists that the acceptance of this doctrine entails:

> That the knowledge of Allah encompasses all things, and that nothing
> escapes His knowledge, be it in the heavens or on the earth. Allah has
> known His creatures before he brought them into existence. He reassigns
> their provisions, term of life, utterances, deeds, actions, movements, their
> internal and external affairs, and who of them is assigned for Jannah [par-
> adise], and which of them is doomed to Hell.
>
> That Allah has pre-decreed what [is] to come into existence. This in
> turn requires believing in the Pen which records all the divine decrees,
> and in the Preserved Tablet on which the decrees are recorded.
>
> That the will of Allah is effective and His capacity is inexhaustible and
> inclusive. Doubtlessly, whatever Allah wills does take place, and whatever

He does not will does not take place due not to incapacity rather to His infinite wisdom. There is nothing that frustrates the capacity of Allah.[13]

Other interpretations are scaled back from this description, but we must keep in mind that the further away we get from this interpretation, the further we are distancing ourselves from what appears to be the most widely held conservative Sunni position.

Thus, a picture emerges that may seem paradoxical but is actually quite rational. On the one hand, we cannot go too far in stressing Allah's transcendence. He is not to be associated with any finite being in the world. On the other hand it is also clear that God not only sees every detail of the world, he also does not permit anything to happen outside of his specific plan. The latter statement leads many Muslims to believe that God directly manages all events.

Here then, is an important distinction to Christian theism. We stated earlier in the book that Christian theism is an open worldview. God has created a universe that incorporates uniform laws, and he has endowed human beings with the opportunity to exercise genuine creativity within the world that he created. Islamic theism, on the other hand, adds another restriction beyond the limits intrinsic to the universe. Whatever creativity creatures may possess, they can exercise it only insofar as Allah permits it according to his inscrutable will. Thus, Islamic theism on the whole leaves us ultimately in a closed universe in which God's will sets the boundary for what any creature can do as a causal agent.

We shall need to come back to the doctrine of *Qadr* in the context of the fifth worldview question, which concerns human knowledge.

3. Worldview Question 3: *Human beings are the pinnacle of God's creation. They have been given abilities of which other creatures, such as angels and jinn, are not capable. However, their high standing also brings with it the responsibility to live up to God's standards.*

The fact that we have emphasized the absolute greatness of Allah in Islam should not mislead us into thinking that therefore Islam has a low view of human beings. The following account follows the events as nar-

---

[13]Mahmoud Murad, *This Message Is for You*, <www.scribd.com/doc/295593/This-Message-is-for-You>.

rated in sura 2 and repeated in other places. According to the Qur'an, when God set out to create Adam, he called a general meeting of all of the spiritual beings he had created heretofore and announced what he was about to do. When the angels learned of his intention, they were offended and actually questioned Allah's wisdom. After all, they claimed, they had been praising God faithfully all along. Why would he now put another creature above them, particularly one who would be prone to mischief?

> Behold, thy Lord said to the angels: "I will create
> A viceregent on earth." They said:
> "Wilt Thou place therein one who will make
> Mischief therein and shed blood?—
> Whilst we do celebrate Thy praises
> And glorify Thy holy (name)?"
> He said: "I know what ye know not." (2:30)

Allah's mysterious reply that he knew something of which the angels were ignorant would soon take on concrete meaning. God personally educated Adam in how to identify the many creatures on earth (presumably plants, animals and objects in nature). He then called another meeting in which he challenged the angels to give the proper labels to various items in creation, but they failed miserably at this task. Then God brought out Adam, and to their amazement, he was able to do the very thing that they could not bring off. They took back their criticism and acknowledged that Allah had not made a mistake in creating such a wonderful being. In order to drive home this point, Allah commanded all of the angels to bow down before Adam.

> And behold, We said to the angels:
> "Bow down to Adam:" and they bowed down:
> Not so Iblîs: he refused and was haughty:
> He was of those who reject Faith. (2:34)

Iblîs[14] thus became Satan or *Shaytan*. Note, then, that in Islam, just as in Judaism and Christianity, the devil is a fallen spiritual being (though in this case a jinn, one of the lower order), who would not obey God. It is significant for our understanding of the position of human beings in Islam that the specific occasion for his rebellion actually occurred not in

---

[14]If you look at the "*bl*" combination of letters in *Iblîs*, it may make sense to you that this name shares the same linguistic root as our word *diabolical*.

rebelling against God's superiority per se, but in refusing to demonstrate the superiority of human beings over him.

Let us pursue this story just a little further, and then we will be able to draw some important conclusions. God now placed Adam and his wife (her name is not mentioned in this sura) into a garden and gave the familiar command not to eat of a certain tree. In a manner that is not specified, Satan was able to persuade them into disobedience, and they were expelled from the garden and deprived of their happiness.

But this version of the story has a relatively quick happy ending.

> Then learnt Adam from his Lord
> Words of inspiration, and his Lord
> Turned towards him; for He
> Is Oft-Returning, Most Merciful. (2:37)

Even while Adam was out of favor with God, he received instructions from Allah, and upon proper penitence, God restored him to fellowship. Thus, there was no permanent curse, Adam did not remain a fallen creature, and humankind was not beset with heritable "original sin."

We have, then, the following preliminary picture of what Islam teaches concerning who we are as humans. We are God's representatives on earth, higher than any other living creatures and (in contrast to Christian belief) with a nature that is not corrupted by Adam's fall. Consequently, we are born in a state of purity and innocence, a fact that implies that any newborn comes into the world as a Muslim.

However, it now becomes our obligation to live up to our standing. To be born pure does not guarantee that we shall remain pure. The Qur'an enjoins,

> O ye people!
> Adore your Guardian-Lord,
> Who created you
> And those who came before you,
> That ye may have the chance
> To learn righteousness.

Privilege implies responsibility, and the stakes are immeasurably high. In the simplest of terms, Islam sees each human being spending a lifetime on probation. It is one thing to acknowledge God as the greatest with mere words, even if they are meant sincerely, it is quite another to live one's entire life in submission to him, and the latter requirement is the test for whether a person will qualify for salvation. To quote John L. Esposito,

> Faith places the Muslim on the straight path; acts demonstrate commitment and faithfulness. In Islam, the purpose of life is not simply to affirm but to actualize; not simply to profess a belief in God but to realize God's will—to spread the message and law of Islam. Faith without works is empty, without merit; indeed, it is the Book of Deeds that will be the basis for divine judgment.[15]

Thus, we need to add one important amendment to the above summary of what it means to be human. We have been given the rank as the second-highest being in the universe, we have been born in the state of purity, we may even have the advantage of living in a culture where Islam is taught and practiced. Nevertheless, none of that means anything unless we devote our lives to the service of Allah and the teachings of Muhammad. If we do not pass the test, then our destination will be hell.

4. Worldview Question 4: *Death is a time of transition between this life and our eternal state, which will consist of either paradise or hell.*

Thus we can make an easy segue to the next topic, which is about what happens to a person at death. If we take this question completely literally, there are two answers, one concerning a person's physical remains and one concerning the soul. However, the two are interrelated. Proper observance of burial customs contributes to the fate of the soul after death. Some time in the future, the deceased will face an interrogation by the two angels Munkar and Nakir,[16] and anything that the survivors can do in order to help the deceased give the proper answers will increase their chances of entering paradise. Therefore it is a good thing to encourage a person right before he dies to say the confession one last time: "There is no God but God, and Muhammad is the prophet of God." If this is no longer possible, those who are gathered at the funeral will repeat it on behalf of the deceased. The corpse must be washed and transformed into a state of ritual purity. Finally, he or she must be buried lying on the right side, facing in the direction of Mecca.

---

[15]Esposito, *Islam: The Straight Path*, pp. 68-69.
[16]Denny, *Introduction*, p. 289.

These outward physical measures have their purpose in guiding the soul into being fully prepared for the upcoming judgment at the end of time. Everyone agrees that eventually there will be the last day on which all the dead will be raised in order to face judgment. In the meantime, what happens in the interval immediately after death and before the resurrection and the judgment is a matter of debate. Some Muslims hold that the soul will simply sleep peacefully until that time; others believe that between death and resurrection there will be a period of spiritual purgation in which postmortem suffering will purify the soul so as to become fit for heaven.[17]

Regardless of these speculations, there is no question of what will happen when the resurrection takes place. All human beings will be called to stand before the divine tribunal, and all of their beliefs and attitudes as well as the record of every last little action that they have performed during their lifetime will become the basis for judgment. Every human being will have accumulated a book of their deeds, both good and evil, during their mortal lives. No one can be fully sure that they have enough good to outweigh any bad, and so be assured of going to paradise. The three notable exceptions to this are martyrs, children before puberty and those who are mentally impaired, the latter two because they are not fully accountable for their actions. For anyone else, one may think that one has a good chance, but, to repeat our earlier observation, to claim assurance for salvation implies that one can dictate to Allah what he must do, and this attitude is considered to be inappropriate. Suzanne Haneef asserts that

> no Muslim, even the best among them, imagines that he is guaranteed Paradise; on the contrary the more conscientious and God-fearing one is, the more he is aware of his own shortcomings and weaknesses. Therefore the Muslim, knowing that God alone controls life and death, and that death may come to him at any time, tries to send on ahead for his future existence such deeds as will merit the pleasure of his Lord, so that he can look forward to it with hope for His mercy and grace.[18]

Still, once the last day arrives, there will no longer be any ambivalence. As

---

[17]Ibid.

[18]Suzanne Haneef, *What Everyone Should Know About Islam and Muslims* (Chicago: Kazi Publications, 1979), p. 37. As we shall point out further below, the word "grace" here is far removed from what Christians mean by the term because in the Islamic context what Haneef calls "grace" is based on our works.

soon as Allah has established his verdict, one of the angels will come up
to the person and hand him the book of his deeds. Without having to be
told anything, the human being will recognize his fate by the hand in
which the angel places the book. If he puts it into his right hand, he knows
that he has experienced Allah's mercy and will be allowed to enter Paradise. In the unfortunate event that the angel places the book into a person's left hand, the time will have come for him to reconcile himself to
living in hell from now on (69:13-37).

Keeping in mind the origin of these beliefs in the desert culture of
Arabia, the tortures of hell are described as something that a desert nomad would think of as being immeasurably horrible. What would be a
worse torture than being in a desert without water? The answer is to be
in the desert and come across a well and think that you will be refreshed,
but then realizing that the water is so polluted that it is impossible for a
human being even to take a little sip of it. In the Qur'anic description, hell
is first of all a place of hot, odiferous, poisonous water in which the unbe-
liever will have to endure numerous tortures.

Heaven, on the other hand, is depicted as a desert nomad's ideal place
of delight. Picture a beautiful oasis with fresh water, luscious green plants,
handsome boys serving all the best to eat and drink, and the beautiful
huri, the enticing, dark-eyed virgins, whose services are perennially available. Now, there is no question that the description of heaven given in the
Qur'an is one that is utterly geared to men. Nonetheless, one should not
infer that women will not be eligible for heaven. The Qur'an says of the
faithful believers that they are headed for

> gardens of perpetual bliss: they shall enter there, as well as the righteous
> among their fathers, *their spouses*, and their offspring: and angels shall
> enter unto them from every gate (with the salutation): "Peace unto you for
> that ye persevered in patience! Now how excellent is the final home!"
> (13:23, emphasis mine)

Thus, even though the descriptions in the Qur'an are very definitely oriented toward male desires, there is no intent of excluding women. Presumably women will receive whatever would be the counterpart of bliss
for their sex.

5. Worldview Question 5: *Allah has endowed human beings with the
capability of knowledge by means of reason and the senses. Thereby, they*

can also know God's revelation. However, God's sovereign decrees limit human knowledge.

We saw earlier in connection with the creation of Adam that humans have greater intelligence than angels and jinn. God has created human beings in such a way that their senses will be reliable sources of information and their reasoning skills are trustworthy. Al-Faruqi goes so far as to begin his entire description of Islam with the statement that "first, Islam is rationalistic."[19] He bases this conclusion on the verse in the Qur'an that forbids conversion by force:

> Let there be no compulsion in religion: *Truth stands out clear from Error:* whoever rejects evil and believes in God hath grasped the most trustworthy hand-hold, that never breaks. And God heareth and knoweth all things. (2:256, emphasis mine)

Human reason is sufficient to discern truth from falsehood. We are capable of a rational approach to the world around us, and we need not abdicate our rationality when it comes to matters of religion. This is a very good thing because, as we saw, we need to utilize all of our potential to prove our devotion to Allah by living up to his standards, and the stakes are extremely high: eternal bliss or eternal torment.

Of course, our reasoning ability, no matter how sharp, would be useless if we did not have the necessary information to apply it, but this is where divine revelation helps us out. Around the globe, every group of people has had one or more messengers from God who taught them the same precepts as Muhammad did. There is no definitive list of all of the prophets prior to Muhammad, but the various listings include numerous Old Testament figures, such as Adam, Noah, Abraham, Lot, David and Jonah, as well as both Isaac and Ishmael, to mention just a few. The prophet with the highest standing other than Muhammad himself is Abraham, followed very closely in importance by Jesus. Although the Qur'an denies both his crucifixion and his divine nature, it vigorously affirms his virgin birth as well as his teaching, healings and miracles. Furthermore, in sura 11, the Qur'an also mentions prophets outside of the Bible, whom God sent to their people in their day: Hud to the A'ad, Salih to the Thamud, and Shu'yeb to the Midianites. Thus, whatever should be known could be known easily by simply listening to the prophets.

---

[19]Al-Faruqi, "Islam," p. 308.

However, human beings are prone to give in to temptations and to fall into unbelief. Sadly, each of the previous prophets encountered that same obstacle. Even though it turned out to be to their own detriment, the people mocked them and rejected them. Every day that Noah spent building the ark, his contemporaries, who should have repented of their sin, mocked him instead. What could be a clearer warning sign than that, along with his words, Noah was publicly building a huge ship, which would be the only escape from the flood? Nevertheless, the people resisted him. Thus the prophets were a clear source of knowledge, and the fact that the people nevertheless did not submit to Allah is due to their evil, not to a lack of sufficient information.

Furthermore, among the prophets were a few who were even more distinguished. These were the "messengers," who also left books of their teachings for posterity: Moses brought the Law, David brought the Psalms, and Jesus brought the Gospel. But the same unbelieving people who did not listen to them in person corrupted their writings in order to suit their idolatrous preferences. As a result, the clear messages from God, which might have survived in writing even if their original bearers had been rejected, became distorted in their written forms as well.[20]

All of that should have changed with the coming of Muhammad. He was considered to be the "seal of the prophets," and what distinguishes him in Islamic eyes is the belief that his message, as recorded in the Qur'an, was preserved free from error or human interference. There is thus no need for any further prophets, and however much the message may have been obscured previously, it should now be clear and accessible to everyone. Therefore Jews and Christians receive special encouragement:

> O People of the Book! Now hath come unto you, making (things) clear unto you, Our Apostle, after the break in (the series of) our apostles, lest ye should say: "There came unto us no bringer of glad tidings and no warner (from evil)." (5:19)

---

[20]Contemporary Muslims have received much aid in this contention by the practice of textual criticism of the Bible, in which even Christians expose the many variants in the biblical manuscripts. However, the claim that the text of the Bible had been altered goes back to the time of Muhammad himself, long before this scholarly discipline emerged. For a Christian response on this issue see Winfried Corduan, *Neighboring Faiths: A Christian Introduction to World Religions* (Downers Grove, Ill.: InterVarsity Press), pp. 81-82, 108.

The particular evidence for the authority of the Qur'an is the Qur'an itself. People who already believe in Islam consider the Qur'an to be self-authenticating:

> Say: "What thing is most weighty in evidence?" Say: "God is witness between me and you; This Qur'an hath been revealed to me by inspiration, that I may warn you and all whom it reaches." (6:19a)

On the other hand, those who reject the prophet Muhammad and claim that the Qur'an is nothing but a forgery are challenged by the nature of the Qur'an itself.

> They say He hath invented it. Say: Then bring ten surahs, the like thereof, invented, and call on everyone ye can beside Allah, if ye are truthful! (11:13)

The message has been delivered, and there should be no excuse not to accept it.

Nevertheless, clear revelation does not imply automatic acceptance of the revelation. In order to make the following point as clear as possible, I shall provide some quotations from the Qur'an, but leave out some phrases that are a part of those verses. Then I will restore the missing pieces, and you will see my point. These verses teach that those who are committed to unbelief will not change their minds, no matter how strong the evidence may be.

> Of them there are some who (pretend to) listen to thee; . . . *[elision 1]*. . . So they understand it not, and deafness in their ears; if they saw every one of the signs, not they will believe in them; in so much that when they come to thee, they (but) dispute with thee; the Unbelievers say: "These are nothing but tales of the ancients." (6:25)

Supernatural indicators would do no good for those confirmed in their unbelief.

> If their spurning is hard on thy mind, yet if thou wert able to seek a tunnel in the ground or a ladder to the skies and bring them a sign,- (what good?) . . . *[elision 2]* . . . (6:35)

and

> Those who reject our signs are deaf and dumb,- in the midst of darkness profound. . . . *[elision 3]* . . . (6:39)

In short, those who do not believe are attached to their unbelief and would not believe if they could. They have only themselves to blame for the consequences of their unbelief. These conclusions are correct, and their truth is not altered by restoring the elisions. Nevertheless, putting back the missing parts certainly complicates the picture.

These are the parts that I left out of the above quotes:

Elision 1: but We have thrown veils on their hearts;

Elision 2: If it were God's will, He could gather them together unto true guidance;

Elision 3: whom God willeth, He leaveth to wander: whom He willeth, He placeth on the way that is straight.

So, now we see that those who do not recognize the truth will also be kept from doing so by God. Here is another verse from the same sura that makes the point that belief and unbelief ultimately depend on God's will.

> Those whom God (in His plan) willeth to guide,- He openeth their breast to Islam; those whom He willeth to leave straying,- He maketh their breast close and constricted, as if they had to climb up to the skies: thus doth God (heap) the penalty on those who refuse to believe. (6:125)

We can know the truth—dependent on our will and God's. If our will is disinclined to believe God's revelation, we can expect little help from God. Allah may be merciful at his preference (as he was to Adam), but as a general rule,

> Even if We did send unto them angels, and the dead did speak unto them, and We gathered together all things before their very eyes, they are not the ones to believe, unless it is in God's plan. But most of them ignore (the truth). (6:111)

Now we can see more directly how *Qadr*, God's predestination, affects human beings. Although human beings have a choice whether to obey Allah or not, the choice is not open-ended. It appears that God classifies each person into one of two groups: those who are believers and those who are his enemies. Once people have fallen into the second category, God will not only refuse to aid them, he will use his power to make sure that they remain deluded in their unbelief.

It is helpful at this point to elaborate on this aspect of Islam by making a distinction to Christianity. In Romans 5:10 the apostle Paul exults:

For if, while we were enemies, we were reconciled to God through the death of His Son, [then how] much more, having been reconciled, will we be saved by His life! (Holman Christian Standard Version)

Even though we already were enemies of God due to our fallen nature, God loved us and made peace with us because of Christ's death on the cross. On the other hand, in the Qur'an we read,

Lo! God is an enemy to those who reject Faith. (2:98b)

Regardless of how much agency we ascribe to God's creatures, all of their actions are bracketed by his will. As a matter of fact, the Qur'an promises occasions in which God will intentionally provide opportunities for believers to demonstrate that they accept his plans as final.

Be sure we shall test you with something of fear and hunger, some loss in goods or lives or the fruits (of your toil), but give glad tidings to those who patiently persevere, Who say, when afflicted with calamity: "To God We belong, and to Him is our return": They are those on whom (Descend) blessings from God, and Mercy, and they are the ones that receive guidance. (2:155-57)

6. Worldview Question 6: *Right and wrong are based on the teachings of the Qur'an, as amplified by the Hadith and interpreted by the schools of law, the shari'a.*

Thus, there is nothing left for us to do than to try our best to follow all of God's commandments. There is no point in speculating on God's will. Rather than search for God's purposes, we should accept whatever he sends our way *bilā kayf,* which means "without asking why."[21] Any statement of intentions on our part should be accompanied by the phrase *"inshallah"*—"if God wills" (18:24), a phrase that can express genuine reliance on God (and is also taught for Christians in James 4:15), but in popular usage can also become either a formula of resignation or a mantra to ward off evil. Our obligation is not to out-think Allah but to do his will.

The source of knowledge about what is right or wrong, as already indicated, is the Qur'an. In case there should be some ambiguity concerning how a particular commandment should be interpreted, one can consult

---

[21]Martin, *Islam,* p. 100.

the hadiths, which are several collections of sayings and actions by Muhammad, as allegedly[22] remembered by those who knew him well. For example, quite a few of these recollections are attributed to Aïsha, his very young wife who turned into a spunky young widow and was not above disputing with the caliphs themselves. Even though it is accepted practice to use the expression *Hadith* in the singular, there is no single authoritative collection, and the various components are of uneven authority. Consequently, there developed among Sunni Muslims four schools of Islamic Law *(shari'a)* that advocated different degrees of strictness in applying the rules of the Qur'an and their relationship to the Hadith. Of the four, the one that adheres most strictly to the most literal applications of the Qur'an is the Hanbalite school. Among its heritage is the Wahhabite reform movement, which, in turn, gave rise to the Taliban in Afghanistan, one of the so-called fundamentalist movements of Islam.[23]

---

[22]There are several collections of hadiths, and they are considered of uneven reliability, even among Muslims. A representative collection is provided by Maulana Muhammad Ali, *A Manual of Hadith* (Lahore, Pakistan: The Ahmadiyya Anjuman Ishaat Islam, 1944), easily accessible at <http://www.sacred-texts.com/isl/hadith/index.htm>.

[23]The first appearance of a "radical" Islamic group came about in the struggle for the successor (caliph) to Muhammad as leader of the new Islamic community, which pitted Muhammad's own family (his son-in-law Ali ben Talib and his grandsons, al-Hassan and al-Hussein) against the Umayyad clan, who believed they were entitled to the position. A group called the *Kharijites* (which means "dissenters") emerged with the message that the person who is most qualified to be caliph should be whoever was the most devoted to Allah and most exemplary in obeying the Qur'an. Anyone who thought otherwise had lapsed from true Islam and deserved to receive the same treatment as unbelievers who fight against Islam. In fact, the Qur'an considers lapsed Muslims and hypocrites to be worse than unbelievers: "They swear by Allah that they said nothing (evil), but indeed they uttered blasphemy, and they did it after accepting Islam; and they meditated a plot which they were unable to carry out: this revenge of theirs was (their) only return for the bounty with which Allah and His Messenger had enriched them! If they repent, it will be best for them; but if they turn back (to their evil ways), Allah will punish them with a grievous penalty in this life and in the Hereafter: They shall have none on earth to protect or help them" (9:74). Furthermore, "The Hypocrites will be in the lowest depths of the Fire: no helper will you find for them" (4:145).

There is a remarkable phenomenon occurring in contemporary scholarship in the social sciences with regard to explaining the nature of "fundamentalism" in its various manifestations, which are usually considered to be Christian fundamentalism, radical Islam and Hasidic Judaism. The underlying question is what these "fundamentalists" have in common and what similar influences they might have in their respective settings. Needless to say, there are many conflicting opinions. See, for example, Bruce Lawrence, *Defenders of God: The Fundamentalist Revolt Against the Modern Age* (New York: Harper & Row, 1989). I would like to suggest that the problem is that these groups have little in common other than that they represent conservatism in their individual contexts. Observers have taken a term that is only appropriate to Christianity, applied it arbitrarily to other religions, and are now trying to explain a phenomenon that they themselves created by their own unreflective use of terminology. In the case of Islam, for example, if groups like the Taliban need to receive a

The obligations for a Muslim begin with the five pillars: to recite the confession (there is no God but Allah), to pray five times a day, to fast during the month of Ramadan, to give the annual contribution for the poor, and to make the pilgrimage to Mecca at least once in a lifetime. But this is only the beginning. Muslim life is strictly regulated. There are three fundamental categories of actions: those that are directly commanded *(fard)*, those that are permitted *(halal)*, and those that are prohibited *(haram)*. Of course, any violation of *halal* is *haram*, and not to carry out the obligations that are *fard* is also *haram*. I am mentioning this logical truism because a negative mindset is the most common result among human beings who believe that their eternal destiny is based on keeping rules. When everything is riding on one's actions, and when there is no assurance of God's indulgence, let alone any grace, avoiding the potentially negative consequences of any sin is bound to become the primary incentive for one's actions rather than the positive motivation of keeping the rules out of gratitude.

7. Worldview Question 7: *Human history has significance in demonstrating the absolute sovereignty of God but, even more so, as the opportunity for people to demonstrate their submission to him.*

Human history is the world's longest final exam, and the test starts right along with the lectures. On a less ultimate level, the goal of history is to subsume the entire world under the *umma*, the Islamic community, which is as much a political entity as a congregation of believers. The significance of this statement can be clarified by drawing another point of contrast. Many religions anticipate a time in which their beliefs and practices will be observed universally around the globe.[24] The question is, what are you expected to do in the meantime? For example, in Christianity believers are exhorted to submit to rulers, even if they are pagan, and even though many Christians look forward to Christ's actual govern-

general label beyond Wahhabite and Hanbalite, the best term would not be "fundamentalist" but "neo-Kharijite." Their preferred self-designation is Salafi, which means "those who follow the prophet."

[24]Judaism looks forward to the Messianic age, Christians wait for the second coming of Christ (frequently along with the expectation of a millennium), and Zoroastrians are counting on Saoshyant to set the world right. Even among the religions where history is a never-ending cycle, Hindus expect Kalki, Buddhists Maitreya, and Jains another whole set of twenty-four Tirthankaras. See Winfried Corduan, *A Tapestry of Faiths: Common Threads Among the World's Religions* (Downers Grove, Ill: InterVarsity Press, 2003), pp. 171-94.

ment on earth during the "millennium," only God himself will bring about this end.[25] Until then, we should do what we can to promote justice and peace while we wait for God to bring things to a conclusion by his own power. Islam, on the other hand, comes with the mandate to set up Islamic governments, and it is never fully implemented unless there is an Islamic state.

> Thus have We made of you an *Ummat* justly balanced,
> That ye might be witnesses
> Over the nations. (2:143)

Yusuf Ali explains in his commentary on this and the preceding verse that the *umma* is a new nation, "an independent people with laws and rituals of their own." In this state there will be no idolatry permitted, but the "people of the book," Jews and Christians, will be tolerated, as long as "they pay the Jizya with willing submission, and feel themselves subdued" (9:27). The *jizya* is a compensation required of Christians and Jews for enjoying the benefits of living in a Muslim community without contributing to it.

Many Muslims believe that shortly prior to the last judgment, the Mahdi will appear. There are several conflicting traditions concerning this figure. In Shi'ite Islam he is the twelfth Imam, who, as a five-year-old child in A.D. 878, went into seclusion in a remote cave, where he has been living ever since, until the time will come for him to disclose himself again. In other divisions his identity is less specific. Many Muslims also believe in the second coming of Christ; specifically that he will descend on the Mosque of the Umayyads in Damascus, Syria. Some believe that Christ is the Mahdi, while others believe that Jesus and the Mahdi are two distinct persons.[26] Still others do not have much use for the idea of a

---

[25]Just as I have been doing with Islam all along, I am here referring to Christianity in what I consider its more representative form and relying more literally on the Bible. The fact that there have been Christians who have attempted to establish God's kingdom on earth by their own power, sometimes even by physical force, does not mean that this perspective is of equal standing with the more biblical view that I am addressing in the text.

[26]An interesting sidelight is provided by the Pakistani group (now actually two groups), called the Ahmadiyya sect. This sect was started in the nineteenth century by Ghulam Ahmad of Qadiyan, who claimed to be the Mahdi, the second coming of Christ, and the fulfillment of Hindu hopes for the return of Krishna (though not, as frequently misrepresented, Krishna himself). Ahmadiyya Islam is consistently pacifistic, and it has now divided into two subgroups, named after the towns of their headquarters. The Qadiyan branch says that Ghulam was only a reformer, whereas the Lahore branch takes the unorthodox view that he was a

Mahdi at all since Muhammad is the final prophet. I am mentioning this debate because it illustrates the fact that Muslim expectations for the end times are not at all unanimous. How history ends is not all that crucial considering that the all-important last judgment follows immediately.

8. Worldview Question 8: *A devout Muslim is grateful to Allah for providing the opportunity to serve him and will strive to follow the divine instructions in even the smallest part of life.*

Obviously, we find among Muslim people the same distribution of degrees of commitment as in all other religions. So, let us focus on the person who is serious in devotion to Allah. Such a man or woman will frequently express gratitude that Allah has provided the chance to enter Paradise. Muslims refer to the teachings of the Qur'an as "good news." Christians may be surprised at this use of the term, which is, of course, synonymous with "gospel," because among Christians the idea of the gospel is tied to our fallen state and our utter inability to improve our standing with God in our own power, and God's grace that saves us apart from our good works. Islam has neither the doctrine of original sin by which all human beings are condemned from birth on, nor is there a doctrine of salvation by grace according to which our works are not instrumental in contributing to our salvation. In fact, Muslims tend to find the idea of free salvation irresponsible, and even without a notion of original sin, they are sufficiently convinced of human sinfulness that they consider any chance at salvation at all to be a true act of mercy on God's part. All but one of the suras (number 9) of the Qur'an begins with the expression "in the name of Allah, the most gracious and most merciful." They see the fact that they must live up to divine standards in order to receive salvation not as a burden but as an opportunity.

Still, Islam demands of the person nothing less than everything. The standards for a truly acceptable life are high and become extremely detailed the more one seeks to implement them according to the Hadith. To mention just a few obvious ones, there are restrictions on food, of course, such as avoiding pork, blood or strangled meat. Not only women but also men must follow principles of clothing and personal decoration on clothing. To be more specific, men must have their limbs covered at least as far

---

prophet as well. Consequently, the latter form of Ahmadiyya Islam is not officially recognized as true Islam in Pakistan.

as their elbows and knees and may not wear gold or garments made entirely of silk. There are rules for every aspect of a normal day, including how to perform common actions and what prayers or formulas to speak alongside them.[27] The earnest Muslim will not chafe at these requirements, but follow them with gratitude to Allah for giving him this chance to demonstrate his allegiance.

Nevertheless, gratitude and hope are not the same things as joy and grace. The weight of the obligations and their consequences are too profound to induce automatic rejoicing (though there are, of course, happy Muslims). On an extreme end, Muhammad Ibn Abd al-Wahhab, the founder of the Wahhabite movement in Saudi Arabia, prohibited music, a rule that was eventually relaxed in its country of origin but was revived by its offspring, the Taliban. But what really makes the picture so poignant is that, all the compliance by a human being notwithstanding, the will of Allah can always override all the good works a person may have accumulated. It is easy to believe that God has it in his power to forgive a person's sins without the need for any atonement. But, as Colin Chapman observes,

> This understanding of forgiveness, however, leaves us open to a frightening uncertainty, since we can never have any assurance about God's verdict for each individual on the day of judgment.[28]

Chapman follows this statement with a reference to the feelings of terror expressed by the first two caliphs (who are considered to be exemplary in their lives, as expressed by the term "rightly guided") on their deathbeds, since even they did not know whether they would be accepted by God.

The true Muslim must assert that God is all-caring, all-forgiving and all-merciful, but he may not draw the implication that therefore God will definitely grant him access to paradise. He has been taught to dismiss the

---

[27]To underscore this point, allow me to extend it a little further, not because it may look exaggerated to non-Muslims, but because it illustrates the reality that I am addressing. The Hadith even includes the proper means of sanitation and which prayers to utter before and after one performs biological acts of necessity. Furthermore, it does so clearly and openly without violating any sensitivities, which are more likely to be the product of Western "Christian" scruples than Islamic attitudes. Maulana Muhammad Ali, *A Manual of Hadith*, chapter 4, section 1: "Natural Evacuations" <http://www.sacred-texts.com/isl/hadith/had07.htm>.

[28]Colin Chapman, *The Cross and the Crescent: Responding to the Challenge of Islam* (Downers Grove, Ill.: InterVarsity Press, 2003), pp. 259-60.

Christian belief in the atonement, but he may not understand that it is precisely because the atonement is the work of God, and not of a human being, that the Christian is able to express assurance of salvation. So, our

---

Mecca Death Toll Is Confirmed; King Calls It Fate

The Saudi Interior Minister, Prince Nayef, said today that 1,426 Muslim pilgrims died in a stampede in a pedestrian tunnel linking this city with a tent camp for pilgrims. Prince Nayef said the stampede was caused when seven pilgrims fell from an overhead bridge near the tunnel. Other officials said a power failure caused the air-conditioning in the 1,500-foot-long, 60-foot-wide tunnel to switch off in 112-degree heat on Monday, setting off the stampede. "It was God's will, which is above everything," King Fahd said of the disaster. "It was fate."

AP News Report, published by the *New York Times*, July 4, 1990

Muslim neighbor is glad to do all he can in order to measure up on the last day, and he knows that Allah is good, but he cannot erase the question mark that always hangs over him when it comes to his eternal destiny. I have heard more than one Muslim tell me that he is sure to go to heaven—as long as he remains conscious of God and his commandments every second of his life. The qualification takes all the certainty out of the stated assurance.

Nevertheless, for millions of people Islam has provided stability. They are convinced that, any uncertainty notwithstanding, they are on the right side. *"Allahu akbar"* is a victory shout over any competing religions. But our look at Islamic theism has revealed a worldview that seems uneven: it is ultimately a closed system that puts humans in a bind between personal accountability and divine determinism. Allah appears to oscillate between mercy and nothing short of hatred toward unbelievers.

But perhaps, to come to a better understanding of the positive role that Islam plays in the lives of its believers, we should not limit our comparison to the two theisms of Christianity and Islam. Let us keep in mind that Islam arose in what Muslims call "the times of darkness." Muhammad's primary message was directed against idolatry and superstition in a society in which justice and power were synonymous, many people were treated worse than animals, and infanticide was a common practice. We need to acknowledge the advances that Islam made at its inception over its contemporary culture, which in some important ways (e.g., women's rights) also put it ahead of European culture at that time. Historically, the origins of Islamic theism are tied to a certain amount of influence from Judaism and Christianity, but this new theism established a culture that brought some improvements to society that did not exist at that time in the cultures established under the insignia of the two older forms of theism. Although the debate on whether early Islam was spread by the sword is still continuing, it is a fact that many localities opened their doors happily to Islam and were glad to be relieved of the rampant corruption of the Byzantine empire. Islam had found some truths and made a great contribution by spreading them.

However, Islam simultaneously walled itself off from the two older forms of theism and declared itself to be the final truth, superior over its two fountainheads from its outset. Whereas Judaism has a millennia-long history of development, and Christianity did not begin to settle crucial questions in its councils until hundreds of years after Christ, Islam for the most part closed its door to any further refinements of its theism, in particular foreclosing the possibility that it could learn any further from Judaism and Christianity. To be sure, the schools of shari'a developed, but these were predominantly schools of jurisprudence, not of theological investigation. Potential innovations in theology, such as those proposed by the Mu'tazilites, even if they received a hearing or public endorsement for a while, were most likely greeted with suspicion and, even if they were not eventually declared to be heretical, they would sooner or later be swallowed up by traditional formulations.

Now, none of the remarks above should be considered to be a criticism per se. I, too, as an evangelical Christian, am leery of innovations in theology. But my point is that, from my perspective, Islam closed the lines of communication, both external and internal, far too soon. Consequently it incorporated the ambiguities and uncertainties that we mentioned above, that could have been resolved if Islamic theism had allowed itself to keep learning and growing in insights over its first few centuries. Islamic theism certainly is an authentic theism, but it is one that unfortunately became truncated before it could reach full maturity.

FOLK ISLAM

For virtually any religion, in addition to its various schools, denominations and sects, it is possible to encounter a wide gulf between the "standard" version of the religion, which is the way it is being taught in the books and by its leaders, and the "folk" version of the religion, which is the way that the religion is actually lived out on a day-to-day basis by the common people. For example, it is fairly easy to discern a "folk" Christianity in the U.S. state of Indiana, where I live.[29] Many authors point out that because Islam stresses the transcendence of God so much, it stands out as a religion in which the gulf between the "standard" form and the "folk" version has become particularly wide. Colin Chapman, for example, makes the point that Sufism developed as a way of addressing "the hunger of the heart" for those who "longed for a faith that has reality for the individual,"[30] and that "folk" Islam can be seen as one further step (albeit perhaps a very large one) in speaking to the same felt needs.[31] (Even though the division can be arbitrary at times, I will now continue on without enclosing the two terms in quotation marks.)

Many accounts of folk Islam tend to depict it as genuine Islam, but lived out with a different attitude than one would expect within the standard version. The people carry out the basic duties of the five pillars and observe other Islamic obligations, but their goal is not the worship of Allah for its own sake but to tap into the sources of power and blessing that Islam provides. For example, a common phenomenon is that people who have manifested a great amount of devotion during their lives may be venerated as saints, and those who admire them visit their tombs in order to receive special blessings. Drawing on my experience in India, it is not at all unlikely that one may walk down the streets of, say, Hyderabad and suddenly encounter a little gap between houses and businesses. In that little open area there may be the tomb of a saint, set up as a concrete prism about the size of an oversize coffin and surrounded by a concrete wall, perhaps about three feet tall. The entire little structure is painted and covered by Islamic symbols and perhaps some other decorations specifically associated with the person buried there. People who need particular spiritual help may visit such a site and say prayers there.

---

[29]Corduan, *Neighboring Faiths*, pp. 37-38.
[30]Chapman, *Cross and Crescent*, p. 122.
[31]Ibid., p. 129.

Life is too large and complicated for individual humans to manage by themselves, and people always look for solutions that will provide immediate aid when the crops fail, relationships are out of kilter, a family member is ill or other problems invade their lives. So-called folk Islam attempts to give such aid. Additionally, practices in Islamic folk religion are frequently geared for spiritual protection from the malicious spirits (the jinn), curses or the "evil eye." In fact, in some areas, this second aspect is so overwhelming that one could conclude that folk Islam really has no place in a chapter on Islamic theism because it seems to be more of a form of animism than theism.

In many areas of the world, folk Islam goes beyond the description of Islam as addressing felt needs with superstitious practices. If we accept the supposition underlying folk Islam that standard Islam does not meet certain needs, and if the Muslim population happens to live in an area where another religion is thriving, and if it appears that this other religion meets that particular need, the result is often a syncretism in which elements of the other religion are incorporated into Islamic practices.

I have seen folk Islam in many different situations in South Asia and Southeast Asia. For example, about an hour's boat ride outside of Singapore is a little island called Kusu Island, or "Turtle Island," which houses a shrine built in honor of a Muslim saint, his wife and his daughter, similar to the tombs mentioned above. In this case, however, the legend holds that they did not die but that in the late nineteenth century they were raptured directly to heaven. Kusu Island is fairly flat, but the devotees built an artificial hill about 100 feet tall on one end of the island. They planted trees on it and erected a wooden shrine, covered with yellow paint, at its summit. There are two different paths, one leading up to the shrine and one leading down, thus enabling an efficient procession of worshipers during the month of October when many Malaysian Muslims observe special days there. But the shrine is always open, and people visit it throughout the year, particularly if they encounter financial problems or are having to deal with wayward children.

As one enters the premises, there is no doubt that it is an Islamic structure, with the crescent moon and star on the signs, the walls and the "tombs." Furthermore, there is a tapestry depicting the ka'aba in Mecca, and there are wall hangings with verses from the Qur'an. But that is not all that we find in the Islamic shrine on Kusu Island. At the foot of one of the tombs is a shelf holding the yin-and-yang-shaped blocks used for Chinese fortune telling, and in one corner of the building there is a big oven of the type that is used to burn paper as an offering to the spirits of Chinese religion. And there is more that does not seem to fit in with standard Islam. After having said prayers and undertaken other rituals, a worshiper may take a small plastic shopping bag, fill it with rocks and hang it on one of the trees along the downward path, thereby having created a "sacred object," which would be a highly questionable action in standard Islam. Then, some time later, when his prayers hopefully have been answered, he will visit the shrine again, express his gratitude and remove the stone-filled bag.

Thus we see that folk Islam is not a somewhat revised version of Islam but, in many places, adapts itself to surrounding non-Muslim cultures and frequently becomes downright syncretistic.

For anyone attempting to learn about the Islamic world and how to encounter Muslims in a real-life setting, it is essential that they learn as much as they possibly can about folk Islam. Still, in many cases, folk Islam is so far removed from standard Islam that, if the goal is to understand Islamic theism and the nature of Islam as it has affected the world in recent years, folk Islam occupies a very different category. Wahhabite Islam, the version of Islam practiced by the Taliban, for example, was founded precisely in order to eliminate the practices of folk Islam. Furthermore, to the best of my knowledge, Muslims in the United States (now close to 7 million strong) are not particularly inclined toward folk Islam. Therefore, it is good to know about it, but it is a different worldview than the one I have attempted to describe in this chapter.

Chapter 11

THE EXAMINED LIFE

CONCLUSION

Across my foundering deck shone
A beacon, an eternal beam./Flesh fade, and mortal trash
Fall to the residuary worm;/world's wildfire, leave but ash:
In a flash, at a trumpet crash,
I am all at once what Christ is,/since he was what I am, and
This Jack, joke, poor potsherd,/patch,
matchwood, immortal diamond,
Is immortal diamond.

GERARD MANLEY HOPKINS,
"THAT NATURE IS A HERACLITEAN FIRE,
AND OF THE COMFORT OF THE RESURRECTION"

We have now examined eight basic worldviews, seven if we don't count nihilism, or nine if we count both forms of existentialism separately.

Or eleven, if we add the briefly mentioned animism and the postmodern perspective. But who is counting? We could multiply worldviews to fit the number of conscious inhabitants of the universe at any one time—or at all times if we take an Eastern twist or if we see the universe from the aspect of eternity. On the contrary, we could say that there is one basic worldview composed of one proposition: Everyone has a worldview!

Still, we may ask, are these the only choices? Where is the Playboy philosophy? And what about the artist who "creates" to bring order out of the chaos of life? These options certainly have adherents. Yet when we examine each option, we find that each is a subdivision or specific version of one or more of those already discussed. Hedonistic Playboy philosophy is an unsophisticated version of naturalism. People are sex machines; oil them, grease them, set them in motion, feel the thrill. Wow! Pure naturalism in which the good is what makes you feel good and, with any luck, doesn't hurt anyone else.

Aestheticism—the worldview of a person who makes art out of life in order to give form to chaos and meaning to absurdity—is considerably more sophisticated and attractive. Its adherents (people like Walter Pater in the late nineteenth century and Ernest Hemingway, Hermann Hesse, James Joyce, Wallace Stevens, Somerset Maugham, Pablo Picasso, Leonard Bernstein in the twentieth) are often personally attractive, even charismatic. But aestheticism is a form of existentialism in which the artist makes value, endowing the universe with a certain formality and order. The code hero of Hemingway is a case in point. His ethical norms are not traditional, but they are consistent. He lives by his own rules, if not the rules of others. The roles Humphrey Bogart played in *Key Largo, Casablanca* and *The Treasure of the Sierra Madre* have given this worldview a more than professional dimension and have taken aestheticism (life as a certain style) into the marketplace. Nonetheless, aestheticism is just a specific type of atheistic existentialism in which people choose their own values and make their own character by their choices and actions. We have seen in chapter six where that leads.

The fact is that while worldviews at first appear to proliferate, they are made up of answers to questions that have only a limited number of answers. For example, to the question of prime reality, only two basic answers can be given: either it is the universe that is self-existent and has always existed, or it is a transcendent God who is self-existent and has always existed. Christian and Islamic theism and deism as well claim the latter; naturalism, Eastern pantheistic monism, New Age thought and postmodernism claim the former. As one theologian put it, either the present universe of our experience has had a personal origin or it is the product of the impersonal, plus time, plus chance.[1]

---

[1] Francis A. Schaeffer, *The God Who Is There* (Downers Grove, Ill.: InterVarsity Press, 1968), p. 88.

Or to take a different example, to the question whether one can know something truly or not there are only two possible answers: one can either know or not know something about the nature of reality. If a person can know something, then language in which that knowledge is expressed in some way corresponds unequivocally to reality and the principle of noncontradiction operates. Postmodernism's rejection of this notion is self-referentially incoherent.

To say that we can know something true does not mean we must know exhaustively what is true. Knowledge is subject to refinement, but if it is true knowledge, there must have been at least a grain of truth in one's unrefined conception. Some aspect of that conception has to remain as it was in the beginning, or it was not knowledge. For example, ancient people observed the sun move in the sky. We know that the sun stands still and the earth turns. But our knowledge includes the truth of the ancients' observation; the sun appears to rise as much to us as it did to them. In any case, if we can know something about reality, this rules out the infinite number of possible explanations suggested by conceptual relativism. In that system we cannot know what is actually the case. We are bound within the borders of our language system. This is essentially nihilism.

There are likewise a limited number of choices regarding the notion of time. Time is either cyclical or linear; it either goes someplace (that is, is nonrepeatable) or eternally returns (and thus does not exist as a meaningful category). And there are a limited number of choices regarding basic ethics and metaphysics and questions about personal survival at death. And so on.

Worldviews, in other words, are not infinite in number. In a pluralistic society they seem to exist in profusion, but the basic issues and options are actually rather small. The field, as I have narrowed it, contains eleven options (or ten, or eight—our counting problem!). Our own personal choice lies somewhere on this field, but if the argument of this book is valid, two conclusions follow. First, our choice need not be blind. There are ways to bring light to the paths from which we choose. Second, whatever choice we make, if we are not going to be hypocritical, we are committed to live by it. As indicated in the very definition of worldview, we "live and move and have our being" in accordance with the worldview we really hold, not the one we merely confess. A fearless honesty should characterize both our self-analysis—where we are now—and our pursuit of truth.

CHOOSING A WORLDVIEW

How, then, should we choose to live? How can we decide among the finite alternatives? What can help us choose between a worldview that assumes the existence of a transcendent, personal God and one that does not? Something of my own view of this matter should certainly have become obvious in the descriptions and critiques of the various options. Now is the time to make this view explicit.[2]

Unless each of us begins by assuming that we are in our present state the sole maker and meaning-giver of the universe—a position held by few even within the New Age worldview—it would be well to accept an attitude of humility as a working frame of reference. Whatever worldview we adopt will be limited. Our finitude as human beings, whatever our humanity turns out to be, will keep us both from total accuracy in the way we grasp and express our worldview and from completeness or exhaustiveness. Some truths of reality will slip through our finest intellectual nets, and our nets will have some holes we have not even noticed. So the place to start is humility. We do tend to adopt positions that yield power to us, whether true or not.

But humility is not skepticism. If we expect to know anything, we must assume we can know something. And with that assumption other elements are entailed, primarily the so-called laws of thought: the laws of identity, noncontradiction and the excluded middle. By following such laws we are able to think clearly and be assured that our reasoning is valid. Such assumptions, then, lead to the first characteristic that our adopted worldview should possess—inner intellectual coherence. Keith Yandell of the University of Wisconsin states this succinctly: "If a conceptual system contains as an essential element a (one or more membered) set of propositions which is logically inconsistent, it is false."[3]

It is on this basis that the worldviews of deism, naturalism, pantheistic monism and so forth were examined in the preceding chapters. Each was found inconsistent at some major points. Naturalists, for example, declare the universe to be closed on the one hand, and yet most naturalists affirm that human beings can reorder it on the other hand. If my argu-

---

[2]I have written at length about why one should choose one worldview over another in *Why Should Anyone Believe Anything at All?* (Downers Grove, Ill.: InterVarsity Press, 1994).

[3]Keith Yandell, "Religious Experience and Rational Appraisal," *Religious Studies*, June 1974, p. 185.

ment is correct, we have seen that for us to be able to shape or reorder our environment, we must be able to transcend our immediate environment. But since naturalism declares we cannot do this, naturalism is inconsistent and cannot be true, at least as it is normally formulated.[4]

A second characteristic of an adequate worldview is that it must be able to comprehend the data of reality—data of all types: that which each of us gleans through our conscious experience of daily life, that which are supplied by critical analysis and scientific investigation, that which are reported to us from the experience of others. All these data must, of course, be carefully evaluated on the lowest level first (is it veridical? is it illusory?). But if the data stand the test, we must be able to incorporate them into our worldview. If a ghost refuses to disappear under investigation, our worldview must provide a place for it. If a man is resurrected from the dead, our system must explain why that could happen. To the extent that our worldview denies or fails to comprehend the data, it is falsified or at least inadequate.

It is just such a challenge to naturalism that has caused some to accept theism as an alternative. The historical evidence for the resurrection of Christ, and for various other "miracles," has been found by many to be so heavy that they have abandoned one conceptual system for another. Conversions to Christianity, especially among intellectuals in our time, are almost always accompanied by changes in worldview, for sin, as seen by the Bible, has an intellectual as well as a moral dimension.[5]

Third, an adequate worldview should explain what it claims to explain. Some naturalists, for example, explain morality by reference to the need to survive. But as we saw, this is explaining the moral quality *(ought)* solely by reference to the metaphysical quality *(is)*. Perhaps the human species must develop a concept of morality in order to survive, but why should it survive? And it is no good responding with B. F. Skinner, "So much the worse" for us if we do not survive, for that just begs the question.

The crucial questions, then, to ask of a worldview are, How does it explain the fact that human beings think but think haltingly, love but hate too, are creative but also destructive, wise but often foolish, and so

---

[4]Each formulation of each worldview must be considered on its own merits, of course. But for each of the worldviews I have weighed and found wanting I know no formulation that does not contain problems of inconsistency.

[5]See, for example, Romans 1:28.

forth? What explains our longings for truth and personal fulfillment? Why is pleasure as we know it now rarely enough to satisfy completely? Why do we usually want more—more money, more love, more ecstasy? How do we explain our human refusal to operate in an amoral fashion?

These are, of course, huge questions. But that is what a worldview is for—to answer such questions, or at least provide the framework within which such questions can be answered.

Finally, a worldview should be subjectively satisfactory. It must meet our sense of personal need as a bowl of hot oatmeal breaks the fast of a long night's sleep. I mention satisfaction last because it is the most ephemeral quality. If it were first, it would suggest that subjectivity is the most important factor, and it would also beg the question. To say an adequate worldview must satisfy is to talk in circles; the question is, how can a worldview satisfy? And the answer, I believe, is clear: a worldview satisfies by being true. For if we think or even remotely suspect that something in our grasp of reality is illusory, we have a crack that may widen into a fissure of doubt and split the peace of our world into an intellectual civil war. Truth is ultimately the only thing that will satisfy. But to determine the truth of a worldview, we are cast back on the first three characteristics above: internal consistency, adequate handling of data, and ability to explain what is claimed to be explained.

Still, subjective satisfaction is important, and it may be lack of it that causes us to investigate our worldview in the first place. The vague, uneasy feeling we have that something doesn't fit causes us to seek satisfaction. Our worldview is not quite livable. We bury our doubt, but it rises to the surface. We mask our insecurity, but our mask falls off. We find, in fact, that it is only when we pursue our doubts and search for the truth that we begin to get real satisfaction.[6]

Where, then, are we today? In terms of possible worldviews, our options are numerous but, as we have seen, limited. Of those we have investigated, all but theism were found to have serious flaws. If my argument has been correct, none of them—deism, naturalism, existentialism, Eastern pantheistic monism or New Age philosophy, nor the postmodern perspective—can adequately account for the possibility of genuine knowledge, the facticity of the external universe or the existence of ethical dis-

---

[6]For a full treatment of the nature of doubt and its contribution to the formulation of an adequate worldview, see Os Guinness, *God in the Dark* (Wheaton, Ill.: Crossway, 1996).

tinctions. Each in its own way ends in some form of nihilism.

Islam poses both an alternative and a separate challenge. Because it is based on a theistic notion of God as creator, sustainer and revealer of the truths of reality, the most foundational worldview notion (the nature of ultimate reality) is similar to that of Christianity. Searchers for truth will need to look more intently at specific details of each worldview—possible internal inconsistencies and, especially, the differing conceptions of the nature and character of Allah and the biblical God, the historical evidence for the nature and character of Jesus, and the reasons for the authority accorded to their two foundational scriptures—the Bible and the Qur'an. This is a task that here must be left to you as readers.[7]

CHRISTIAN THEISM REVISITED

There is one worldview that offers both a firm intellectual foundation and a route out of such nihilism. For those who follow the decline of religious certitude through its trek from the seventeenth to the twenty-first century, the way forward is not to go beyond nihilism. It is rather to return to an early fork in the intellectual road.

It may seem strange to suggest that we throw off modern and postmodern thought and return to the seventeenth century. But we should be reminded that Christian theism as I have defined it was culturally abandoned not because of its inner inconsistency or its failure to explain the facts, but because it was inadequately understood, forgotten completely or not applied to the issues at hand. Moreover, not everyone abandoned theism three centuries ago. There remain at every level in society and in every academic discipline—in science and the humanities, in technology and the business world—those who take their Christian theism with complete intellectual seriousness and honesty.[8]

Questions and rough edges—indeed theism has those. And there are

---

[7]See, for example, Colin Chapman, *The Cross and the Crescent: Responding to the Challenge of Islam* (Downers Grove, Ill.: InterVarsity Press, 2003); and Chawkat Moucarry, *The Prophet and the Messiah: An Arab Christian's Perspective on Islam and Christianity* (Downers Grove, Ill.: InterVarsity Press, 2001).

[8]See, for example, two collections of personal essays by philosophers who are openly Christian: Kelly James Clark, ed., *Philosophers Who Believe: The Spiritual Journeys of 11 Leading Thinkers* (Downers Grove, Ill.: InterVarsity Press, 1993); Thomas V. Morris, ed., *God and the Philosophers: The Reconciliation of Faith and Reason* (New York: Oxford University Press, 1994); and Paul M. Anderson, *Professors Who Believe: The Spiritual Journeys of Christian Faculty* (Downers Grove, Ill.: InterVarsity Press, 1998).

problems. Finite humanity, it would seem, must be humble enough to recognize that any worldview will always have those. But theism explains why we have such questions and problems. Its ground is neither the self nor the cosmos, but the God who transcends all—the infinite-personal God in whom all reason, all goodness, all hope, all love, all reality, all distinctions find their origin. It provides the frame of reference in which we can find meaning and significance. It stands the fourfold test for an adequate worldview.

Gerard Manley Hopkins, a nineteenth-century Jesuit poet whose own intellectual journey provides a fascinating study of how a searching mind and heart can find a resting place, has left us a rich vein of poems that embody the Christian worldview. None, I think, better captures the tone of Christian theism than "God's Grandeur," and it will put a fitting personal close to our rather intellectual consideration of worldviews:

The world is charged with the grandeur of God.
 It will flame out, like shining from shook foil;
 It gathers to a greatness, like the ooze of oil
Crushed. Why do men then now not reck his rod?
Generations have trod, have trod, have trod;
 And all is seared with trade; bleared, smeared with toil;
 And wears man's smudge and shares man's smell: the soil
Is bare now, nor can foot feel, being shod.
And for all this, nature is never spent;
 There lives the dearest freshness deep down things;
And though the last lights off the black West went
 Oh, morning, at the brown brink eastward, springs—
Because the Holy Ghost over the bent
 World broods with warm breast and with ah! bright wings.[9]

Of course, there is much more to be said about the personal and theological dimensions of this way of looking at life.[10] To accept Christian theism only as an intellectual construct is not to accept it fully. There is a deeply personal dimension involved with grasping and living within this worldview, for it involves acknowledging our own individual dependence

[9]Gerard Manley Hopkins, "God's Grandeur," in *The Poems of Gerard Manley Hopkins*, 4th ed., ed. W. H. Gardner and N. H. MacKenzie (New York: Oxford University Press, 1967), p. 66.
[10]The New Testament is the primary text for Christian theism, but I also recommend John R. W. Stott, *Basic Christianity*, rev. ed. (Downers Grove, Ill.: InterVarsity Press, 1973), and J. I. Packer, *Knowing God*, rev. ed. (Downers Grove, Ill.: InterVarsity Press, 1993).

on God as his creatures, our own individual rebellion against God and our own individual reliance on God for restoration to fellowship with him. And it means accepting Christ as both our Liberator from bondage and the Lord of our future.

To be a Christian theist is not just to have an intellectual worldview; it is to be personally committed to the infinite-personal Lord of the universe. And it leads to an examined life that is well worth living.

Index

Bold type indicates major discussions.

Finding the Textbook You Need

The IVP Academic Textbook Selector
is an online tool for instantly finding the IVP books
suitable for over 250 courses across 24 disciplines.

ivpacademic.com